MW01031748

TO GROW IN WISDOM

TO GROW IN WISDOM

An Anthology of
Abraham Joshua Heschel

Edited by
Jacob Neusner
with
Noam M. M. Neusner

MADISON BOOKS
Lanham • New York • London

Published by Madison Books
4720 Boston Way
Lanham, Maryland 20706

3 Henrietta Street
London WC2E 8LU England

Distributed by National Book Network

Library of Congress Cataloging-in-Publication Data

Heschel, Abraham Joshua, 1907–1972.
To grow in wisdom : an anthology of
Abraham Joshua Heschel / edited by
Jacob Neusner with Noam M.M. Neusner.
p.   cm.
Includes bibliographical references.
1. Judaism.
2. Man (Jewish theology).
3. Life.
I. Neusner, Jacob, 1932–   .
II. Neusner, Noam M.M. (Noam Mordecai Menahem).
III. Title.
BM45.H4547   1989
296.3—dc20   89–13110 CIP

ISBN 0–8191–7464–5 (alk. paper)

British Cataloging in Publication Information Available

For
Samuel H. Dresner

Heschel's greatest disciple and
continuator

CONTENTS

Part III: An Afterword: Heschel Remembered

ACKNOWLEDGEMENTS

3. A Time of Renewal

From *Midstream,* November, 1972, pp. 40–48. © 1972 by Theodor Herzl Foundation. Reprinted by permission.

4. The Holy Dimension

From *The Journal of Religion* 1943, 23:117–124. © 1943 The University of Chicago Press. Reprinted by permission.

5. A Preface to an Understanding of Revelation

From *Essays Presented to Leo Baeck on the Occasion of His Eightieth Birthday.* London, 1954: Horovitz Publishing Co. Ltd. pp. 28–35, © 1954 East and West Library. Reprinted by permission.

6. Prophetic Inspiration: An Analysis of Prophetic Consciousness

From *Judaism* 1962, 2:3–13. © 1962 American Jewish Congress. Reprinted by permission.

7. Architecture of Time

From *Judaism* 1952, 1:44–51. © 1952 American Jewish Congress. Reprinted by permission.

8. Space, Time, and Reality: The Centrality of Time in the Biblical World-View

From *Judaism* 1952, 1:262–269. © 1952 American Jewish Congress. Reprinted by permission.

9. The Concept of Man in Jewish Thought

From S. Radhakrishnan and P. T. Raju, eds. *The Concept of Man.* London, 1960: Allen and Unwin Ltd., pp. 108–157 © 1960 Allen and Unwin Ltd. Reprinted by permission.

10. The Religious Message

From John Cogley, ed. *Religion in America: Original Essays on Religion in a Free Society*. New York, 1958: Meridian Books, pp. 244–271 © 1958 The Fund for the Republic. Reprinted by permission.

11. The Religious Basis of Equality of Opportunity: The Segregation of God

From Mathew Ahmann, ed. *Race: Challenge to Religion*. Chicago, 1963: Henry Regnery, pp. 55–71 © 1963 Henry Regnery. Reprinted by permission.

12. To Grow in Wisdom

From *Congressional Record* 1961 107:A1973-A1975. Not subject to copyright.

13. A Daughter's Memory

© 1987: Jason Aronson, Inc. Reprinted by permission.

PREFACE

A braham Joshua Heschel, 1907–1972, has a message to deliver to the twenty-first century. The purpose of this anthology is to help make the man accessible by providing a selection of his profound thought. This is not the final anthology of his work or the first. But we hope it will serve its purpose, which is to show some of the many dimensions of Heschel, as we can know him in writing. Part of the range and variety of his types of thought and expression are placed on display here. If readers work their way through these papers and conclude, as we have, that Heschel set the standard not for scholarship alone, or for piety alone, or for theology alone, or for moral conscience alone, but for all of these things and more, then we shall have made possible for a new generation, that cannot know the man, to understand and appreciate, at least, that part of the human achievement that is in the permanent condition of writing—and it is all there is, and all there needs to be. For it was through intellectual and religious expression such as we offer here that Heschel defined the measure of Judaism as a living religion in this century now speaks to the coming century as well—a considerable claim, amply demonstrated in the papers we have collected and arranged. The cooperation and collaboration of father and son, the one who knew Heschel well, the other who has only heard about him, formed the critical tension in choosing and arranging the papers. To papers in which the son found resonance of a voice of truth, the father gave preference for presentation in these pages.

This anthology covers only a small part of what we believe are those essays of Heschel that enjoy enduring value. We anticipate that further anthologies will be required to lay before the coming generations what we conceive to be his important work. We have made our contribution, and we anticipate that others in due course will make their choices as well. Ours is not to complete the task, but we also are not free to neglect it. The papers presented here include some not before anthologized. But the criterion for selection is not prior inaccessibility, but the capacity of each paper to join together with all the others and so to show us, in its way, how diverse and yet cogent were Heschel's intellectual initiatives. The papers show us in action a religious thinker, a theologian working toward a systematic account of religion, a public figure—but above all, a human being, a very particular human being: a Jew, bearing in spirit and flesh the mark of standing in a covenanted relationship, through holy Israel, the Jewish people, with God who made heaven and earth and gave the Torah. When we follow the flow of Heschel's thought, as these papers portray it, we find ourselves in a single stream. That is what makes Heschel remarkable, and these papers exemplary. Heschel drew together the history and the religion, the inner life and the worldly presence, of Israel, the Jewish people, and said in a few words what he thought that Israel stood for and should do, wherever and whenever that Israel took place. And that applies to the century that will read this book, long after its editor, and even his son, have joined Heschel among all who have gone before. *Many have drunk, many will drink:* God's rule endures.

The copyright holders who have supplied permission to reprint work subject to their original copyright are listed in the acknowledgements. The work of actually finding and assembling the papers and the entire editorial management of the project was carried out by Noam Mordecai Menahem Neusner, my No. 3 son, and a major in the writing seminars at The Johns Hopkins University. That accounts for his sharing in co-editorship of this book. May he produce many more, in his own time, in his own way, and on subjects that he has made his own.

In twenty years at Brown University, difficult and disappointing years in the aspect of this particular corner of the academy, I have found strength and solace in remarkable co-workers, colleagues and, as a matter of fact, also friends. My colleagues at Brown University, Professors Ernest S. Frerichs, Wendell S. Dietrich, and Calvin Goldscheider, discussed this project with me and made useful suggestions. Professor Dietrich, himself a specialist in modern and contemporary theology of Judaism and "Jewish thought," has taught me much about Heschel in his theological context. Professor William Scott Green served as consultant for this analogy; he is certainly the best maker of books we know today, for he simply flows with good ideas.

Jacob Neusner
Noam Mordecai Menahem Neusner

July 28, 1988
My fifty-sixth birthday

Program in Judaic Studies
Brown University
Providence, Rhode Island
U.S.A.

Part I

INTRODUCING HESCHEL

Chapter 1

ABRAHAM JOSHUA HESCHEL:
THE MAN

braham Joshua Heschel, 1907–1972, was the greatest religious
thinker in Judaism, east or west, in the twentieth century and
certainly the most profound and weighty theologian of Judaism ever to
work in North America. He also produced major works of scholarship.
Furthermore, he played a critical role in the public affairs of both the
Jewish community and the American people in the last decades of his
life. There was none like him, none near him, none who approached his
power to join together intellectual achievement in analysis and advocacy
and public service. In his lifetime he gained the position of the single
most influential Judaic thinker in public life and within the community
of Judaism, and, after his death, he has found an enduring and engaged
audience for his thought.

And that is how it should be, for his was Torah and human greatness
in a single person. That explains why, nearly two decades after his death,
he continues to speak to new generations, and it accounts for this
anthology as well. Here we collect and set forth a selection of his essays
that bear continuing interest in the intellectual life of the world of Judaism
and relevance to public policy and discourse. The purpose of this
anthology is not merely to preserve writings to make the man accessible
through a sizable selection of his profound thought. It was through
intellectual and religious expression such as we offer here that Heschel
defined the measure of Judaism as a living religion in this century and

now speaks to the coming century as well—a considerable claim, amply demonstrated in the twenty-nine papers we have collected and arranged.

Let me begin on a personal note, to explain why planning and carrying out this anthology was important to me, a labor of not love but consecration. Apart from Harry Austryn Wolfson and Erwin R. Goodenough, Heschel was the only senior scholar of Judaism, gentile or Jewish, whom as a student and then a junior colleague I admired for *Menschlichkeit,* and not only for learning, (if truth be told, there were few enough in my time to admire just for the learning). In Heschel's power of the spirit and will, his capacity to persuade by person and gesture and by speech, as much as by the appeal to sound reasoning, compelling argument, well-crafted premises, accurate knowledge of the entire range of evidence and prior study of the evidence, he was, and remains, unique among scholars of Judaism. The learning, the sheer erudition, certainly were exhibited by many others. One thinks of the correctly celebrated learning, for example, of Saul Lieberman, with his prodigious feats of memory and his capacity to throw this together with that to come up with something else. But while Lieberman in his day was erudite, learned but not very interesting, rich in knowledge of this and that but lacking insight and perspective, Heschel as a scholar showed imagination, insight, wit, and intellectual vigor, none of the sloth masquerading as precision in which Lieberman took pride. Heschel was certainly a productive scholar. But Heschel's industry, the productivity, these too have their match. Solomon Zeitlin, for instance, wrote a lot of books. But Zeitlin is a mere curiosity in the footnotes of sour scholarship, forgotten by all but his aging claque. And Lieberman and Zeitlin, like many in their day, treated learning as a blood sport, and hated other scholars more than they loved learning. Along with Wolfson and Goodenough, Heschel was the opposite: a great spirit, a beautiful *Mensch,* and brilliant among the mere *idiot-savants.*

But that does not explain why Heschel is as interesting today as he was when he died. That is a mark that the combination of erudition and intelligence, productivity and breadth of vision, is unique to Heschel, and unique is a word I use about once a decade. When reviewing the principal articles of Heschel in preparation for making this anthology, I found surprising not how much, but how little, of Heschel's total *ouevre* is now known. Since his books are in print, I took for granted that people have access to pretty much everything of consequence. The opposite is the case. He produced numerous monumental articles, land-marks on their subjects, that until now have attracted little interest. Many of the chapters of this anthology mark the first reprinting in three or more decades of some of Heschel's greatest intellectual achievements. While, as his student assistant, I typed the manuscript of *God in Search of Man,* I thought I knew well a larger chapter in Heschel's thought, I have now found I know only the outlying reefs of a vast and unknown continent. If, therefore, this anthology wins for Heschel a fresh hearing, it is also for what is essentially fresh and hitherto unknown or unappre-ciated writing. And that renders likely the requirement of yet another anthology, when the full dimensions of Heschel's intellectual achieve-ment are taken and understood. Now let us begin with Heschel, and then turn to these first steps, the chapters of Heschel's thought that are presented here.

For these personal reflections do not explain why the particular rele-vance of Heschel for the twenty-first century requires explanation. In the world today, and in the coming generations as well, live many Jews whose lives are shaped by the teachings of Judaism, Jews who, in various ways and settings, seek to live lives of holiness, to learn the Torah and to carry out and stand for its teachings. Whether women or men, whether Orthodox or Reconstructionist, Conservative or Reform, Israeli or dias-poran, these Jews testify, in American Israel and in the State of Israel alike, to an authentic vision. They understand that the Torah conveys whatever we shall ever know of what it means to be "in our image, after our likeness," that is, to be like God. So they look for God in the Torah and in the life that the Torah in God's name commands. And in how they live they show us what they have found out. Heschel in his lifetime and in the written record he left as heritage is a principal figure among those exemplary Jews—thirty-six is the received number of them—who form living exemplars of the Torah of Moses our Rabbi, handed down by God at Mount Sinai.

Abraham Joshua Heschel was born in Poland in 1907, came to America in 1940, leaving Warsaw under German rule and losing most of his family in the murder of the Jews of Europe. He taught at Hebrew Union College, the Reform rabbinical seminary, in the early 1940s and in the Jewish Theological Seminary of America, the Conservative one, in the later 1940s, 1950s, and 1960s, until his death in 1972. He wrote many important works of Jewish thought and Jewish learning, covering every important classic from biblical and Talmudic times to the great mystics of the eighteenth and nineteenth centuries, from philosophers such as Judah Halevi and Moses Maimonides to mystics such as the Master of the Good Name, founder of Hasidism, not to mention the great figures of nineteenth century Jewish thought in the West. Heschel mastered whatever there was to know. But that is not what matters. What counts is that he made it his own, and made himself over through his learning. That is why he stands for Judaism in our place and in our time. He stands for us because he passed through the great formative experiences of our three American generations of Jews.

He was an immigrant, like my grandmother. When I took her to meet him, they spoke in Yiddish, hers simple and unadorned, his poetic and unadorned. To this day, thirty-five years later, I remember hearing them talk, though I understood little of what they said, because of the sweetness of the moment, in which my past and my hopes for the future came together. But he also made himself into an American, like my father. He took an active part in Jewish community life, lecturing everywhere people wanted to hear him, traveling endlessly. And, as has the third generation, he became a critical moral figure in American life, who marched with Martin Luther King and in his day opposed the war in Viet Nam. He stood for Judaism in an address to the Pope, spoke for world Jewry in the crisis of 1967, rejoiced at the unification of Jerusalem, and in his writings and his addresses spoke an authentic message of Torah, drawing upon resources of spirituality constantly fed and renewed through learning in Torah and through living in Torah. His was the model of a life of Judaism of our day. That is why he is important to any picture of Israel in America. He lived it all—past and present—and pointed the way to the future as well.

Let me explain, first and most important, why I believe Heschel stands as one of the great minds of American Judaism, a model for generations to come. What then did he try to do, and what makes his intellectual work of lasting importance? Heschel attempted to create a "natural theology" for Judaism, a theology which would begin where people actually are, in all their secularity and ignorance, and carry them forward to Sinai. He did not define his task in cultural or philosophical terms. That is to say, he did not announce "his" position or "his" doctrine of evil. He did not evade the theological task by announcing his "definition of the God-concept," as if by defining matters, you solve something. What had come before him were two sorts of Judaic theologizing.

First were "scholarly" accounts of the "mind of the rabbis" and other efforts at a historical account of what some interesting Jews have thought in the past. These accounts exhibit many conceptual flaws, but chief among them is their unrelenting historicism. So far as the "scholarly" theologians have a theological agendum, it is to describe what those they regard as normative have had to say. The unstated corollary is that since the biblical or Talmudic authorities indeed are authoritative, when we have found out what they said, we have an account of Jewish theology— what we are supposed to affirm. That is why, in Heschel's days at Jewish Theological Seminary, the course in "theology" consisted of Louis Finkelstein's comments on *The Fathers According to Rabbi Nathan,* rabbinic text probably of medieval origin. By contrast Heschel was reduced to teaching elementary courses in medieval biblical exegesis to beginning students in the Seminary's Teachers Institute, a college-age program, but not allowed to teach his own theology in the Rabbinical School. To make this point clear, let me compare it to permitting a great brain surgeon to teach only comparative zoology to college sophomores. Heschel was not allowed to teach the subject of which he was the international master.

The then-*doyen* of Talmud-studies, Saul Lieberman, time and again belittled Heschel's work, both to his face and behind his back. But Lieberman never understood the difference between objective scholarly judgment and his private (and mean-spirited) feelings against other scholars, old and young. In the range of Lieberman's sharp tongue, Heschel was the most distinguished, but not the sole, target. But Heschel was close at hand. So, as "rabbi" of the Jewish Theological Seminary synagogue, Lieberman refused for decades to give to Heschel a certain liturgical honor that, to Heschel alone, bore deep personal meaning, in the context of Heschel's own liturgical tradition. It is a mark of the character of a whole generation of Jewish scholars of Judaism that Heschel suffered the abuse, both personal and intellectual, that he received. But he suffered it with dignity, because he knew who he was, and who, and what, the other side was too. He went about his work. Today nearly all of those who hated him and could not appreciate his achievement are dead and en route to complete oblivion. Their work is consulted occasionally, but studied never, providing no model for future generations. Heschel lives on in work that enriches one generation after another. Still,

Heschel's career at that school permanently stains the honor and good name of the school and condemns the second-rate and small-minded people who treated him in that way. Long after they are forgotten, Heschel will serve as a rich resource for Jewish thought and self-understanding. Their work where it bore any value at all now passes onward through the works of those who use it. His work will continue to stand on its own, to instruct in its terms for its purposes.

The second kind of theology that preceded him was done primarily by people trained in philosophy, particularly philosophy or religion, sometimes also social thought. They would posit a static, concrete, one-dimensional "thing" called "Judaism." They would produce a set of propositions, "Judaism and . . ." statements, to show often, as in the case of Herman Cohen, that "Judaism and German culture" constitute the highest achievement of man. In the instance of Mordecai Kaplan, knowledge of philosophy of religion in the model of John Dewey led to abandoning the effort to think within, and through, the classical litera-ture of Judaic religious experience, though Kaplan knew this literature and has given evidence of deeply understanding it. Other Jewish theolo-gians had and have a much less satisfactory knowledge of the classical literature to begin with. Heschel told me that Martin Buber, for instance, received his first copy of the Talmud from Heschel on the occasion of his 60th birthday, and thanked Heschel, saying: "I've always wanted one." For a person to claim to be a Jewish authority and not to know the Talmud is simply a contradiction in terms. Rosenzweig, much more celebrated than Heschel, exhibits a very thin Jewish education indeed, which accounts for the external, homiletical and evangelical quality in his writing. He had to convert to Judaism at a mature age. He knew why he affirmed, but he had to learn what. His writing, in contrast to Heschel's, exhibits little profound learning. That is not to diminish the achievement of Buber and Rosenzweig, except in the comparison with Heschel. For they drew upon shallow pools but he upon the deepest springs of the Judaic spirit.

What is remarkable is that Heschel knew everything he had to know to do what he wanted to do. First, let us survey simply the subjects on which he composed interesting books: the prophets, Talmudic theology of revelation, medieval philosophies (many), medieval mysticism, Has-idism, American Jewish community life, Zionism, the life of Jewish piety (Sabbath, prayerbook). In point of fact, there is not a single record of

Jewish religious experience, not a single moment in the unfolding of the Jewish spirit, which Heschel did not take into his own being and reshape through the crucible of his own mind and soul. Heschel also knew the main issues of modern and contemporary philosophy of religion and followed Protestant theology. He knew and respected Tillich and Niebuhr, and they knew and respected his work. (I do not think he was equally close, in the period of his active theological work, down to the early 1960s, to any Catholic theologian, though later on, primarily on a political basis, several entered his life. I cannot find in Heschel's major writings, however, an equivalent interest.) Much of Heschel's theology constituted a post-Kantian exercise, through the medium of Judaic religious experience, in a solution of the problems raised by Hume and answered by Kant.

Heschel's argument was intended, as I said, to move from philosophy of religion, relevant everywhere, to natural theology, deriving from the sources of the being of humanity in general (ontology), and upward to Judaic theology, revealed by God in the Torah to Moses, our rabbi. Heschel proposed to demonstrate that this way that was natural to humanity led not merely to God or generalized religiosity, but *specifically* to Sinai and to Torah—yet not through a leap of faith. What philosophy of religion did not attempt was the apology for the specific claims of revealed religion. What theology did not dare to do was to join natural theology to Torah. This is what Heschel proposed to accomplish—a very brave venture. His argument begins in this world, with that part of men and women left untouched by the critique of the Enlightenment: emotions and responses. He reaches into the inner life and looks for those elements which, present and accepted in a this-worldly framework, speak of the next world and testify to God, to the image of God impressed upon man and woman. People exhibit the capacity for wonder and awe. How so? It means that not everything can be explained. The opposite of religion is taking things for granted. Wonder is a "form of thinking," an act that goes beyond knowledge.

The next stage is to take seriously the awesomeness of our very capacity to think and to respond, to wonder: "The most incomprehensible fact is the fact that we comprehend at all." Out of wonder comes awe, out of awe, wisdom: "Awe is an intuition for the creaturely dignity of all things . . . a realization that things not only are what they are, but also stand for something absolute. Awe is a sense for the transcendence, for the reference everywhere to Him who is beyond all things." Awe precedes faith and is at its root—but itself testifies to its implication: "The ineffable is there before we form an idea of it. Yet what we affirm is the intellectual certainty that in the face of nature's grandeur and mystery we must respond with awe. What we infer from it is not a psychological state but a fundamental norm of human consciousness." This I take to be the ontological response to Kant. This mode of argumentation is striking, for it combines two things. First, Heschel looks for natural experiment accessible to everyone. But second, he claims that the experience constitutes the experiential aspect of the supernatural, of Torah. Therefore all things are to be linked to the Hebrew Scriptures, to Talmudic literature, to the holy writings of Judaism, above all to the experience of Torah in life.

Heschel thus proposes to move from the shared experience of ordinary people to the distinctive truth of Torah. This constitutes his primary effort to locate the foundations of natural theology and to endow them with supernatural and revelatory meaning. When I offered this two-stage interpretation of his thinking to Heschel, he said, "Yes, you're right. But there is a third stage." I asked, "What is left out?" He said: "I won't tell you. I'm working on it now. But you're right as far as you go." Now, alas, we shall never know. Clearly, his theology was an exploration of ontological issues, not epistemological ones. But where he would have gone had he lived, I cannot say.

The Christian world knew Abraham Joshua Heschel chiefly in his roles of the 1960s as a holy man and politician. In his day he was a hero to the religious sector of the left, which knew nothing of the man or the intellect, but found in Heschel an evocative symbol, a kind of authentic prophet. Heschel himself fostered that impression and enjoyed the adulation of circles responsive to his political stance, even though along with the adulation came exploitation. That his trip to Selma in the civil rights cause of the 1960s proved a disaster to the Jewish communities of Alabama and Mississippi hardly registered within his liberal and radical constituency; they were safe at home and able to enjoy a clean conscience. The Jews in the South paid a heavy price in renewed anti-Semitism. To Heschel, however, in the place and time in which he lived out his days, these were critical, important, prophetic actions. They were expressions of his religious faith no less than his putting on of tefillin in the morning and reciting the creed, *Hear, Israel, the Lord, our God, is the one God*. The opposition to the war in Viet Nam, in which he followed Martin Luther King as well, derived from the same profound religious feeling. Heschel's good heart and good will led him, in the 1960s, to ignore the complexities of social issues and the difficulty of discovering, in political life, the entirely moral or the entirely immoral position. Those of us who see the issues of his time differently, knowing as we do how it all ended—with the ruin of Viet Nam and the boat people and the murder of half of the population of Cambodia—can blame him and the many for whom he spoke for everything but a sullied spirit. He and those he embodied believed in a redeemed world, but all about were the stigmata of unredemption. It was his glory to be wrong, but—we now know—he was profoundly wrong in the greater part of his politics.

The Heschel that—we now know—endures is in his books, and that is exactly as it should be. For Heschel spent most of his time in his study, not on the political platform or in dramatic symbolic gestures of protest, and he was above all else a very serious intellectual. None of this shows in the public Heschel, but it will endure. Heschel's authentic existence, not his public role as a shaman for the left, focused upon his theological and scholarly enterprise. He was an exceptionally poor teacher in the classroom, but a brilliant teacher in his study. As guide, counselor and friend, he raised up many disciples, now prominent on the right and on the left as well. In the classroom he was on the public platform, and this brought out the worst in him, a kind of second-rate academic showmanship. In his study he was fully himself, a good talker, a good listener, with wellsprings of sympathy and, above all, infinite learning. He stood for theology in a Jewish community which then did not know the importance of theology. To the Jews "theology" is defined in the narrowest way, as "proofs for the existence of God" or, at most, discussion of the nature of God. For the many larger religious questions subsumed, for Christians, under "theology," the Jews have different words. They speak of "Jewish thought" or "philosophy of Judaism," and very commonly of "ideology"—all of them highly secular words. And, in Conservative Judaism today, they still do, and in consequence still rehearse stupefying banalities set forth in words dead before they hit the page. Heschel insisted on calling his work theology and bravely did so in the midst of secular and highly positivistic scholars, who measured the world in terms of philological learning and thought of theology as

something you do on Purim, when you're drunk. It somehow is not
Torah—only philology and other safe, antiseptic subjects are Torah.

This made Heschel's life as a theologian difficult and sometimes bitter.
He had not only to establish the legitimacy of his endeavor and to
vindicate its value, but also to do it—define the work, carry it out,
defend it and change the entire context in which it is to be received. No
wonder he found his political role so easy. He did not have to define the
task, or create the audience, or establish the occasion. He had only to
come and radiate sanctity. By contrast, his everyday task was exceedingly
challenging. Anyone who thinks that I exaggerate should read the
reviews of his theological books. I doubt that, in his lifetime, any
important theologian has found so little understanding of his task, let
alone of his achievement of it, as Heschel. He was called a poet and a
mystic, "un-Jewish," and dismissed as a vapid rhetorician. I cannot recall
a single review (though there may have been some) which both understood what he was about and offered interesting critical comment. Either
he was dismissed or he was given uncritical, often unintelligent, praise.
But after death, much has changed for Heschel, as he grows in stature
precisely because of those writings that, in his lifetime, found so slight a
comprehending hearing, and still less appreciation.

It is the frailty of the man that makes his achievement great. His
extraordinary learning was no birthright. He worked hard. His writings
were not dictated into his ear by a kindly angel. He struggled. His ideas
were born in anguish and intellectual daring and courage. He was tough-
minded, and his was a luminous intelligence. This should not be obscured by the public, and more easily accessible, personality. For those
within the Jewish tradition, holiness comes of learning, the luminous
stands before and points toward the numinous. Heschel knew this: he
spent the largest part of his life in his study because he was a rabbi and
knew what a rabbi was meant to be and do. In a Jewish community by
and large indifferent to Judaism and hermetically closed to learning and
religiosity, led by men of wealth among the laity, or of an attentuated
and false, manufactured charisma among the clergy, Heschel stood for
something alien and authentic. To remember him by encountering his
words once more is to learn what we are not, but might become—"in
our image, after our likeness."

Chapter 2

THE INTELLECTUAL ACHIEVEMENT OF ABRAHAM JOSHUA HESCHEL

L et us examine a single book. It is his *Theology of Ancient Judaism (TORAH MIN HASHSHAMAYIM BEASPAKLARIA SHEL HAD-DOROT, volume II.* (London and New York: Soncino Press, 1965. 440 pp.)), which appeared nearly twenty-five years ago. This work continued Heschel's study of the major trends of thinking in rabbinic Judaism. As we noted in connection with his theology, Heschel devoted most of his scholarly and theological career to the problem of revelation and inspiration. Indeed, if that fact is understood, one can penetrate into the heart of both Heschel's scholarship and his theology. His major works (dealing with the prophets, rabbinic Judaism, Saadia, Ibn Gabirol, Maimonides, Hasidism, modern philosophy of religion and philosophy of religion and philosophy of Judaism) centered upon the theme, narrowly defined, of religious knowledge, but broadly viewed, of the encounter between the human being and God in real, as opposed to (merely) intellectual life.

As I have stressed in Chapter One, Heschel's was both a theological and a scholarly enterprise. If he had not chosen to pursue scholarly themes, such as the one before us, he could have made an extraordinary contribution to philosophical theology alone. Indeed, many of his readers are quite unaware of his scholarship in biblical, talmudic and Hasidic themes. Similarly, if Heschel had chosen the way of systematic historical scholarship alone, he would have reached great heights. He sought both to recover the historical theology of Israel, and to contribute to Judaism's philosophical theology.

In order to appreciate what Heschel achieved in this work, one must keep in mind that until then we had no really adequate explanation of the thought, of theology, behind the numerous sayings of talmudic rabbis dealing with matters of faith. We had a number of jerry-built structures, which impose upon talmudic Judaism alien categories borrowed from other traditions (as in the case of Moore, in the preceding essay). We had some excellent anthologies. There also were rather confused and functionally almost useless "harmonies" of talmudic ideas which, speaking from a historical viewpoint, never in fact existed in the mind of any one human being, or in any one time or place. These studies all assumed that the literature of a period of five or six hundred years may be expounded as a whole, as if everyone who said anything used language and possessed ideas that remained constant over the whole period. If you can take seriously the proposition that from Chaucer to Joyce we can speak meaningfully of "the English literary mind," then you can work with such categories.

Until Heschel produced these volumes we were in the situation of medieval Ptolemaic astronomy. We had a great deal of data, very accurately understood, and some obviously unsatisfactory, cumbersome theories for explaining them. The cycles and epicycles have multiplied beyond belief. We had no simple realistic, historically verifiable and economical way of explaining our data. Like Copernicus, therefore, Heschel tried to set the world on its head. He assumed, first of all, that certain central figures should be made the focus of a historical-theological study, to see whether in a tentative fashion we may come to an adequate principle underlying and unifying their sayings and disputes. He therefore cited numerous teachers, but stayed (in Volume I) mainly within the framework of the issues commented on by Akiba and Ishmael. Secondly, he allowed the disputes of Akiba and Ishmael to provide the substance of his discussion, and did not claim to explain all of "talmudic Judaism." He looked behind and beyond the details of their immediate discussions, however, to discover general interpretive principles not only to explain one or another detail, but to illuminate the central underlying issues separating two seminal men.

Heschel found such a hermeneutical principle, outwardly a deceptively simple one, but one which is most helpful. Heschel held that the disputes

between Akiba and Rabbi Ishmael are based upon a fundamental disa-
greement on the nature of revelation and religion. Ishmael held that the
religion comes from God to the human being, and therefore lays stress
upon the realities of language known to the human being. Religion is a
matter which the human being's reason can comprehend, and his life
express. Its terms are the language of this world, and its vocabulary is
the raw material of daily life. God is transcendent, beyond the world,
and all that we can know of God and God's will is its this-worldly
manifestation. Akiba, on the other hand, held that God is immanent,
and that this world, as much as the next, contains the Presence. Therefore, revelation may speak in a language not wholly human in origin or
intention, and speak not only of the world as the human being commonly understands it, but also of mysteries, of realities beyond those we
can see and touch. Religion is a matter not only for the human being's
comprehension, but stands in some measure beyond his capacity to
understand. The Torah speaks of a reality that may transcend the world.
Thus immanental religion stands opposed to transcendental religion,
mysticism to rationalism, neo-Platonism to Aristotelianism, and Akiba
to Ishmael.

This brief description can mean nothing to readers if they think that
all Heschel did is to impose upon two Tannaim some category other than
any yet tried. What is extraordinary is that, working within these
categories, Heschel was able to organize and to make sense out of the
great mass of otherwise discrete and sometimes arcane material. He did
not try to impose an external and irrelevant heuristic principle, but
demonstrate over and over again that in one concrete dispute after
another there are to be located the abstract principles of immanentalism
versus transcendentalism. What is astonishing is that after a while, the
participating reader can easily and accurately predict the position on a
specific question to be taken by Akiba and Ishmael and their followers,
given merely a statement of the question.

In Volume I of this project, Heschel treated the interpretation of
revelation, the nature of miracles, sacrifices, the Presence, suffering,
theological language, and so forth. At each point he examined not only
the numerous relevant sayings of the two chief figures, but those of
others in their respective schools. Some readers of Volume I may have
found excessive the many quotations provided by the author, but in
establishing his thesis, completeness, order and precision were essential.

Without actually examining the evidence, one can hardly be aware of how intrinsically valid was Heschel's hermeneutical principle. Without seeing how thorough and well-disciplined has been his study of talmudic literature, one cannot fully appreciate his achievement in bringing some order and sense to it. The more interesting critique of volume I lay in its subject-matter, called "aggadah," that is, theology. Some argued that *aggadah,* meaning here religion and theology as these words are understood today, is irrelevant. Judaism has no dogma, only *halakhah*— which means a law, a pattern of actions.

However, Heschel maintained, Jews are not robots, contented with mindless, thoughtless repetition of meaningless action. They have always, even the most stupid among them, been thoughtful people, who acted because of a faith, however naive or primitive or uncritical, and not in a spiritual or intellectual vacuum. Hence the aggadic parts of the Talmud and cognate literature have been included in our tradition, not because ancient academicians could not find a better entertainment for their idle hours, as some exceptionally dull-souled expositors have maintained.

Heschel demonstrated in these volumes that the rabbis were just as serious, just as penetrating, and just as self-consistent in theology as in law, for precisely the same reason, and in much the same the human being. He showed that just as the talmudic Rabbis were men of formidable consistency in their legal opinions, so were they rational and fully sensible in their theological ones. And he accomplished this not by preaching or argument, but by a close and careful study of sources. Until Heschel we had to accept the judgment that the Rabbis were not really interested in ideas, only in law. That their main interest in law was shown by their lack of principled thought on other issues. After Heschel we no longer had need to take seriously such a shallow opinion, for he demonstrated with truly halakhic precision that the Rabbis of the Talmud were at least as concerned with theology as they were with law. That represents his greatest contribution in the work on ancient theology.

In Volume II, Heschel concentrated upon the major issues of revelation as they emerge in rabbinic theology. Having established the existence of two great and contrary principles by which revelation could be conceived, those of Akiba and of Ishmael, he traced how the Rabbis thought about revelation in concrete and mostly exegetical images, stressing the specific tests which embody their basic theses. In many places, moreover, he moved far beyond the central theses themselves, in order to provide a fuller and richer account of rabbinic ideas on revelation. He was not, therefore, bound by the limits of his original presupposition, however fruitful and penetrating it is. The major themes of this volume are first, the idea of Torah in heaven, its pre-existence, its form, how it was written. Second, he speaks of Moses' ascent to heaven. Akiba's view was that Moses actually went up, to heaven, and Heschel treats not only his ascent but the ascents of Enoch and Elijah. Third, he examines the idea of the descent of the Kavod. He considers fruther the idea of "Torah from heaven," carefully analyzing rabbinic ideas on the substance of Torah, and on the Ten Commandments as the whole Torah. He shows how the concept of Torah was broadened and extended in the Akiban school. He considers the views which the Rabbis declared to be heretical, such as that Moses made it up himself, that less than the whole Penta-teuch was revealed, and the like. He examines the two approaches to Mosaic Revelation. Ishmael's school held that Moses often paraphrased God's will in his own words. In the Akiban school everything was believed to be in the precise form spoken by the divinity, without exception.

Heschel turns to a very elaborate analysis of the figure of Moses, including attention to what he himself, by contrast to the Lawgiver, was believed to have said, the school of Ishmael tending to delimit, and that of Akiba to extend the role of the divinity in revelation. He shows that the two schools differed fairly consistently on whether the prophet was a partner in, or merely an inert vessel of, revelation, with the Akibans holding the latter view. The greatness, prophecy and literary achieve-ments of Moses produced varying schools of thought, which are traced, in general, to the underlying principles elucidated in Volume I. Heschel discussed the prophetic foundations of other books, such as Job; proph-ecies which were lost or suppressed, and the like. This is clearly a work of gigantic proportions, for Heschel not merely demonstrated that the Rabbis were as serious about and as consistent in theological as in legal issues, but he recovered from the vast literature of ancient and medieval Judaism just how those issues were shaped concretely in their exegetical and heuristic setting. Sometimes the reader may feel that in trying to prove that the Rabbis were "talmudic" even about aggadah, Heschel himself has composed a highly "talmudic" account, but mostly he does not.

However, I found a number of difficulties in first studying this volume, and it is now clear that, within Heschel's lasting legacy and enduring contribution, his work on talmudic theology will not take a primary place. Indeed, even now it is a mere curiosity, and that is for a number of reasons, some minor, some not. First are the minor ones, which are still worth noting. The publisher is responsible for one of them. Specifically, it was, and remains, deplorable that the publisher did not prepare an index, a list of sources quoted or cited (of which there are hundreds), a survey of sages mentioned and a complete bibliography. Heschel should have done it, with student help, on his own. The absence of these normally commonplace aids greatly diminishes the usefulness of the volume for reference and research. However carefully we may study it, we cannot remember every place where Heschel treats a given text or idea, and since this work will remain absolutely essential for all future studies of rabbinic theology, the human beingy future students are going to regret the failure to provide these basic tools.

Second, and equally minor if more than merely annoying, I think Heschel quoted in full far too many sources. It was one thing to prove, in Volume I, that the sources said what Heschel said they said. In Volume II, it becomes a burden. The book has the quality of a scrapbook; Heschel did not really assimilate the mass of materials. While they are not all easily available, that is no reason to quote each and every one verbatim. Some could have been summarized; some paraphrased briefly; some merely cited. Many sources make the same point. Indeed, whole chapters or sections merely provide new illustrations of an idea already quite adequately set forth and abundantly demonstrated. Since this is a relatively long book, one might have expected that it would seek to treat tangential or minor points with some brevity. This unfortunately is not the case. In many places the narrative simply stands still; no new ideas emerge, and one merely reconsiders what the author has already made quite clear. Perhaps Heschel thought that he would prove to his detractors by quoting lots of sources that he, too, knew lots of sources, and since, for the other side's part, that is what theological and legal studies consisted of—citation and paraphrase with unsystematic observations on this and that, called hiddushim—he did the same thing. But the upshot is an unreadable book.

Alas, it is also not a very easy book. I wish Heschel had provided a more extensive abstract presentation of the basic issues and ideas of

Volume II. He very frequently assumed that the main idea comes across quite clearly from the text he is quoting and briefly commenting on. This is not the case. The felicitous presentation of the basic theses of Volume I is not duplicated here. Much is quoted; little is spelled out in thoughtful, one might say theological, detail. The introduction, by contrast to the fifty-nine pages in Volume I, is only six pages long, and consists mainly of a polemic on the importance of theology. No one who doubts that is going to study this book. In all, this was not a very professional undertaking.

These technical problems troubled me far less than the more fundamental methodological issues unresolved in Volume II. Volume I is both a theological and a historical work. Heschel was interested both in exposing the inner elements of a major complex of ideas, and in finding their historical settings in the great academies. On the whole, the line between theology and history was clearly drawn and almost never violated. Here, by contrast, I found a frequent confusion of historical and theological language. Heschel rightly treats the medieval and early modern exemplars of the basic principles under study, showing how the issues elicited continuing attention and hermeneutical dispute in later times. This is a thoroughly valid, historical-theological investigation. He also pays some attention to discussions of these same problems in late antiquity, but here I found the treatment most inadequate. He discusses Philo, but I could find slight evidence that he had made a close and careful study of Philonic *scholarship*. Like many other scholars of his day, Heschel had a tendency to think that scholarship began with his own work, and in his discussion of Philo he was simply ignorant.

A major concern is the figure of Moses. Yet, how Moses was described in contemporary Christian thought, which had to confront the same theological issues concerning revelation as did the Rabbis, is never considered. The figure of Moses in the Fourth Gospel, for example, presents a most complex and subtle problem. One should imagine that men practically contemporaneous with the Rabbis and living in the same country, touched upon themes which concerned the "philosophers" of Judaism as well. The Samaritans, who were certainly a major element in Jewish Palestine in this period, actually centered their religious thought upon the figure of Moses. Indeed, Heschel's stress on the Mosaic figure recalls more than anything else that of the fourth century Samaritan teacher Marqah. When discussing the state of theological ideas in a given period, one must, I think, pay close attention to how kindred groups treated these same ideas. Here one ought to consider whether the Rabbis were influenced by the conceptions of those living close at hand, such as, in this instance, the Samaritans and the Christians.

Heschel treats a great mélange of medieval philosophical and Kabbalistic works in the very context of his historical and theological investigation, but never makes explicit the relations between them. He seems to suppose that the theological issue is what makes it possible to compare the Zohar and the Talmud, and this may well be so; but I do not see how the Zohar (or Maimonides for that matter) can be used historically to illuminate the theology of late antiquity. This is thoroughly unhistorical, confusing, and hopelessly uncritical. It renders the book a mere curiosity, as I said, though, I hasten to add, it is hardly the only book on the bookshelves that we preserve mainly as a record of how not to do things.

The simplest flaw is what renders the book beyond all use. Within talmudic materials, Heschel mostly ignores serious historical issues, accepting as completely factual accounts about the Rabbis which by no means reveal what was happening, but only what later figures thought had happened earlier. I was disappointed to learn, for example, that Heschel regards as quite historical the accounts of Yohanan ben Zakkai's disputes with the Sadducees, which are almost certainly very late and imaginative at best. If one is elucidating an idea, he or she need not pay much attention to the historical setting in which the idea was manifested. However, if, like Heschel, he wants to trace the development of that idea by specific schools and teachers, he cannot very well ignore major historical issues inherent in the sources. Using historical language requires adherence to the canons of historical inquiry. Heschel did not really know those canons and did not try to learn them. That is why this work will not make the contribution that Heschel's genuinely interesting and original ideas ought to have gained for it.

A pioneering work such as this was bound to reveal not only new information but also new methodological issues. In noting the chief of these, namely the unsatisfactory state of Heschel's thought on the relationship between historical and theological research, I do not wish to leave a false impression. This book had to be written, for Volume I required a sequel such as this, in which the great issues would be not merely set forth, but spelled out. If Heschel had only isolated the exegetical issues in which major theological principles could be discerned, as he does here, Volume II would have been an exceptionally important book. Having seen that the two great theologies of revelation held by rabbinic schools would yield numerous concrete problems, he has provided an exemplary demonstration of painstaking research concerning precisely what was said and why. I do not think he has overstated his case, nor has he transformed a very fine insight into a blunt axe, with which to chop apart and mechanically rearrange the sources. The richness of this volume testifies to the subtlety and sensitivity of his mind. But it also tells us one of the principal flaws in Heschel's scholarly work, which was inattention to issues of method.

Let me now conclude with a general judgment. Heschel's theological and scholarly articles and books are as vivid and important today as they were when he wrote them, not because they contain information, though they do in abundance, but because they preserve and transmit wit, intelligence, imagination, daring, intellectual honesty. All of his books are now in print, and those originally in other languages are now being translated into Enlish. True, it is easy to find fault with aspects of his scholarship, not only in detail but in a fundamental way, and in the area in which I work, I have done so. His scholarship on history of ideas in talmudic times rests on premises that are undemonstrated and uncritical and hopelessly wrong. In his work on Hasidic masters, Heschel gathered and arranged information but lacked the conceptual tools to produce a work of analytical quality. His writing on mysticism in Judaism laid somewhat heavier stress on appreciation than on the framing of interesting questions for study. In these and other ways, Heschel's extraordinary range of interest carried him beyond his intellectual depth and the capacity of his mental equipment. But that is what marks the greatness of the *ouevre:* the power of wit, daring, imagination, the intellectual courage, the ambition, and, above all, the love for Israel, the Jewish people, that reaches full and complete expression in love for the learning of Israel in the aspect of eternity. And it is that profound and animating love that comes to expression in the papers gathered here.

That is why, as a scholar, Heschel will be remembered long after other scholars of the mid-twentieth century have been forgotten, the great and the mighty, the influential and important, the pretentious and the pompous, God love them all, God forgive them all. Heschel gave his life for love of Israel, and because of that, Heschel's life work endures. It is because Heschel set the standard—humanly and intellectually—by which all others are found to be wanting, some in this, some in that.

Yes, I remember you, Abraham Heschel. I remember you in death as in life. You are the one, the only one, who in this field of learning vindicated the scholarly life of learning as an exercise in the art of being human, mortal in God's image, after God's likeness. For you learning formed the arena for the expression of conscience and character and also as a challenge to the human will and intelligence. Not for you was scholarship confused with mere power-politics let alone the celebration of personalities through the celebration of mere knowledge. Yours was, and therefore still is, the quest for understanding in search of faith, and faith in the service of God, and so it is for us all. That is why those of us who understand appeal to your example in validation of the things for which we have lived our lives too.

Part II

HESCHEL SPEAKS

Chapter 3

A TIME OF RENEWAL

Who is a Jew? A witness to the transcendence and presence of God; a person in whose life *Abraham* would feel at home, a person for whom *Rabbi Akiba* would feel deep affinity, a person of whom the Jewish martyrs of all ages would not be ashamed.

Who is a Jew? A person whose integrity *decays* when unmoved by the knowledge of wrong done to *other* people.

Who is a Jew? A person in travail with God's dreams and designs; a person to whom God is a challenge, not an abstraction. He is called upon to know of God's stake in history; to be involved in the sanctification of time and in building of the Holy Land; to cultivate passion for justice and the ability to experience the arrival of Friday evening as an event.

Who is a Jew? A person who knows how to recall and to keep alive what is holy in our people's past and to cherish the promise and the vision of redemption in the days to come.

How to assure the survival of the Jews? The best prophet of the future is our past. How did we meet the assaults and challenges of change and decay, of persecution and contempt, and survive as a people down through centuries? We had no might, no allies, no friends, no territory, no visible establishment to keep us intact, loyal, whole. The answer often given that we were held together by the strength of the concept or idea of One God, and that allegiance to it overcame the power of kings and tyrants as well as the contempt and hatred of neighbors, is a fume of fancy. The Jews were often attacked in the name of other attractive and powerful myths and ideas, and still resisted the temptations of conversion and assimilation. Moreover, man is made of flesh and blood, he has a heart as well as a mind. Could man live by abstraction alone?

What kept our integrity alive was a commitment of heart and soul, love that goes with character and conviction.

The wisest answer to the enigma of our survival may be found in the famous saying that God, Israel and Torah are one. The three realities are inseparable, interdependent, and the commitment to these realities is appreciation and love.

A life in which one of these commitments is missing becomes a tripod with two legs. And yet the three are not of equal standing and must be seen in the proper order of importance. Confusion in the order—a malady that often occurs in history—results in distorting fundamental perspectives, vital values.

Classical Reform Judaism concentrated on ethical monotheism as the essence of Judaism, disregarding Torah and Israel. Secular nationalism has made the people of Israel its central concern, disregarding God and Torah. While modern ultra-orthodoxy, in its eagerness to defend obser-vance, tends to stress the supremacy of the Torah, equating Torah with *Shulhan Aruch,* in disregard of God and Israel, frequently leading to religious behaviorism.

Implicit in my opening statements about Abraham and Rabbi Akiba is the necessity of living in accord with our tradition; of living as much as possible—and perhaps a little more than possible—according to the discipline of faith and halacha.

The Zionist idea embraces not only the land but also the people, and by people we mean both the biological reality as well as the essential thoughts and commitments it stands for. *"Der Zionismus ist die Heimkehr zum Judentum noch vor der Ruckkehr ins Judenland,"* "Zionism is the return to Judaism even before returning to the land of the Jews," said Herzl, in his opening-address at the first congress. Indeed, Judaism without *halacha* is like a tree cut off at its roots. In fact, the disparagement of faith and Halacha threatens the very existence of our people. There is danger which calls for most urgent attention. For more than 1800 years we were a people without a land. Now we face the possibility of a land without a people.

Today all we have are either individuals rummaging for leftovers of the heritage of a people perished, of communities extinguished, or of individuals untroubled by agony over a thousand years vanished, over countless souls cut off from us, thinking that the present moment is the whole, that the self can live without a past.

And yet what we know about Abraham and of Rabbi Akiba is not only law. In fact, most of what is contained in the *Chumash* or *Tenach* is non-legal ideas or tales. Similarly rabbinic literature contains both *halacha* and *agada,* and the thinking of Judaism can only be adequately understood as striving for a synthesis between receptivity and spontaneity, a harmony of *halacha* and *agada.*

There is a general assumption that the Rabbis were naïve, simple minded, and unreflective people. How such an assumption can be generalized in regard to such a galaxy of men whose subtle and profound judgments in *halacha* have remained an intellectual challenge to all future students is difficult to see. It is refuted by any unbiased analysis of their *agadic* sayings, which clearly indicate that their inner life was neither simple nor idyllic.

Halacha represents the strength to shape one's life according to a fixed pattern; it is a form-giving force. *Agada* is the expression of man's ceaseless striving which often defies all limitations. *Halacha* is the rationalization and schematization of living; it defines, specifies, sets measure and limit, placing life into an exact system. *Agada* deals with man's ineffable relations to God, to other men, and to the world. *Halacha* deals with details, with each commandment separately; *agada* with the whole of life, with the totality of religious life. *Halacha* deals with the law; *agada* with the meaning of the law. *Halacha* deals with subjects that can be expressed literally; *agada* introduces us to a realm which lies beyond the range of expression. *Halacha* teaches us how to perform common acts; *agada* tells us how to participate in the eternal drama. *Halacha* gives us knowledge; *agada* exaltation.

Halacha gives us norms for action; *agada* vision of the ends of living. *Halacha* prescribes, *agada* suggests; *halacha* decrees, *agada* inspires; *halacha* is definite; *agada* is allusive.

The terminology of *halacha* is exact, the spirt of *agada* is poetic, indefinable. *Halacha* is immersed in tradition, *agada* is the creation of the heart.

Halacha, by necessity, deals with the laws in the abstract, regardless of the totality of the person. It is *agada* that keeps on reminding us that the purpose of performance is to transform the performer, that the purpose of observance is to train us in achieving spiritual ends. "It is well known that the purpose of all *mitzvot* is to purify the heart, for the heart is the essence." The chief aim and purpose of the *mitzvot* performed with our body is to arouse our attention to the *mitzvot* that are fulfilled with the mind and heart, for these are the pillars on which the service of God rests.

The *halachot* refine man's character, *agadot* "sanctify the name of the Holy One blessed be He among us."

To maintain that the essence of Judaism consists exclusively of *halacha* is as erroneous as to maintain that the essence of Judaism consists exclusively of *agada*. The interrelationship of *halacha* and *agada* is the very heart of Judaism. *Halacha* without *agada* is dead, *agada* without *halacha* is wild. Pan-*agadic* Judaism is doomed to extinction.

Halacha is the body of Torah, and the Torah of Israel was preserved only by the power of *halacha,* by the power of the forms of *mitzvot* and good deeds; and all of the poetry and mysticism, thoughts and beliefs, survived only by its merit. *Agada* cleaves, is linked to *halacha,* and has no existence without *halacha. Agada* is as a flame which depends upon the hot coal of the *halacha,* and he who separates the two extinguishes the light of Judaism which burns in the flame. To sum up: He who says, I cherish only *agada,* will eventually forfeit what he cherishes.

"If it is your will to know Him who spoke and the world came into being, learn *agada.* For by doing so you will perceive Him who spoke and the world came into being and cleave to His ways." The voice of *halacha* is powerful, its voice breaks the cedars; *agada* is still a small voice. *Halacha* is like a flow of mighty waters; *agada* is the spirit of God hovering over the face of the waters.

And so, *halachic* authorities, due to historical and sociological factors, not only gained the upper hand but even frequently fostered disparagement of *agada*. In many periods of history acumen stood higher than intuition, *pilpul* suppressed poetry. While *halacha* triumphed, *agada* declined.

The land where halachic acumen reached its climax was Babylonia, while the most exquisite and profound *agada* came into full bloom in the land of Israel.

Wtih the renewal of Jewish life in the Holy Land there was hope for a renewal of the creative power of both *halacha* and *agada*. Indeed, was it not in Safed where a renaissance of spiritual insight came to pass? Was it not in modern history that we were blessed with the marvelous flowering of *agada* in the form of hasidism?

Yet many leaders today, whose learning and zeal evoke respect, remain unaware that some of their decisions contain an element of a pan-*halachic* heresy.

This land was rebuilt by those who lived continuous renunciation of luxuries and careers for the sake of the people—*mesirat nefesh* as a way of living, not an occasional episode; renunciation not because of a negation and contempt for life, but because of love and enthusiasm for a goal.

The Zionist idea did not originate in law, in *halacha,* it originated in the soul, in love of Israel, in *agada.* Most of those who were guided exclusively and rigorously by *halacha* raised serious objections to the Zionist movement.

Modern Zionism came into being as an outburst of insight, first as a dream then as a poetic vision and finally as action. For two thousand years the Jewish soul was filled with longing, with waiting, until it responded to a call and translated two thousand years of prayer into deeds of heroic quality.

Were the men of *halacha* the only people engaged in rebuilding the land? Indeed, it was the mysterious will of God that non-observant Jews should have been the leaders endowed with foresight and the charisma to awaken our people. Saving so many lives, they led our people to the land of our Fathers.

This historic fact is of far-reaching importance in understanding the nature of Jewish existence.

From the day of the prophet Malachi, who says of Elijah that God will send him before "the great and dreadful day," Elijah was regarded as the precursor of the Messiah. The helper in distress, he also appears in our legends to sages and saints, assisting them in solving spiritual problems.

One such problem was faced by one of our great men of the past.

"Two things I love wholeheartedly: Torah and Israel. However, I am not sure which one I love more."

The response of Elijah was:

"The accepted opinion seems to suggests that the Torah is most important, as the verse reads, with regard to the Torah, The Lord made me as the beginning of his way (Prov. 8:22). However, I think that not the Torah but Israel is most important. For the prophet has said: Israel is holy to the Lord; the first fruits of his harvest (Jer. 2:3)."

Those who bless the Lord for the miraculous achievement of the Zionist goal, should seriously ponder the response of Elijah: "I think that not the Torah but Israel is most important."

One of the greatest authorities of rabbinic tradition, Rabbi Simon ben Yohai of the second century said, "It is written, For as the days of a tree shall be the days of my people (Isa. 65:22). A 'tree' signifies the Torah, as it is stated. It (e.g. the Torah) is a tree of life to them that lay hold upon it (Prov. 3:18). Now which was created for the sake of which? Was the Torah created for the sake of Israel or vice versa? Surely, the Torah was created for the sake of Israel."

One of the marvels of Jewish history is the development in our people of a quality rarely paralleled in the world: love of Torah. Yet in many of today's scholars' love of Torah, a passionate intoxication is leading to a replacement of the love of God, even suppressing love of Israel.

One gains the impression that ultra orthodoxy sometimes falls into the trap of placing the Torah above God, of placing deeds higher than reverence for God.

Yet what does our tradition teach us? It is a duty to study Torah. While it is also a duty to love God, one often gets the impression that love of Torah has replaced loved of God. And love of God involves love for his children, even children who went astray, rather than hatred of Israel which we witness in many places.

The spirit of the Rabbi of Satmar hovers over our rabbinic authorities, while the spirit of Rabbi Levi Izhak of Berditshev is taboo.

The time calls for renewal, self-purification, rejuvenation. Yet ultra orthodox establishment remains like a medieval castle, with most of its leaders engaged in building fences and walls instead of homes. As a result, the spirit of Judaism is felt by vast multitudes of young people to be a jail, not a joy. When they are forced to visit the establishment, they feel like inmates waiting to be released. The walls have many guards but there are too few windows.

The beginning of piety is compassion; the death of piety is in public demonstrations. The only way to create an atmosphere of faith is to grow spiritually in privacy.

Much of religious Judaism consists of boxes of make-up. Prayer comes from the hearts, not from politics. Before our eyes conduct and soul grow coarse. "Is there no balm in Gilead? Is there no physician there?

Why then is not the health of the daughter of my people recovered?"
(Jeremiah 8:22)

There is a rather substantial step to take: the question the exclusive
ultimacy of *halacha*. But take the step we must not only to prevent its
alienation from our people, but primarily because it is an act of seeing
the truth of our traditions.

It is a time to act for God, set aside the Torah (or the uncompromising
rigidity of some of our laws).

There was a time when we could assume the absoluteness of rigid
halachism, a time when such a stance was constructive and holy. But we
live today in a world filled with unprecedented demands on our conscience, cruel challenges to human dignity and compassion; to hide
exclusively behind the walls and fences of rigorism is to suppress our
love of Israel and understanding of God.

Many wonderful minds continue to spend their time on evolving
sophisticated pilpulistic solutions to illusory legal problems while the
burning issues are: What to do with leisure time; how to abstain from
labor on the Sabbath and not be bored; how to stop the exemption of
girls from volunteering for service in the hospitals, where people often
die because there is no nurse to offer help? I am grateful to God that in
the official establishments and hotels kashruth is observed. But what
hurts is the question why it is only required for butcher-stores to be
under religious supervision? Why not insist that banks, factories, and
those who deal in real estate should require a *hechsher* and be operated
according to religious law? When a drop of blood is found in an egg we
abhor the idea of eating the egg. But often there is more than one drop
of blood in a dollar or a lira and we fail to remind the people constantly
of the teachings of our tradition.

In the classical rabbinic decision-making the flexible human condition
not infrequently served as a factor in reaching a *halachic* decision. *Agadic*
considerations served as a basis for legal judgment.

There may be a modicum of truth that the secret of our survival is a
will to live. But the will to live only persists if there is a meaning to live
by.

There is a passion that animates the Jewish soul: a craving for ultimate
meaning. Sacred and precious as it is to fight for our people living in
dignity and security, the question that vexes the young people is: What
is the ultimate meaning of living in security and dignity? What direction

should determine our way of living? What values to cherish? What qualities to cultivate?

I believe that the ultimate meaning of existence is to be a *religious witness*.

Why a witness? Because the reestablishment of the State of Israel is an unprecedented incredible event in man's spiritual history. Its sheer existence is an exclamation of the power of the Jewish spirit over the chaos of history. Those who are present at the unfolding of such a marvel must bear witness to the world, to generations to come.

What do I mean by a religious witness? Compassion for God and reverence for man, celebration of holiness in time, sensitivity to the mystery of being a Jew, sensitivity to the presence of God in the Bible.

The most radical change that occurred in our century is the elmination of the Hebrew Bible from the greater part of the world. It is no accident that Russia, China and India are opposed to us.

Whether the people of America, England, France will retain authentic friendship for the state of Israel will depend upon whether the vision of the Prophets and the voice of the God of Israel will not completely vanish from their minds.

For the sake of God, for the sake of Israel and the world, the people of Israel must emerge as religious witnesses, to keep the consciousness of the God of Abraham and the reverence for the Bible alive in the world. Yet, this is our task. We Jews are messengers who forgot the message. How to recall the message? How to proclaim it? How to live it?

This is a golden hour in Jewish history. Young people are waiting, craving, searching for spiritual meaning. And our leadership is unable to respond, to guide, to illumine. With Zion as evidence and inspiration, as witness and example, a renewal of our people could come about.

Chapter 4

THE HOLY DIMENSION

I

To look upon religion as upon a star, sublime, distant, and inaccessible, while at the same time handling it as if it were a bank account, a matter of calculation, wherein every detail is explainable and every transaction a computable operation, is an extravagant inconsistency. To apply a paleontological method to religion as if it were a fossil, chiseled from the shale, is intellectual violence. Indeed, the routine of our scientific procedure threatens to confine living religion in a frozen system of concepts, treating it as if it were a plant brought home by an expedition from exotic lands. But will observations made on a plant that is uprooted from its soil, removed from its native winds, sunrays, and vegetal surroundings, and kept in a hothouse disclose its primordial nature? The growth in the inwardness of man that reaches and curves toward the light of God can hardly be transplanted into the shallowness of mere reflection. When taken out of the depths of piety, it exists mostly in a symbiosis with other values like beauty, justice, or truth. Torn out of its medium in human life, it is metamorphosed like a rose pressed between the pages of a book. Reduced to terms and definitions, to concepts and moral principles, religion is like a desiccated remnant of a living reality.

Religion should be studied in its natural habitat of faith and piety, in a soul where the divine is within reach of all its thoughts. From the point of view of a critical mind, to which the enigmatic holiness of religion is not a certainty but a problem, we can hardly expect more than a telescopic examination, a glimpse from afar of what is to the pious man compellingly present and overwhelmingly close. A questionnaire submitted to a chance audience will not yield the evidence we need. It is fallacious to idealize neutral and indifferent informants. Vacancy of experience cannot be compensated for by lack of bias. How do we gain an adequate concept of history or astronomy? We do not turn to the man in the street but to those who devote their life to research, to those who are trained in scientific thought and have absorbed all the data about the subject. For an adequate concept of religion, we likewise should turn to those whose mind is bent upon the spiritual, whose life *is* religion, and who are able to discern between truth and happiness, between spirit and emotion, between faith and self-reliance. Only those will apprehend religion who can probe its depth with unhalting precision, who can combine the intuition of love with rigor of method, who are able to translate the ineffable into thought and to forge the imponderable into words. It is not enough to describe the given content of religious consciousness. We have to press the man of piety with questions, compelling him to understand and unravel the meaning of what is taking place in his life as it stands at the divine horizon. While penetrating the consciousness of the pious man, we may conceive the reality behind it.

Every investigation springs out of a basic question, which sets the rudder of our mind. Yet the number of questions available for our research is limited. They are conventionally repeated in almost every scientific investigation. Like tools, they are handed down from one scholar to another. Not through our own eyes but through lenses ground by our intellectual ancestry do we look at the world. But our eyes are strained and tired of staring through spectacles worn by another generation. We are tired of overlooking entities, of squinting at their relations to other things. We want to face reality as it is and not ask only: What is its cause? What is its relation to its sources? To society? To psychological motives? We are tired of dating and comparing. Indeed, when the questions that were once keen and penetrating are worn out, the investigated object no longer reacts to the inquiry. Much depends upon the driving force of a new question. The question is an invocation of the enigma, a challenge to the examined object, provoking the answer. A new question is more than the projection or vision of a new goal; it is the first step toward it. To know what we want to know is the first prerequisite of research.

Modern man seldom faces things as they are. In the interpretation of religion our eyes are bent toward its bearing upon various realms of life rather than upon its own essence and reality. We investigate the relation of religion to economics, history, art, libido. We ask for the origin and development, for its effect upon psychical, social, and political life. We look upon religion as if it were an instrument only, not an entity. We forget to inquire: What is religion itself? In our contemplations religion as such is left in the background. In the foreground looms large and salient its subjective supplement, the human response to religion. We heed the resonance and ignore the bell, we peer into religiousness and forget religion, we behold the experience and disregard the reality that antecedes the experience. But to understand religion through the analysis of the sentiments it instills is as if instead of describing the inner value of a work of art we were to apprehend it by its effects on our mind or feelings. The essence of a thing is neither tantamount to nor commensurable with the impression it produces; what is reflected in the imagination of an individual is something altogether different from the original. The stratum of inner experience and the realm of objective reality do not lie on the same level.

II

It is hard to dismiss the popular concept that religion is a function of human nature, an avenue in the wide estate of civilization. We have been indoctrinated with the idea that religion is man's own response to a need, the result of craving for immortality, or the attempt to conquer fear. But are we not like the dwellers in the desert, who, never having seen rivers, presume that they are canals devised and constructed by man for navigation? It is true that economic needs and political factors have taught him to exploit the riverways. But are the rivers the product of human genius?

Most people assume that we feed our body to ease the pangs of hunger, to calm the irritated nerves of the empty stomach. As a matter of fact, we do not eat because we feel hungry but because the intake of food is essential for the maintenance of life, supplying the energy necessary for the various functions of the body. Hunger is the signal for eating, its occasion and regulator, not its true cause. Let us not confound the river with navigation, nutrition with hunger, or religion with the use which man makes of it.

To restrict religion to the realm of human endeavor or consciousness would imply that a person who refuses to take notice of God could isolate himself from the Omnipresent. But there is no neutrality before God; to ignore means to defy him. Even the emptiness of indifference breeds a concern, and the bitterness of blasphemy is a perversion of a regard for God. There is no vacuum of religion. Religion is neither the outgrowth of imagination nor the product of will. It is not an inner process, a feeling, or a thought, and should not be looked upon as a bundle of episodes in the life of man. To assume that religion is limited to specific acts of man, that man is religious for the duration of an experience, meditation, or performance of a ritual, is absurd. Religion is not a cursory activity. What is going on between God and man is for the duration of life.

We do not see the forest for the trees. We hear, see, feel, and think, but are unaware of our soul; we devise systems of ideas and we organize society and nature but do not comprehend the purpose of our life. Our life seems to be a confused jumble of spasmodic and disconnected events. The overwhelming desire of yesterday is forgotten today, and the monumental achievement of today will be obliterated tomorrow. Does our soul live in dispersion? Is there nothing but a medley of facts unrelated to one another, chaos camouflaged by civilization?

The pious man believes that there is a secret interrelationship among all events, that the sweep of all we are doing reaches beyond the horizon of our comprehension, that there is a history of God and man in which everything is involved.

Religion is the light in which even the momentous appears as a detail. It is the ultimateness in the face of which everything seems premature, preliminary, and transitory. The pious man lives in esteem for ultimateness, in devotion to the final amid the mortal and evanescent. Religion to him is the integration of the detail into the whole, the infusion of the momentary into the lasting. As time and space in any perception, so is the totality of life implied in every act of piety. There is an objective coherency that holds all episodes together. A man may commit a crime now and teach mathematics perfectly an hour later. But when a man prays, all he has done in his life enters his prayer.

His own heart is not the source of that light in which the pious man sees his simple words becoming signals of eternity. Hands do not build the citadel in which the pious man takes shelter when all towers reared by man are tottering. Man does not produce what is overwhelming and holy. The wonder occurs to him when he is ready to accept it.

Religion is neither a state of mind nor an achievement of the intellect. It does not rule hearts by the grace of man; its roots lie not in his inwardness. It is not an event in the soul but a matter of fact outside the soul. Even what starts as an experience *in* man transcends the human sphere, becoming an objective event outside him. In this power of transcending the soul, time, and space, the pious man sees the distinction of religious acts. If prayer were only the articulation of words, of nothing but psychological relevance and of no metaphysical resonance, nobody would in an hour of crisis waste his time by praying in self-delusion.

Religion is a bestowal, a divine grant to man. It did not come into existence to console the desperate, to guarantee immortality, or to protect society. It is a reality in itself, not a function of man.

Religion is not an exclusive event in the course of time but a permanent condition, an invisible continuity. It is not a conclusion, won from an inquiry into the nature of the universe, not an explanation of a riddle, but the living in the riddle, the effort to be the answer to the riddle one's self.

The domain of religion is the entire world, all of history, the vast as well as the tiny, the glorious as well as the trite. Everything in the universe throws its weight upon the scales of God's balance. Every deed denotes a degree in the gauge of the holy, irrespective of whether the man who performs it is aiming at this goal or not. It is just the nonritual, the secular conditions, which the prophets of Israel regarded as being a divine concern. To them the totality of human activities, social and individual, all inner and external circumstances, are the divine sphere of interest.

The desire of a pious man is not to acquire knowledge of God but to abide by him, to dedicate to him the entire life. How does he conceive the possibility of such devotion? How can man be near to God?

III

Religion, in itself, the state which exists between God and man, is neither produced by man nor dependent upon his belief; it is neither a display of human spirit nor the outgrowth of his conscience. Religion exists even if it is in this moment not realized, perceived, or acknowledged by anybody, and those who reject or betray it do not diminish its validity. Religion is more than a creed or a doctrine, more than faith or piety; it is an everlasting fact in the universe, something that exists outside knowledge and experience, an *order of being,* the *holy dimension* of existence. It does not emanate from the affections and moods, aspirations, and visions of the soul. It is not a divine force in us, a mere possibility, left to the initiative of man, something that may or may not take place, but an actuality, the inner constitution of the universe, the system of divine values involved in every being and exposed to the activity of man, the ultimate in our reality. As an absolute implication of being as an ontological entity, not as an adorning veneer for a psychical wish or for a material want, religion cannot be totally described in psychological or sociological terms.

All actions are not only agencies in the endless series of cause and effect; they also affect and concern God, with or without human intention, with or without human consent. All existence stands in a holy dimension. All existence stands before God—not only men—here and everywhere, now and at all times. Not only a vow or conversion, not only the focusing of the mind upon God, engages man to him. Life is enlistment in his service; all deeds, thoughts, feelings, and events become his concern.

Religion is, as it were, the space for the perpetual contact between God and the universe. This condition outlasts catastrophies and apostasies and constitutes God's covenant with mankind and the universe.

Man does not possess religion; he exists *in* religion. This religious existence precedes his religious experience. Creed and aspiration are the adjustments of consciousness to the holy dimension. Religion is not an election; it is the destiny of man.

Man can know God only because God knows him. Our love of God is a scant reflection of God's love for us. For every soul is a wave in the endless stream that flows out of the heart of God.

Man is an animal at heart, carnal, covetous, selfish, and vain; yet spiritual in his destiny: a vision beheld by God in the darkness of flesh and blood. Only eyes vigilant and fortified against the glaring and superficial can still perceive God's vision in the soul's horror-stricken night of falsehood, hatred, and malice.

We are prone to be impressed by the ostentatious, the obvious. The strident caterwaul of the animal fills the air, while the still small voice of the spirit is heard only in the rare hours of prayer and devotion. From the streetcar window we may see the hunt for wealth and pleasure, the onslaught upon the weak, faces expressing suspicion or contempt. On the other hand, the holy lives only in the depths. What is noble retires from sight when exposed to light, humility is extinguished in the awareness of it, and the willingness for martyrdom rests in the secrecy of the things to be. Walking upon clay, we live in nature, surrendering to impulse and passion, to vanity and arrogance, while our eyes reach out to the lasting light of truth. We are subject to terrestrial gravitation, yet we are faced by God.

In the holy dimension the spiritual is a bridge flung across a frightful abyss, while in the realm of nature the spiritual hovers like the wafted clouds, too tenuous to bear man across the abyss. When a vessel sails into a typhoon and the maw of the boiling maelstrom opens to envelop the tottering prey, it is not the pious man, engrossed in supplication, but the helmsman who intervenes in the proper sphere with proper means, fighting with physical tools against physical powers. What sense is there in imploring the mercy of God? Words do not stem the flood nor does meditation banish the storm. Prayer never entwines directly with the chain of physical cause and effect; the spiritual does not interfere with the natural order of things. The fact that man with undaunted sincerity pours into prayer the ichor of his soul springs from the conviction that there is a realm in which the acts of faith are puissant and potent, that there is an order in which things of spirit can be of momentous consequence.

There are phenomena which appear irrelevant and accidental in the realm of nature but are of great meaning in religion. To worship violence, to use brutal force, is natural, while sacrifice, humility, and martyrdom are absurd from the point of view of nature. It is in the domain of religion that a thought or a sentiment may stand out as an everlasting approach to truth, where prayers are steps toward him that never retreat.

Just as man lives in the realm of nature and is subject to its laws, so does he find himself in religion; and, just as it is impossible to take leave of nature, so it is impossible to escape the bounds of religion. Whatever happens to man, he will sever himself from the dimension of the divine neither by sin nor by stupidity, neither by apostasy nor by ignorance.

It has become a general habit to denote religion as the relationship between God and man. However, relationship expresses only a particular aspect in the existence of a subject, while religion is an essence, the meaning and totality of existence. Relationships do not touch the quick of life. Man's being related to state, society, family, etc., does not penetrate all strata of his personality. In his final solitude, in the hour of approaching death, they are blown away like chaff. It is in religion, in the holy dimension, that he abides whatever befalls him.

There is no relationship *ex nihilo,* no relationship in a void. Every relationship presupposes a setting, in which it can take place, the common ground to those associated in it. In this setting the relationship is potentially contained even before it comes into effect. It is the setting, origin, and possibility of the relationship between God and man that we call religion.

Man's life is not imprisoned in a realm wherein causality, struggle for existence, will to power, *libido sexualis,* and the craving for prestige are the only springs of action. Life is not permanently enslaved to these variable motives. It is woven into relations which run far beyond that realm. Besides the struggle for physical existence there is an effort to acquire meaning and value, an endeavor to preserve what is lasting in man, to maintain the essential in all the vicissitudes and changes. But what is the lasting in man? What is the meaning of the whole life, not of particular actions or of single episodes which happen now and then, but of existence as such?

IV

What do we mean by the concept of existence? In ascribing existence to a person, we imply that the person is more than a mere word, name, or idea and that he exists independent of us and our thinking, while what is denoted as a product of our imagination, like the chimerical Brobdingnags or the Yahoos, depends entirely on our mind; it is nonexistent when we do not think of it. However, existence so described is a negative concept, asserting what the existing is not or indicating the relation of the existing to us. What is the positive and direct meaning of existence? Even if we add that existence always implies some minimum of continuity or permanence, we gain nothing but an insight into the relation between existence and time, saying that the existing has some sequence in time. The concept of what is most fundamental is thus impregnable to analysis. It is even immune to a question, for to ask what *is* existence is almost a tautology. However, we may ask: What does existence mean to us? How do we understand our own existence?

We usually ignore the problem; it is an intellectual adventure that few dare. Yet we are harrowed with wonder and awe when swept by the awareness of our existence. When death wipes away what has once been dear, mighty, and independent, the rock and riddle of life fall upon us, and we learn that life is not a matter of course, that it cannot be taken for granted. Why are we in existence instead of nothing? Is life the offspring of nothingness or the germ of immortality? What is the course of the shuttle that runs but once between birth and death?

Our existence seesaws between what is more and what is less than existence. Death stands behind each of us, while before us in the open door of the divine exchequer where we lay up the sterling coin of piety and spirit, the immortal remains of our dying lives. We are constantly in the mills of death, while for a limited time the contemporaries of God.

The island of existence is washed by the two oceans of eternity and nothingness, eroding it into what is less and elevating it into what is more than existence, into nothingness and into a higher reality, namely, the identity of event and value, the unity of being and meaning.

Existence, the domain of things and facts, is not the ultimate realm. There is a reality of spirit. The realm of values that illumine our lives— justice, beauty, goodness, purity, holiness—did not evolve from nature. Values cannot be derived from being nor can being be derived from nature. Both originate in a higher source. Values are ideals that ought to be realized, a challenge to nature, not a part of nature. Values are not laws of being that express a regularity in the life of nature like the laws of physics. They never fully agree with natural reality. Being as such is neutral and indifferent to values. The physician is not concerned with the question whether the heart of his patient is "good" or "bad" in a moral sense. He is only interested in a diagnosis of the physical condition. The cosmic tragedy is the abyss between being and value. It is incumbent upon us to build the bridge, to invade life with spirit, and to anoint the slaves of selfishness princes of spirit.

The universe, the apex of our abstractive thinking, is a concept of totality that implies not only the sum of parts but some sort of unity or system, in which each part has its specific function, in which each particular is related to the whole. Totality, the arrangement of being according to a purpose, is neither a quantity nor a relation; it is a quality *sui generis* that is not contained in the parts. "The human body contains a sufficient amount of fat to make seven cakes of soap, enough iron to make a medium-sized nail, a sufficient amount of phosphorus to equip two thousand match-heads; enough sulphur to rid one's self of one's fleas." But man as such is more than the mere addition of these elements. The parts did not exist prior to the whole; their character is derived from and conditioned by the whole. Totality is an essence, a value. But being valuable, it points toward something that is beyond itself. Things can only be valuable for something or somebody. The universe has a value that transcends its being; its totality is prior to its parts.

There is a connection between being and value. No being is without relation to value. The universe is not without windows. But where do they lead if not to God? Religion is the value of the universe, the inner unity of all being, a cosmic disposition toward what is more than being and value. As totality is implied in every part, so is the value of the universe involved in every event, in every phenomenon. The care for the universal in the particular, for the complete in the part, is the essence of piety. Piety is emancipation from the absurdity of the particular.

There is no existence in itself. Existence always belongs to an existing but is not identical with it. Every existence belongs to something that is by itself less than existence. But this relationship between existence and existing is transitory, mortal. All beings are perishable, passing, and always dependent upon external conditions. The very essence of existence reveals the inner impotence of being qua being. For existence implies, as we have seen, belonging to somebody as well as permanence and independence; but there is neither independence nor true permanence in the existence of an existing. This want manifests the dualism of being and value. Independence and permanence are values, the freedom from what is less than being, namely, nothingness. Existence as such is devoid of value and borders on nothingness. Hence existence must also imply another relationship that is permanent and independent; it must stand in a relationship to something that is devoid of nothingness. Existence without what is more than existence is an abstraction.

To exist is to belong to an existing as well as to something that is more than existence. Existence has two sides: one is directed to us; the other is open to God. To be means to belong to God and to man. This dual ownership is the value of life. In visions of wisdom, in devotion to the good, in submission to beauty, and when overwhelmed by the holy, we awake to behold existence in this relationship. In reverence, suffering, and humility we discover our existence and find the bridge that leads from existence to God. And this is religion.

Life is something that visits matter. It is a transcendent loan, hidden to man and faced by God. Since it is present in our body, we are inclined to take it for granted. To the unbiased mind it is a revelation of a transcendent sphere. Being neither physical nor emotional, neither material nor rational, it remains a mystery in spite of its reality. Human will never creates life. In generating life, man is the tool, not the master. Science can produce a machine but not an organism. The old dream of a homunculus, a man produced artificially, has been renounced by science. We know that something animates and inspirits a living body. But how? And whence does life come?

Nothing can exist or be conceived of as being apart from the holy dimension. Through our very existence we possess duration in the divine knowledge. Existence is our contact with God. In existence man discovers God. We do not infer ourself through a syllogism or through any reasoning but through our existence. So we approach God not only through our thoughts but, first of all, through our life.

Religion is the interest of God in man, his covenant with the universe. Our task is to concur with his interest, to live in accordance with God's vision of man. Piety is the response of man to the holy dimension, the subjective correlative of objective religion.[1]

We live not only in time and space but also in the knowledge of God. The events in the world reflect in him, and all existence is coexistence with God. Time and space are not the limits of the world. Our life occurs here and in the knowledge of God.

Note

1. Cf. the author's "Analysis of Piety," *Review of Religion,* VI (1942), 293–307.

Chapter 5

A PREFACE TO AN UNDERSTANDING
OF REVELATION

We have never been the same since that day on which Abraham crushed his father's precious symbols, since the day on which the Voice of God overwhelmed us at Sinai. It is forever impossible for us to retreat into an age that predates the Sinaitic event. Something unprecedented happened. God revealed His name to us, and we are named after Him. There are two Hebrew names for Jew: *Yehudi,* the first three letters of which are the first three letters of the Ineffable Name, and *Israel,* the end of which, *el* means in Hebrew God.

If other religions may be characterized as a relation between man and God, Judaism must be described as a relation between *man with Torah* and *God.* The Jew is never alone in the face of God. The Torah is always within him. A Jew without the Torah is obsolete.

The Torah is not the wisdom but the destiny of Israel; not our literature but our essence. It was produced neither by way of speculation nor by way of poetic inspiration but by way of revelation. But what is revelation?

The Mistaken Notion

Many people reject the Bible because of a mistaken notion that revelation has proved to be scientifically impossible. It is all so very simple: there is no source of thought other than the human mind. The

Bible is a book like any other book, and the prophets had no access to sources inaccessible to us. 'The Bible is the national literature of the Jewish people.' To the average mind, therefore, revelation is a sort of mental outcast, not qualified to be an issue for debate. At best, it is regarded as a fairytale, on a par with the conception that lightning and thunder are signs of anger of sundry gods and demons, rather than the result of a sudden expansion of the air in the path of an electric discharge. Indeed, has not the issue been settled long ago by psychology and anthropology as primitive man's mistaking an illusion for a supernatural event?

We Forgot the Question

The most serious obstacle, however, which we encounter in entering a discussion about revelation does not arise from our doubts, whether the accounts of the prophets about their experiences are authentic; the most critical vindication of these accounts, even if it were possible, would be of little relevance. The most serious obstacle is *the absence of the problem.* An answer, to be meaningful, presupposes the awareness of a question, but the climate in which we live today is not genial to the growth of questions which have taken centuries to bloom. The Bible is an answer to the supreme question: What does God demand of us? Yet the question has gone out of the world. God is portrayed as a mass of vagueness behind a veil of enigmas, and His voice has become alien to our minds, to our hearts, to our souls. We have learned to listen to every ego except the 'I' of God. The man of our time may proudly declare: nothing animal is alien to me but everything divine is. This is the status of the Bible in modern life: it is a great answer, but we do not know the question any more. Unless we recover the question, there is no hope of understanding the Bible.

Is It a Meaningful Problem?

Revelation is a complex issue, presupposing first of all certain assumptions about the existence and nature of God who communicates His will to man. Even granting the existence of a Supreme Power, the modern man, with his aloofness to what God means, would find it preposterous to assume that the Infinite Spirit should come down to commune with the feeble, finite mind of man, that man could be an ear to God. With the concept of the Absolute so far removed from the grasp of his mind, man is, at best, bewildered at the claim of the prophets like an animal when confronted with the spectacle of human power. With his relative sense of values, with his mind conditioned by circumstances and reduced to the grasp of the piecemeal, constantly stumbling in his efforts to establish a system of universally integrated ideas, how can it be conceived that man was ever able to grasp the unconditioned?

The first thing, therefore, we ought to do is to find out whether, as many of us seem to think, revelation is an absurdity, whether the prophetic claim is an intellectual savagery.

Is It a Meaningful Question?

Is it meaningful to ask: Did God address Himself to man? Indeed, unless God is real and beyond definitions that confine Him; unless He is unfettered by such distinctions as transcendence and immanence; unless we feel that we are driven and pursued by His question, there is little meaning in starting our inquiry. But those who know that this life of ours takes place in a world that is not all to be explained in human terms; that every moment is a carefully concealed act of His creation, cannot but ask: Is there any event wherein His voice is not suppressed? Is there any moment wherein His presence is not concealed?

True, the claim of the prophets is staggering and almost incredible. But to us, living in this horribly beautiful world, God's thick silence is incomparably more staggering and totally incredible.

Why Study the Problem?

Is it historical curiosity that excites our interest in the problem of revelation? As an event of the past that subsequently affected the course of civilization, revelation would not engage the modern mind any more than the battle of Marathon or the Congress of Vienna. However, it concerns us not because of the impact it had upon past generations, but as something which may or may not be of perpetual, unabating relevance. Thus, in entering this discourse, we do not conjure up the shadow of an archaic phenomenon, but attempt to debate the question whether to believe that there is a voice in the world that pleads with man at all times or at some times in the name of God.

It is not only a personal issue, but one that concerns the history of all men from the beginning of time to the end of days. No one who has, at least once in his life, sensed the terrifying seriousness of human history or the earnestness of individual existence can afford to ignore the problem. He must decide, he must choose between Yes and No.

Is Revelation Necessary?

In thinking about the world, we cannot proceed without guidance, supplied by logic and scientific method. Thinking about the ultimate, climbing toward the Invisible, leads along a path on which there are countless chasms and very few ledges. Faith, helping us take the first steps, is full of ardour but also blind; we are easily lost with our faith in misgivings which we cannot fully dispel. What could counteract the apprehension that it is utter futility to crave for contact with God?

Man in his spontaneity may reach out for the hidden God and with his mind try to pierce the darkness of His distance. But how will he know whether it is God he is reaching out for or some value personified? How will he know where or when God is found: in the ivory-tower of space or at some distant moment in the future?

The certainty of being exposed to a Presence which is not the world's is a fact of human existence. But such certainty does not result in esthetic indulgence in meditation; it stirs with a demand to live in a way which is worthy of that Presence.

The beginning of faith is not a feeling for the mystery of living or a sense of awe, wonder or fear. The root of religion is the question what to do with the feeling for the mystery of living, what to do with awe, wonder or fear. Religion, the end of isolation, begins with a consciousness that something is asked of us. It is in that tense, eternal asking in which the soul is caught and in which man's answer is elicited.[1] Who will tell us how to find a knowledge of the way? How do we know that the way we choose is the way He wants to pursue?

What a sculptor does to a block of marble, the Bible does to our finest intuitions. It is like raising the dead to life.

Metaphysical Loneliness

The ideals we strive after, the values we try to fulfil, have they any significance in the realm of natural events? The sun spends its rays upon the just and the wicked, upon flowers and snakes alike. The heart beats normally within those who torture and kill. Is all goodness and striving for veracity but a fiction of the mind to which nothing corresponds in reality? Where are the spirit's values valid? Within the inner life of man? But the spirit is a stranger in the soul. A demand such as 'love thy neighbour as thyself' is not at home in the self.

We have all a terrible loneliness in common. Day after day a question goes up desperately in our minds: Are we *alone* in the wilderness of the self, alone in this silent universe, of which we are a part, and in which we also feel like strangers?

It is such a situation that makes us ready to search for the voice of God in the world of man: the taste of utter loneliness; the discovery that unless the world is porous, the life of the spirit is a freak; that the world is a torso crying for its head; that the mind is insufficient to itself.

Saying No to Man

Modern man used to think that the acceptance of revelation was an effrontery to the mind. Man must live by his intelligence alone; he is capable of both finding and attaining the aim of his existence. That man is not in need of superhuman authority or guidance was a major argument of the Deists against accepting the idea of prophecy. Social reforms, it was thought, would cure the ills and eliminate the evils from our world. Yet, we have finally discovered what prophets and saints have always known: bread and beauty will not save humanity. There is a passion and drive for cruel deeds, which only the fear of God can soothe; there is a suffocating sensuality in man, which only holiness can ventilate.

It is, indeed, hard for the mind to believe that any member of a species which can organize or even witness the murder of millions and feel no regret should ever be endowed with the ability to receive a word of God. If man can remain callous to a horror as infinite as God, if man can be bloodstained and self-righteous, distort what the conscience tells, make soap of human flesh, then how did it happen that nations did not exterminate each other centuries ago?

Man rarely comprehends how dangerously great he is. The more power he attains, the greater his need for an ability to master his power. Unless a new source of spiritual energy is discovered commensurate with the source of atomic energy, a few men may throw all men into final disaster.

What stands in the way of accepting revelation is our refusal to accept its authority. Liberty is our security and to accept the word of the prophets is to accept the sovereignty of God. Yet our understanding of man and his liberty has undergone a serious change in our time. The problem of man is more grave than we were able to realize a generation ago. What we used to sense in our worst fears turned out to have been a utopia compared with what has happened in our own days. We have discovered that reason may be perverse, that liberty is no security. Now we must learn that there is no liberty except the freedom bestowed upon us by God; that there is no liberty without sanctity.

Unless history is a vagary of nonsense, there must be a counterpart to the immense power of man to destroy, there must be a voice that says NO to man, a voice not vague, faint and inward, like qualms of conscience, but equal in spiritual might to man's power to destroy.

From time to time the turbulent drama is interrupted by a voice that says 'NO' to the recklessness of heart.

The Voice speaks to the spirit of prophetic men in singular moments of their lives and cries to the masses through the horror of history. The prophets respond, the masses despair.

The Bible, speaking in the name of a Being that combines justice with omnipotence, is the never-ceasing outcry of 'No' to humanity. In the midst of our applauding the feats of civilization, the Bible flings itself like a knife slashing our complacency, reminding us that God, too, has a voice in history. Only those who are satisfied with the state of affairs or those who choose the easy path of escaping from society rather than of staying within it and keeping themselves clean of the mud of vicious glories will resent its attack on human independence.

How did Abraham arrive at his certainty that there is a God who is concerned with the world? Said Rabbi Isaac: "Abraham may be compared to a man who was travelling from place to place when he saw a *palace in flames*. 'Is it possible that there is no one who cares for the palace?' he wondered. Until the owner of the building looked out and said, 'I am the owner of the palace.' Similarly, Abraham our father wondered, 'Is it conceivable that the world is without a guide?' The Holy One, blessed be he, looked out and said, 'I am the Guide, the Sovereign of the world.' "[2]

The world is in flames, consumed by evil. Is it possible that there is no one who cares?

Is God Concerned?

There is an abyss of not knowing God in many minds, with a rumor floating over it about an ultimate Being, of which they only know: it is an immense unconscious mass of mystery. It is from the perspective of such knowledge that the prophets' claim seems preposterous.

Let us examine that perspective. By attributing immense mysteriousness to that Ultimate Being, we definitely claim to know it. Thus, the Ultimate Being is not an unknown but a known God. In other words: a God whom we know but one who does not know, the great Unknower. We proclaim the ignorance of God as well as our knowledge of His being ignorant!

This seems to be a part of our pagan heritage: to say, the Supreme Being is a total mystery, and even having accepted the Biblical God of creation we still cling to the assumption: He who has the power to create a world is never able to utter a word. Yet why should we assume that the endless is forever imprisoned in silence? Why should we *a priori* exclude the power of expression from the Absolute Being? If the world is the work of God, isn't it conceivable that there would be within His work signs of His expression?

The idea of revelation remains an absurdity as long as we are unable to comprehend the impact with which the reality of God is pursuing man. Yet, as those moments in which the fate of mankind is in the balance, even those who have never sensed how God turns to man, suddenly realize that man—who has the power to devise both culture and crime,

who is able to be a proxy for divine justice—is important enough to be
the recipient of spiritual light at the rare dawns of his history.

Notes

1. Man Is Not Alone, vol. I, p. 68 f.
2. *Genesis Rabba,* ch. 39.

Chapter 6

PROPHETIC INSPIRATION: AN ANALYSIS OF PROPHETIC CONSCIOUSNESS

Content and Form

The problem to which we wish to turn our attention is the *how* of prophetic experience. What form does the prophet's experience assume?[1]

To the consciousness of the prophet, the prophetic act is an act of communication, in which a message is conveyed to him by means of words or signs. Decisive is not only his understanding or appropriation of the content but also his awareness of their being communicated to him. Decisive is not only the message but also the intercourse or encounter between him and the Divine, namely the form in which the message comes to his attention. It is the encounter which lends the character of prophecy to the experience.

In order to comprehend the form or the essential structure of that encounter, it will be necessary to subtract from it its accidental aspects, or whatever does not belong indispensably to it. In other words, we must disregard all features, the omission of which would not make revelation unthinkable. We are, therefore, excluding from our present consideration not only the substantial elements (e.g., the pathos motive), but also all contingent formal elements, such as the outward form of the experience (e.g., whether it was an act of hearing or of seeing).

The usual definitions seek to understand revelation and inspiration from the psychological or at best the anthropological standpoint. Yet an intelligent understanding of the prophetic consciousness of inspiration will never be possible as long as the immanent meaning of inspiration is overlooked. Our question, then, is: What is, to the mind of the prophets, the ultimate, irreducible form or essential structure of the prophetic act?

The prophetic act comprises a transpersonal fact which we call *inspiration* and a personal fact which we call *experience*. We will not be able to apprehend the meaning of the experience before gaining an insight into what inspiration meant to the prophet. For it is the certainty of the objective or transpersonal aspect of the act upon which the meaning and relevance of the experience depend. From a phenomenological point of view, we can do justice to the essence of the experience only when we include in our discussion the transpersonal element, sensed or understood as something staggeringly real. We must, therefore, examine the structure of the inspiration in its objectivity which is a given fact for experience in order that we may be in a position to grasp the character of the experience which it initiates.

In accordance with our procedure in the analysis of prophetic experience, we shall take as our point of departure *the form of inspiration* corresponding *to the form of experience*. What does the prophet—apart from all factual content—view and experience as the essentially characteristic form of the act of inspiration?

Inspiration—An Event

To the consciousness of the prophet, the prophetic act is more than an experience; it is an objective *event*. This is its essential form. Whatever be the mode in which inspiration is apprehended, there remains always its character as an event, not as a process. What is the difference between process and event? A process happens regularly, following a relatively permanent pattern; an event is extraordinary, irregular. A process may be continuous, steady, uniform; events happen suddenly, intermittently, occasionally. Processes are typical; events are unique. A process follows a law; events create a precedent.

Inspiration then, is not a process that goes on all the time, but an event that lasts a moment. The heavens declare the glory of God evermore; the word of God comes to the prophet at *some* moments. The prophet has to wait some time before a revelation comes to him; Jeremiah on one occasion waits ten days, but he does not anticipate the desired moment (42:7).

The term used in the Bible to describe general events in history, *va'yehi* ("it happened"), is employed to describe prophetic inspiration (*va'yehi d'var Adonai eilai*), particularly in Jeremiah and Ezekiel.

God is not simply available once and for all, so that whenever man may feel like seeking Him, He would be found by him. There is an alternative to God's presence, namely, His hiding. God may withdraw and detach Himself from history. While exposed to the overwhelming presence, the prophets predict the absence.

> With their flocks and their herds
> They shall go seek the Lord,
> But they will not find Him;
> He has withdrawn from them.
>
> Hosea 5:6

> Then they will cry to the Lord,
> But He will not answer them;
> He will hide His face from them at that time,
> Because they have made their deeds evil.
>
> Micah 3:4

> I will wait for the Lord, who is hiding His face from the house of Jacob, and I will hope in Him.
>
> Isaiah 8:17

Precious is the word of God, and the prophets do not take it for granted. It is given to them now, but a time will come when it will not be given.

> Behold, the days are coming, says the Lord God,
> When I will send a famine on the land;
> Not a famine of bread, nor a thirst for water,
> But of hearing the words of the Lord.
> They shall wander from sea to sea,
> And from north to east;
> They shall run to and fro, to seek the word of the Lord,
> But they shall not find it.
>
> Amos 8:11–12

Prophetic experience, then, is not the perception of vistas nor the perception of sounds that persist all the time. It is not a discovery, a coming upon something permanently given by the mind of the prophet. What the prophet encounters is not something given, a timeless idea, *mishpat,* justice, a law, but something dynamic, an act of giving; not an eternal word but a word spoken, a word expressed, springing from a Presence, a word in time, a pathos overflowing in words. His experience is a perception of an act that happens rather than a perception of a situation that abides.

An Ecstasy of God

There is another sense in which prophetic inspiration must be described as having been an event—to the consciousness of the prophet. It is in the sense of having been more than an inner experience. What happened in the decisive moments in the life of the prophet does *not* burst *out of* him but *upon him,* and what is more: inspiration is an act that *happens to him* and also *beyond him.*

To the prophet the supremely real is not his experience, but that which is given *to* his experience, that which surpasses his power of experience. To him God is not an object but a subject, and his perceiving matters less than God's uttering His word. He is not the agent, the moving force; he stands within the event, not above it.

No perception is as plain, direct and infallible as eating food. What we see or touch remains away from us, what we consume becomes a part of us. "Thy words were found, and I ate them . . ." (Jeremiah 15:16). His is not an experience of God but an experience of a divine experience.

Prophecy is a personal event. It happens to the divine Person Who does not merely send forth words, but becomes involved and engaged in the encounter with man.

Thus to the prophetic consciousness inspiration is more than an emotional experience, a consciousness of inner receptivity. It is experienced as a divine act which takes place not *within* but *beyond,* as an event which happens in his view rather than in his heart. The prophet does not merely feel it; he faces it.

The decisive mark of the prophetic act is in its *transcendent aspect.* To the prophet, the overwhelming fact is not only that he hears but that

God speaks; something happens to him, and something happens to God. What makes possible a prophetic act within his consciousness is an act that happens beyond his consciousness, a transcendent act, *an ecstasy of God*. To the prophet, it is as though God stepped forth out of the silence, aloofness and incomprehensibility of His being to reveal His will to man. In its depth and intensity the act takes place in the transcendent subject but is directed toward the experiencing prophets.

Prophecy cannot be forced. The prophet does not assume that abandonment of consciousness brings about inspiration, as though one had only to leave "the self" in order to be able to receive the Word. Prophecy comes about by the grace of God.

Ecstasy is something which happens to the person; inspiration happens to the human person as well as to the Inspirer. Ecstasy is a psychological process; prophecy, to the mind of the prophet, has its origin in the transcendent act.

Being Present

Little did the prophets tell us how the Divine word came to them or how they knew it to be the word of the very God. Perhaps it was the discovery of being present at a Divine event, "of standing at the council of the Lord" that was the essence of their experience and the source of evidence. Prophetic inspiration involved participation, not only receptivity to communication.

The term "visions," generally applied to some of the descriptions of prophetic experience, is a metonymy. Seeing is but a part of the experience. What stands out as essential, unique, and decisive is *the prophet's participation,* his affecting and witnessing the thinking of the Lord. Witness some of the visions that came to Amos. Once a cloud swept down and devoured every blade of grass in the fields; again a fire appeared so fierce that it licked up the great deep and threatened the land. That was the vision. The people were ripe for severe punishment. Had the record finished here, its meaning would be limited to foreseeing a coming disaster. Yet, the prophet does not accept what he sees; he does not say, Thy will be done. He prays:

> O Lord God, forgive (or: cease), I beseech Thee!
> How can Jacob stand?
> He is so small!

and:

> The Lord repented concerning this;
> It shall not be, says the Lord . . .
> This also shall not be, says the Lord.
>
> Amos 7:1–6

Others may have been granted ultimate insights, may have perceived the imperceptible. What the prophet speaks of is not a personal experience but a startling event, the least important aspect of which is its effect upon the prophet. What he speaks of is an event that must affect heaven and earth.

> Hear, O heavens, and give ear, O earth
> For the Lord has spoken. . . .
>
> Isaiah 1:2

> The Lord roars from Zion,
> And utters His voice from Jerusalem
> And the heavens and earth shake.
>
> Joel 4:16

> Hear, you peoples, all of you:
> Hearken, O earth, and all that is in it.
>
> Micah 1:2

It takes a great inner power to address a nation; it takes Divine strength to address heaven and earth.

> For who among them has stood in the council of the Lord
> To perceive and to hear His word,
> Or who has given heed to His word and listened? . . .
> I did not send the prophets,
> Yet they ran;
> I did not speak to them,

Yet they prophesied.
But if they had stood in My council,
Then they would have proclaimed My words to My people,
And they would have turned them from their evil ways,
And from the evil of their doings.

Jeremiah 23:18, 21–22

By implication these words convey Jeremiah's claim to be among those who stand "in the council of the Lord to perceive and they hear His word." Indeed, there was a moment when the word of the Lord came to him, saying:

> Before I formed you in the womb I knew you,
> Before you were born I consecrated you;
> I appointed you a prophet to the nations.

Jeremiah 1:5

They speak not in the name of a personal experience, of an inner illumination. *They speak in the name of a divine experience, of a divine event.* Inspiration is more than an act that happens to the prophet; inspiration is *a moment of the prophet's being present at a divine event.*

"The mouth of the Lord has spoken" (Isaiah 1:20; 40:5; Micah 4:4). "The Lord has spoken this word" (Isaiah 24:3; Jeremiah 46:13), "has sworn in my hearing" (Isaiah 5:9), "has revealed Himself in my ears" (Isaiah 22:14).

The Event and Its Significance

Two subjects are involved in the act of inspiration—a giver of revelation and a recipient. In order to grasp the essential character of inspiration, its significance for both partners must be elucidated. Principally: how did the prophet conceive the significance of the revelational event for the divine being? Before attempting to answer this question, it should be explained what significance the idea of divinity has in prophetic thought.

The prophets rarely speak of God as He is in Himself, as ultimate being. It is God in relation to humanity, in relation to the world, who is the theme of their words.

It is improper to employ the term *self-revelation* in regard to Biblical prophecy. God never reveals His self. He is above and beyond all revelation. He only discloses a Word. He never unveils His essence; He only communicates His pathos, His will. Consequently the question of significance which we raised must be framed in the following terms: what does the event of revelation imply as regards divine pathos?

At the same time the question must be asked: what does the event of revelation signify for the prophetic partner? Here again the qualification must be made that we are not now concerned with the entire existence of the prophet but with the significance for his own understanding of his experience.

Analysis of the Event

Every event is essentially made up of two phases. Since an event is limited in time, it must have a beginning, and since it is not indefinitely continuous, it must run a certain course. The beginning and the course of development together constitute the characteristic structure of every event. The first phase is effected by a change in the prior, original condition; the second, by a tendency to evolve according to certain momentum. In the first phase we have an interruption and ceasing, in the second a continuance and progress. The first we term *a turning,* or *a decision,* the second *a direction.* Thus there are two aspects of inspiration as seen from the prophet's point of view: a moment of *decision* or *a turning,* and a moment of expression, *a direction.*

What do we mean by *turning* or *decision?*

Every event starts out as a change, as a turning-point; a turning away from a stable condition must take place for the event to happen. In the change lies the transition from motive to initiative, the birth of the event out of the motive.

The moment of turning is that which has an immediate nexus with what precedes the event; it is that which takes place at the source: the origination of an event. Because it introduces or is the genesis of the event, it is rooted in the interior intimate life of him who bears the event. At this stage the event carries a maximum of motivation and a minimum of happening.

In the critical turning we see the initiating and generating factor behind the event, we see the dynamic and potential quality of the latter: the impulse to the opening up of a new direction. The act of turning is the first result of the initiative. At that point we have to grasp the principle which shapes the total structure of the event before the latter is completely realized as fact.

As a rule, God is silent; His intention and design remain hidden from the mind of man. What comes to pass is a departure from the state of silence and aloofness, God's turning from the conditions of concealment to an act of revealment.

This change brings about the transition from a state or a condition which seems permanent and timeless to a moment of encounter which is always unique in time. *Eternity enters a moment.* The uniqueness of the latter interrupts what at a distance seems to be uninterrupted uniformity. Timeless silence we can only conceive in the image of impersonality. It is an order, perhaps a principle, unrelated; it has no face and no regard. Turning is personal; it involves initiative, will. It is the beginning of communion.

A turning is always pivoted upon the will. The prophets know no manifestation of God which is passive, unwilled or unintentional. It is not thought of as proceeding out of God like rays out of the sun. It is an act proceeding from this will and brought about by a decision to disclose what otherwise would remain concealed. In this sense, it is an act within the life of God, so to speak.

Revelation was more than a miracle or an acting upon the prophet. The word was not spoken the way the world came into being. God did not say "Let there be a word!" and there was a word reaching the prophet's ear. He did not create the word out of nothing: He spoke it, as it were, out of His own being.

Turning

The prophetic event impresses itself on the prophet as a happening that springs exclusively from the will and initiative of God. He cannot himself control or call forth inspiration; it must proceed from God and therefore depends utterly on God's willing it. He is unable to conjure it up by human means, not even by prayer. Jeremiah must wait ten days for inspiration, and knows that he cannot induce its coming.

The fact that inspiration is independent of the will of the prophet expresses negatively and indirectly its transcendent nature. Positively, the moment of turning is understood as an expression of *God's will to communicate.* The statement, "Surely the Lord does nothing without revealing His secret to His servants the prophets" (Amos 3:7), contains a thought which lies at the very root of Biblical religion: "The Lord said: Shall I hide from Abraham what I am about to do?" (Genesis 18:17).

The decision to communicate is an event in the life of God. It arises directly from divine motivation: for it belongs to the very nature of God to declare His thoughts to the prophets. Inspiration as a crucial event is conditioned both by the history of man and the character of God.

What do we mean by *direction*?

A personal event is an act of communication in which an intention is conveyed to another person. It means addressing a person. An act of communication has a direction. The turning is the genesis of the event; the direction, its realization. It is a moment in which an act within a person becomes an act for the sake of another person. A relationship is established, the event has reached its end; it has assumed form; it is a maximum of eventuation.

A distinction must be made between a divine manifestation and a divine communication. A divine manifestation which may be either direction evident[2] or may be sensed in its effects upon nature and history,[3] is not directed to the prophet and does not accost him. An essential moment in prophecy is direction. Amos' word—"The Lord roars from Zion, and utters His voice from Jerusalem; the pastures of the shepherds mourn, and the top of Carmel withers" (1:2)—describes a call not directed to any particular person.[4] Likewise, the call in Isaiah's inaugural vision—"And I heard the voice of the Lord saying: 'Whom shall I send, and who will go for us?' " (6:8a)—is not directed to any particular person; it contains a decision, not a direction. It is in verse 9 that the address begins: "And He said: 'Go and say to this people. . . .' " Yet it is those words of decision that suggest how much the mission of the prophet means to God Himself.

Revelation is not a voice crying in the wilderness, an act of communication. It is not simply an act of disclosing, but an act of disclosing *to* someone, the bestowal of a content, God addressing the prophet. There is no intransitive aimless revelation in prophecy. His word is directed to man.

Unlike the voice spoken of in old Rabbinic literature, the *Bat Kol,* the prophets hear a voice calling upon them. It is only marginal to the prophet's experience to overhear words not addressed to him.[5] The word is always spoken to him, addressed to him. The standard formula is: *The word of the Lord came—to me."* It is placed in his mouth (Jeremiah 1:9).

The call that comes to the prophet to accept the prophetic mission[6] is the outstanding example of anthropotropism. Such a call is not reported of the Buddha who attains insight through personal striving, but is claimed by prophetic men like Mohammed or Zarathustra; it belongs to the fundamental features of their religious consciousness. This is an essential characteristic of the prophetic act: that not only does the act come from the initiative of God but that it is directed toward man.

The idea of God's turning (*tropos*) to man is a fundamental presupposition of Biblical prophecy. The idea of pathos is only an answer to the question of content, not to that of form, and does by no means imply the event of revelation. Pathos is the object of communication but does not necessarily of itself engender the latter. The need to reveal itself is by no means intrinsic to it.

Hence in some other category must we seek the primary presupposition of prophecy. This category is to be inferred from the act itself, from the character of eventuation. It is the inclination to *tropos,* the *tropos*-tendency of the Eternal, which is the ultimate ground of prophecy.

Here Am I, Here Am I . . .

Indeed, all of human history as seen by the Bible is the history of God *in search of man.* In spite of man's failure, over and over, God does not abandon His hope to find righteous men. Adam, Cain, the generation of the flood, the generation of the Tower of Babel—it is a story of failure and defiance. And yet, God did not abandon man, hoping against hope to see a righteous world. Noah was saved in the expectation that out of his household generations would not corrupt their ways, and a covenant was established with him and his descendants after him. But it was Noah himself who planted a vineyard and then became drunk. It was Noah himself who set brother against brother, blessing Shem and Japheth, and cursing Canaan to be a slave to his brothers. The arrogance of those who built the Tower of Babel paved the way for greater tension and confusion.

But the Lord did not abandon man and in His search determined to choose Abraham, so that in him, "all the families of the earth be blessed."

Israel's faith is not the fruit of a quest for God. Israel did not discover God. Israel was discovered by God. The Bible is a record of God's approach to man.

> Like grapes in the wilderness,
> I found Israel;
> Like the first fruit on the fig tree,
> I saw your fathers.
>
> Hosea 9:10a

> He found him in a desert land,
> In the howling waste of the wilderness;
> He encircled him, He cared for him,
> He kept him as the apple of His eye.
>
> Deuteronomy 32:10

This is the Biblical conception of God's relationship to man: He would call, and man would answer. God is longing for the work of His hands. That relationship is distorted when the call goes out, and man fails to answer.

> Why, when I came, was there no man?
> When I called, was there no one to answer?
>
> Isaiah 50:2

> I was ready to be sought by those who did not ask for Me;
> I was ready to be found by those who did not seek Me.
> I said: "Here am I, here am I,"
> To a nation that did not call on My name.
> I spread out My hands all the day
> To a rebellious people,
> Who walk in a way that is not good,
> Following their own devices. . . .
>
> Isaiah 65:1–3[7]

I sought for a man among them
who should build up the wall and
stand in the breach before
Me for the land, that I should
not destroy it; but I found none.

                                                    Ezekiel 22:30

Anthropotropism and Theotropism

In the light of these structural categories, religious events must be divided into two types. They are experienced either as a turning of a transcendent being toward man, or as a turning of man toward a transcendent being. The first may be called *anthropotropic,* the second *theotropic.*

To the first category corresponds the consciousness of being approached by God, directly or indirectly, of receiving either teaching or guidance, either a word or an intimation; the consciousness of living under a God Who calls upon man, turns to him, is in need of him. In anthropotropic experience man is affected by the impact of events which he does not initiate, but which are addressed to him or relate to his existence, and in which he feels a transcendent attentiveness focused upon himself.

Prophetic inspiration as a pure act may be defined as anthropotropism, as a turning of God toward man, a turning in the direction of man.

The unique quality of the awareness that characterizes Biblical religion goes beyond what Schleiermacher called "absolute dependence." It is rather an awareness of a God who helps, demands, and calls upon men. It is a sense of being reached, being found, being sought after; a sense of being pursued: *anthropotropism.*

While the prophets of Israel may be regarded as the classical example of anthropotropism, not all anthropotropic experiences are prophetic in character; they occur, in a variety of forms, in the lives of individuals who lay no claim to prophecy, and seem to be at home particularly in theistic religions.

Theotropism, man's turning to God, is a structure of experience that may be attained through the performance of ritual acts, prayer, meditation. It is characteristic of exercises performed in order to induce the state of ecstasy and communion with God; of efforts of a magic nature aimed at establishing contact with the sphere of the Divine.

For prayer, too, is an act consisting of a moment of decision or turning, and of a moment of direction. For to be engaged in prayer and to be away from prayer are two different states of living and thinking. In the depth of the soul there is a distance between the two. The course of consciousness which a person pursues, the way of thinking by which he lives most of the time, are remote from the course and way of thinking peculiar to prayer. To be able to pray one must alter the course of consciousness, one must go through moments of disengagement, one must enter another course of thinking, one must face in a different direction.

For the focus of prayer is not the self. A man may spend hours meditating about himself, or be stirred by the deepest sympathy for his fellow man, and no prayer will come to pass. Prayer comes to pass in a complete turning of the heart toward God, toward His goodness and power. It is the momentary disregard of our personal concerns, the absence of self-centered thoughts, which constitute the art of prayer. Feeling becomes prayer in the moment in which we forget ourselves and become aware of God. When we analyze the consciousness of a supplicant, we discover that it is not concentrated upon his own interests, but on something beyond the self. The thought of personal need is absent, and the thought of divine grace alone is present in his mind. Thus, in beseeching Him for bread, there is one instant, at least, in which our mind is directed neither to our hunger nor to food, but to His mercy. This instant is prayer.

In prayer we shift the center of living from self-consciousness to self-surrender. God is the center toward which all forces tend. He is the source, and we are the flowing of His force, the ebb and flow of His tides.[8]

Just as the prophet is the supreme example of anthropotropism, so is the priest the outstanding exponent of theomorphism. The difference between them must be understood in terms of the different experiences they represent. The prophet, speaking for God to the people, must disclose; the priest, acting for people before God, must carry out the will of God. The prophet speaks and acts by virtue of divine inspiration; the priest performs the ritual by virtue of his official status. In the earliest times non-priests could perform cultic actions.[9] If subsequently, this privilege became confined to the priest, it was rarely assumed that the priest was called by God to perform this task. The transference of the control of the cultic domain to the priest was based not upon a consideration of his calling but upon a consideration of his gifts. This is confirmed by the fact that the priestly vocation was hereditary.[10] Magic and exorcism, the art of healing and divination, sacrifices and prayer— are acts which proceed from man and are directed towards God.

The two types differ not only in inner experience, but also in outward action, in the modes of service. The sphere in which theotropism finds expression is *the cult;* the emotions with which it is charged are those of aspiration and devotion, the soul's longing for God; the course of its piety proceeds from man to God. The point of departure is the sphere of man; the end is in the sphere of the divine. What is hoped for is Divine aid, protection, or intervention. God is called upon to answer, to send relief in distress. Conversely, the sphere in which prophetic anthropotropism finds expression is *history;* the emotions with which it is charged are sympathy for God, sympathy for man; the course of its piety runs from God to man. The point of departure is the divine pathos; the end is the sphere of man. What is hoped for is repentance, human action. Man is called upon to answer, to mend his ways.

Theotropic experience may be an end in itself, whereas anthropotropism is only a means to an end. The former is conceivable as an isolated episode in the life of man, the latter happens as a part of a relationship embracing all of life.

Anthropotropism finds its supreme expression in *prophecy,* theotropism in *psalmody.* Characteristic of the former is *the election* or *the call* that comes to a prophet from above; characteristic of the latter is *repentance* and *conversion.* One must not assume, however, that both types are mutually exclusive. The existence of the prophet, for example, is sustained by both kinds of events. And conversion, the structure of which is theotropic, is often accompanied by an anthropotropic experience as though "a higher power streamed in from without and attained the mastery within man.[11]

Anthropotropism and theotropism are far more than categories describing formal structures of inner events; they affect and shape the substance of religious thinking.

Anthropotropism, the thought of God approaching man, willing, needing and requiring his work, carries not only a supreme affirmation of values encountered here and now, but also the assurance of the ultimate significance of history. The directedness of the Divine upon man sets forth the supreme relevance and urgency of what man must do, of how man may fail, or how his acts affect the course of history.

Where theotropic moments determine the ultimate image of existence, directedness of the mind upon the Divine may become, in extreme cases, the exclusive standard and principle of judgment. Focused upon the Beyond, the mind begins to disregard the demands and values of here and now, sliding into resignation and withdrawal from action, moral indifference and world denial.

To sum up, these seem to the the outstanding features of prophetic inspiration, as seen from the perspective of the prophetic consciousness.

1. It is not brought about by the prophet, but comes about without and even against his will. It presupposes neither training nor the gradual development of a talent. It comes about as an act of election and grace.

2. It is not an absolutely mysterious, numinous, wholly other source from which inspiration comes to the prophet; it proceeds from the known God.

3. It is an event, not part of a process; it is not, it happens.

4. It is an event in the life of God; it happens in God in relation to the prophet; it is an event in which both decision and direction come upon a person as a transcendent act.

5. It is not an act of imparting general information. Prophecy is God's personal communication to man. It deals with what concerns God intimately.

Notes

1. The separation of form and content which we assume in regard to inspiration as well as in regard to experience is not something which can be accepted as a matter of course. From the standpoint of dogmatic theology, every revelation is indivisible. Even in modern discussions of the philosophy of religion any divisibility of revelational experience is not seldom denied. And when we purpose such an analysis, it is not because of the logical dogma of the correlation of content and form. Rather the idea was inferred from a phenomenological examination of the prophet's accounts of their experiences.

2. Exodus 24.9–11.

3. Judges 5:4 ff; Habakkuk 3:3.

4. Cf. Joel 3:16.

5. "And I heard the voice of the Lord saying: 'Whom shall I send, and who will go for us?' " (Isaiah 6:8). The statement "The Lord of hosts has sworn in my ears" (Isaiah 5:9), is ambiguous. Compare also Isaiah 5:9, I Kings 22:18–24. Apocalyptic visionaries read the words written in heavenly books.

6. Amos 7:14 ff; Isaiah, ch. 6; Jeremiah 1:3 ff; Ezekiel 9:2 ff; compare Hosea 1:2.

7. "Here am I" is a phrase of humble readiness and consent, uttered by Abraham (Genesis 22:1), Jacob (Genesis 46:2), Moses (Exodus 3:5), Samuel (I 3:4).

8. See A. J. Heschel, *Man's Quest for God*, New York, 1954, pp. 7, 15, 24.

9. In ancient Israel one was not required to be specially consecrated in order to perform sacrificial functions; anyone might approach the altar and offer sacrifices, cf. Judges 6:26 ff; 13:16, 19; I Samuel 2:13–16; II Samuel 24:25.

10. Exodus 28:1. Compare A. Erman, *Die egyptische Religion,* 2nd ed., Berlin, 1909, p. 67.

11. W. Jumer, *The Varieties of Religious Experience.*

Chapter 7

ARCHITECTURE OF TIME

Technical civilization is man's conquest of space. It is a triumph frequently achieved by sacrificing an essential ingredient of existence, namely, time. In technical civilization, we expend time to gain space. To enhance our power in the world of space is our main objective. Yet to have more does not mean to *be* more. The power we attain in the world of space terminates abruptly at the borderline of time. But time is the essence of existence.

To gain control of the world of space is certainly one of our tasks. The danger begins when in gaining power in the realm of space we forfeit all aspirations in the realm of time. Time is a realm where the goal is not to have but to be, not to own but to give, not to control but to share, not to subdue but to be in accord. Life goes wrong when the control of space, the acquisition of things of space, becomes our sole concern.

Nothing is more useful than power, nothing more frightful. We have often suffered from degradation by poverty; now we are threatened with degradation through power. There is happiness in the love of labor; there is misery in the love of gain. Many hearts and pitchers are broken at the fountain of profit. Selling himself into slavery to things, man becomes a utensil that is broken at the fountain.

Technical civilization stems primarily from the desire of man to subdue and manage the forces of nature. The manufacture of tools, the arts of spinning and farming, the building of houses, the craft of sailing: all go on in man's spatial surroundings. The mind's preoccupation with space to this day affects all activities of man. Even religions are frequently dominated by the notion that the deity resides in space, within particular localities like mountains, forests, trees, or stones, which are, therefore, singled out as holy places; the deity is bound to a particular land; holiness is a quality associated with things of space, and the primary question is: Where is the god? There is much enthusiasm for the idea that God is present in the universe, but that idea is taken to mean His presence in space rather than in time, in nature rather than in history; as if He were thing, not spirit.

Even pantheistic philosophy is a religion of space: the Supreme Being is thought to be the infinite space. *Deus sive natura* has *extensio,* extension or space, as its attribute, not time; time to Spinoza is merely an accident of motion, a mode of thinking. And his desire to develop a philosophy *more geometrico,* in the manner of geometry, which is the science of space, is significant of his space-mindedness.

To this day, the primitive mind finds it hard to realize an idea without the aid of imagination, and it is the realm of space where imagination wields its sway. Of the gods it must have a visible image; where there is no image, there is no god. The reverence for the sacred image, for the sacred monument or place, is not only indigenous to most religions; it has been retained by men of all ages, all nations, pious, superstitious, even anti-religious; they all continue to pay homage to flags and banners, to national shrines, to monuments erected to kings or heroes. Everywhere the desecration of holy shrines is considered sacrilege, and the shrine may become so important that what it stands for is consigned to oblivion. The memorial becomes an aid to amnesia; the means stultify the end. For things of space are at the mercy of man. Though too sacred to be polluted, they are not too sacred to be exploited. To retain the holy, to perpetuate the presence of the god, his image is fashioned. Yet a god who can be fashioned, a god who can be confined, is but a shadow of man.

We are all infatuated with the splendor of space, with the grandeur of things of space. *Thing* is a category that lies heavy on our minds, tyrannizing all our thoughts. Our imagination tends to mold all concepts in its image. In our daily lives, we attend primarily to that which the senses spell out for us—to what the eyes perceive, to what the fingers touch. Reality to us is thinghood, consisting of substances that occupy space; even God, is conceived by most of us as a thing.

The result of our thinginess is blindness to all reality that fails to identify itself as a thing, as a matter of fact. This is obvious in our understanding of time, which, being thingless and insubstantial, appears to us as if it had no reality.[1]

Indeed, we know what to do with space but do not know what to do about time, except to make it subservient to space. Most of us seem to labor for the sake of things of space. As a result, we suffer from a deeply rooted dread of time and stand aghast when compelled to look into its face.[2] Time to us is sarcasm, a slick, treacherous monster with a jaw like a furnace consuming every moment of our lives. Shrinking, therefore, from facing time, we escape for shelter to things of space. The intentions we are unable to carry out we deposit in space; possessions become the symbols of our repressions, jubilees of frustrations. But things of space are not fireproof; they only add fuel to the flames. Is the joy of possession an antidote to the terror of time which grows into a dread of inevitable death? Things, when magnified are stubborn forgeries of happiness; they are a threat to our very lives. We are more harassed than supported by the Frankenstein monsters of spatial things.

Most of us succumb to the magnetic property of things and evaluate events by their tangible results. We appreciate things that are displayed in the realm of space. The truth, however, is that the genuinely precious is encountered in the realm of time rather than in space. Monuments of bronze live by the grace of the memory of those who gaze at their form, while monuments of the soul endure even when banished to the back of the mind. Feelings, thoughts, are our own, while possessions are alien and often treacherous to the self. To be is more essential than to have. Though we deal with things, we live in deeds.[3]

The higher goal of spiritual living is not to amass a wealth of information but to face a sacred moment. In religious experience, for example, it is not a thing that is experienced but a spiritual presence. What is retained in the soul is the moment of insight rather than the place where the act came to pass.[4] A moment of insight is a fortune, transporting us beyond the confines of measured time. Spiritual life begins to decay when we fail to sense the grandeur of what is eternal in time.

Our intention here is not to depreciate the world of space. To disparage space and the blessing of things of space is to disparage the works of creation, which God beheld and saw that "it was good." The world cannot be seen exclusively *sub specie temporis*. Time and space are interrelated. To overlook either of them is to be partially blind. What we plead against is man's unconditional surrender to space, his enslavement to things. We must not forget that it is not a thing that lends significance to a moment; it is the moment that lends significance to things.

Time to us is a measuring device rather than a realm in which we abide. Our consciousness of it comes about when we begin to compare two events and to notice that one event is later than the other; listening to a tune, we realize that one note follows the other. Fundamental to the consciousness of time is the distinction between earlier and later.

But is time only a relation between events in time? Is there no meaning to the present moment, even regardless of its relation to the past? Moreover, do we only know what is *in* time, namely, events that have an impact on things of space? If nothing happened that is related to the world of space, would there be no time?

A special consciousness is required to recognize the ultimate significance of time. We all live it and are so close to being identical with it that we fail to notice it. The world of space surrounds our existence; time is the core of our existence. Space is but a part of living, the rest is time. Things are the shore, the voyage is in time. Existence is never explicable through itself but only through time. When we close our eyes in moments of intellectual concentration, we are able to have time without space, but we can never have space without time. To the spiritual eye, space is frozen time, and things are petrified events.

There are two points of view from which time can be sensed: from the point of view of space and from the point of view of spirit. Looking out of the window of a swiftly moving railroad car, we have the impression as if the landscape were moving while we ourselves were sitting still. Similarly, when gazing at reality while our souls are carried away by spatial things, time appears to be in constant motion. However, when we learn to understand that it is the spatial things that are constantly running out, we realize that time is that which never expires, that it is the world of space which is rolling through the infinite expanse of time. Thus temporality may be defined as the relation of space to time.

The boundless, continuous, but vacuous entity which, realistically, we call space is not the ultimate form of reality. Our world is a world of space moving through time: from the Beginning to the End of Days.

To the common mind the essence of time is evanescence, temporality.

The truth, however, is that the fact of evanescence flashes upon our minds when poring over things of space. It is the world of space that communicates to us the sense of temporality. Time, that which is beyond and independent of space, is everlasting; it is the world of space which is perishing. Things perish within time; time itself does not change. We should not speak of the flow or passage of time, but of the flow or passage of space through time. It is not time that dies; it is the human body which dies in time. Temporality is an attribute of the world of space, of things of space. Time which is beyond space is beyond the division into past, present and future.

Monuments of stone are destined to disappear; days of spirit never pass away. About the arrival of the people at Sinai we read in the book of Exodus: "In the third month after the children of Israel were gone forth out of the land of Egypt, on this day they came into the wilderness of Sinai" (19:1). Here was an expression that puzzled the Masters: "*on this day*"? It should have said: "*on that day*." This can only mean that the day of giving the Torah can never become past; that day is *this* day, *every* day. The Torah, whenever we study it, should be to us "as if it were given us today."[5] The same applies to the day of the Exodus from Egypt: "In every age, man must see himself as if he himself went out of Egypt."[6]

The worth of a great day is not measured by the space it occupies in the calendar. Exclaimed R. Akiba: "All of time is not as worthy as the day on which the Song of Songs was given to Israel, for all the songs are holy, but the Song of Songs is the holiest of the holies."[7]

In the realm of spirit, there is no difference between a second and a century, between an hour and an age. R. Judah and Patriarch cried: "There are those who gain eternity in a lifetime, others who gain it in one brief hour."[8] One good hour may be worth a lifetime; an instant of returning to God may restore what was lost in years of escaping from Him. "Better is one hour of repentance and good deeds in this world than the whole life in the world-to-come."[9]

Civilization is, as we have seen, man's triumph over space. Yet time remains impervious. We can overcome distance but can neither recapture the past nor dig out the future. Man transcends space, and time transcends man.

Time is man's greatest challenge. We all take part in a procession through its realm that never comes to an end but are unable to gain a foothold in it. Its reality is apart and away from us. Space is exposed to our will; we may shape and change the things in space as we please. Time alone is beyond our reach, beyond our power. It is both near and far, intrinsic to all experience and transcending all experience. It belongs exclusively to God.

Time, then, is *otherness*, a mystery that hovers above all categories. It is as if time and the mind were a world apart. Yet it is only within time that there is fellowship and *togetherness* of all beings.

Every one of us occupies a portion of space. He takes it up exclusively. The portion of space which my body occupies is taken up by myself in exclusion of anyone else. Yet no one possesses time. There is no moment which we possess exclusively. This very moment belongs to all living men as it belongs to me. We share time; we own space. Through my ownership of space, I am a rival of all other beings; through my living in time, I am a contemporary of all other beings. We pass through time; we occupy space. We easily succumb to the illusion that the world of space is for our sake, for man's sake. In regard to time, we are immune to such an illusion.

Immense is the distance that lies between God and a thing. For a thing is that which has separate or individual existence as distinct from the totality of being. To see a thing is to see something which is detached and isolated. A thing is, furthermore, something which is and can become the possession of man. Time does not permit an instant to be in and for itself. Time is either all or nothing. It cannot be divided except in our minds. It remains beyond our grasp. It is almost holy.

It is easy to pass by the great sight of eternal time. According to the book of Exodus, Moses beheld his first vision "in a flame of fire, out of the midst of a bush; and he looked, and, behold, the bush burned with fire, and the bush was not consumed" (3:2). Time is a burning bush. Though each instant must vanish to open the way to the next, time itself is not consumed.

Time is of independence, ultimate significance, of more majesty and more provocative of awe than even a sky scattered with stars. Gliding gently in the most ancient of all splendors, it tells so much more than space can say in its broken language of things, playing symphonies upon the instruments of isolated beings, unlocking the earth and making it happen. Every instant is itself a revelation, intimate, immediate, and yet imperceptible, vanishing while we are about to become aware of it.

Time is the process of creation, and the things of space are that which is being created. When looking at space, we see the products of creation; when listening to time, we hear the process of creation. Things of space exhibit a deceptive independence. They show off a veneer of limited permanence. Things created conceal the Creator. It is the dimension of time wherein man meets God, wherein man becomes aware that every instant is an act of creation, a Beginning opening up new roads for ultimate realizations. Time is the presence of God in the world of space, and it is within time that we are able to sense the unity of all things.

Creation, we are taught, is not an act that happened once upon a time, once and for all. The act of bringing the world into existence is a continuous process.[10] God called the world into being, and that call goes on. There is this present moment because God is present. Every instant is an act of creation. A moment is not a terminal but a flash, a signal of Beginning. Time is perpetual innovation, a synonym for continuous creation. Time is God's gift to the world of space.

A world without time would be a world without God, a world existing in and by itself, without renewal, without a Creator. A world without time would be a world detached from God, a thing in itself, reality without realization. A world in time is a world going on through God, realization of an infinite design, not a thing in itself, but a thing for God.

To witness the perpetual marvel of the world's coming into being is to sense the presence of the Giver in the given, to realize that the source of time is eternity, that the secret of being is the eternal within time.

We cannot solve the problem of time through the conquest of space, through either pyramids or fame. We can only solve the problem of time through sanctification of time. To man alone, time is elusive; to man with God, time is eternity in disguise.

Creation is the language of God, time is His song, and things of space the consonants in the song. To sanctify time is to sing the vowels in unison with Him.

This is the task of men: to conquer space and sanctify time.

The Bible is more concerned with time than with space. It sees the world in the dimension of time. It pays more attention to generations and events than to countries and things; it is more concerned with history than with geography. To understand the teaching of the Bible, one must accept its premise that time has a meaning for life which is at least equal to that of space, that time has a significance and sovereignty of its own.

There is no equivalent for the word "thing" in Biblical Hebrew. The word *dabar,* which in later Hebrew came to denote thing, means in Biblical Hebrew speech, word, message, report, tidings, advice, request, promise, decision, sentence, theme, story, saying, utterance, business, occupation, act, good deed, event, way, manner, reason, cause—but never "thing". Is this a sign of linguistic poverty, or rather an indication of an unwarped view of the world, of refusing to equate reality (derived from the Latin word *res,* thing) with thinghood?

Pagans project their consciousness of God into a visible image or associate Him with a phenomenon in nature, with a thing of space. In the Ten Commandments, the God of Israel identifies Himself by an event in history, by an event in time—the liberation of Israel from Egypt—and proclaims: "Thou shalt not make unto thee any graven image or any likeness of any thing that is in heaven above, or that is in the earth, or that is in the water under the earth."

What is the most precious thing that has ever been on earth? The gold of Sheba? The crown of Solomon? The breastplate of Aaron? The Holy Ark? It was the Two Tablets of stone which Moses received upon Mount Sinai; they were priceless beyond compare. He had gone up into the Mount to receive them; there he abode forty days and forty nights; he did neither eat bread nor drink water. And the Lord delivered unto him the Two Tablets of stone, and on them were written the Ten Commandments, the words which the Lord spoke with the people of Israel in the Mount out of the midst of fire. And yet when, on coming down the Mount at the end of forty days and forty nights—the Two Tablets he had just received in his hands—Moses saw the people dancing around the Golden Calf, he cast the Tablets down and smashed them before their eyes!

"Every important cult-center of Egypt asserted its primacy by the dogma that it was the *site* of creation."[11] In contrast, the book of Genesis speaks of the days rather than of the site of creation.[12] In the myths there is no reference to the time of creation, whereas the Bible speaks of the creation of space in time.

Everyone will admit that the Grand Canyon is more awe-inspiring than a goat. Everyone knows the difference between a worm and an eagle. But how many of us have a similar sense of discrimination for the diversity of time? The historian Ranke claimed that every age is equally near to God. Yet Jewish tradition maintains that there is a hierarchy of moments within time, that all ages are not alike. Man may pray to God equally at all places, but God does not speak to man equally at all times. At a certain moment, for example, the spirit of prophecy departed from Israel.

One of the most important facts in the history of Judaism is the transformation of agricultural festivals into commemorations of historical events. The festivals of ancient peoples were intimately linked with nature's seasons. They celebrated what happened in the life of nature in the respective seasons. Thus the value of the festive day was determined by the things nature brings forth. In Judaism, however, Passover, originally a spring festival, became a celebration of the Exodus from Egypt; the Feast of Weeks, an old harvest festival at the end of the wheat harvest (*Hag HaKatzir,* Exodus 23:16, 34:22), became the celebration of the day on which the Torah was given at Sinai; the Feast of Booths, an old festival of vintage (*Hag Ha-Asif,* Ex. 23:16), commemorates the dwelling of the Israelites in booths during their sojourn in the Wilderness (Lev. 23:42f). To Israel, the unique events of historic time were spiritually more significant than the repetitive processes in the cycle of nature, even though physical sustenance depended on the latter. While the deities of other peoples were associated with places or things, the God of Israel was the God of events: the Redeemer from slavery, the Revealer of the Torah, manifesting Himself in events of history rather than in things or places. Thus, the faith in the unembodied, in the unimaginable was born.

Judaism is a religion of time aiming at the sanctification of time. Unlike the space-minded man to whom time is unvaried, iterative, homogeneous, to whom all hours are alike, qualityless, empty shells, the Bible senses the diversified character of time. There are no two hours alike. Every hour is unique and the only one given at the moment, exclusive, and endlessly precious.

Judaism teaches us to be attached to holiness in time, to be attached to sacred events rather than to sacred places, to learn how to consecrate sanctuaries that emerge from the magnificent stream of a year. The Sabbaths are our great cathedrals, and our Holy of Holies is a shrine that neither the Romans nor the Germans were able to burn, a shrine that even apostasy cannot easily obliterate—the Day of Atonement. According to the rabbis, it is not the observance of the Day of Atonement, but the Day itself, "the essence of the Day," which, with man's repentance, atones for the sins of man.

Jewish ritual may be characterized as the art of significant forms in time, the *architecture of time*. Most of its observances—the Sabbath, the new moon, the festivals, the sabbatical and the jubilee year—depend on a certain hour of the day or season of the year. It is the evening, morning, or afternoon that brings with it the call to prayer. The source of faith lies in the realm of time. We remember the day of the Exodus from Egypt, the day when Israel stood at Sinai; and our messianic hope is the expectation of a day, of the End of Days.

While the Jewish festivals celebrate events that happened in time, the date of the month assigned to each festival in the calendar is determined by life in nature. Passover and the Feast of Booths, for example, coincide with the full moon, and the date of all festivals is a day in the month, and the month is a reflection of what goes on periodically in the realm of nature, since the Jewish month begins with the new moon, with the reappearance of the lunar crescent in the evening sky.[13] In contrast, the Sabbath is entirely independent of the month and unrelated to the moon.[14] Its date is not determined by any event in nature, such as the new moon, but by the act of creation itself.

The meaning of the Sabbath is to celebrate time rather than space. Six days a week we live under the tyranny of things of space. On the Sabbath, we try to become attuned to holiness in time. It is a day on which we are called upon to share in what is eternal in time, to turn from the results of creation to the mystery of creation, from the world of creation to the creation of the world.

What is the Sabbath? *Spirit in the form of time.* With our bodies we belong to space; our spirit, our souls, are rooted in eternity, in the holy. The Sabbath is return to the roots. It gives us the opportunity to sanctify time, to raise the good to the level of the holy, to behold the holy by abstaining from profanity.

There is a world of things and a world of spirit. Sabbath is a microcosm of spirit, as if combining in itself all the elements of spirit.

Just as the physical world does not owe its existence to the power of man—it is simply there—so does the spirit not owe its existence to the mind of man. The Sabbath is not holy by the grace of man. It was God who sanctified the seventh day.

The world was brought into being in the six days of creation, yet its survival depends upon the holiness of the seventh day. Great are the laws that govern the processes of nature. But without holiness there would be neither greatness nor nature.

Notes

1. According to Bertrand Russell, time is "an unimportant and superficial characteristic of reality . . . A certain emancipation from slavery to time is essential to philosophic thought . . . To realize the unimportance of time is the gate to wisdom" (*Our Knowledge of the External World,* pp. 166–7).

2. "Time is an evil, a mortal disease, exuding a fatal nostalgia. The passage of time strikes a man's heart with despair, and fills his gaze with sadness" (N. Berdyaev, *Solitude and Society,* p. 134).

3. A. J. Heschel, *The Earth is the Lord's,* pp. 13f.

4. This is one of the aspects which distinguishes the religious from the aesthetic experience.

5. Tanhuma (ed. Buber), vol. II, p. 76; see Rashi to Ex. 19:1, Deut. 26:16.

6. M. Pesahim 10.5; Passover Haggadah.

7. M. Yadaim 3.5.

8. B. Abodah Zarah 10b, 17a, 18a.

9. M. Abot 4.17.

10. In the daily morning service, we read: "The Lord of marvels, in His goodness He renews the wonders of creation every day, constantly."

The preservation of the world, or the laws that account for the preservation of the world, are due to an act of God: "Thou art the Lord, even Thou alone. Thou hast made heaven, the heaven of heavens with all their hosts, the earth and all things that are thereon, the seas and all that is in them, and *Thou preservest them all"* (Nehem. 9.6). "How manifold are Thy works, O Lord . . . All of them wait for Thee, that Thou mayest give them their food in due season . . . Thou hidest Thy face, they vanish . . . Thou sendest forth Thy spirit, they are created" (Psalms 104:24, 27:29, 30). Note the present tense in Isaiah 48:13, 42:5; see also 48:7; Job 34:14–16; Judah Halevi, *Kusari* 3.11. On seeing the wonders of nature, we pray: "Blessed art Thou . . . who doest the wonders of creation" (M. Berakot 9.2; see Resh Lakish, B. Hagigah 12b, and Rashi *ad locum*). The idea of continuous creation seems to have been the theme of an ancient controversy. According to the School of Shammai, the benediction over the lights which is said at the outgoing of the Sabbath is: "Blessed art Thou who *didst create* the lights of fire," whereas according to the school of Hillel, we recite: "Blessed art Thou . . . who *createst* the lights of fire" (M. Berakot 7.5; see Joseph Salomo Delmedigo, *Taalumot Hokmah,* Nobelot Hokmah [Basel, 1629], p. 94a).

11. J. A. Wilson, "Egyptian Myths, Tales and Mortuary Texts", in *Ancient Near Eastern Texts,* p. 8.

12. The legend of the *Eben Shetiyah* is of post-biblical origin, cp. Louis Ginzberg, *The Legends of the Jews,* vol. V, pp. 14–16.

13. Each revolution, from one new moon to the next, constitutes a lunar month and measures about 29 days and 12 hours.

14. The Babylonian seventh day was observed on every seventh day of the lunar month. See J. Barth, "The Jewish Sabbath and the Babylonians", *The American Israelite,* Nov. 20, 1902; see also H. Webster, *Rest Days* (New York, 1916), pp. 253f.

Chapter 8

SPACE, TIME, AND REALITY: THE CENTRALITY OF TIME IN THE BIBLICAL WORLD-VIEW

I

"What, then, is time? If nobody asks me, I know . . ., but if I try to explain it to one who asks me, I do not know." Thus wrote Augustine more than fifteen hundred years ago.[1] Alfred North White-head found it "impossible to meditate on time and the creative passage of nature without an overwhelming emotion at the limitations of human intelligence".[2]

Speaking of a famous school of Arabic thinkers, Maimonides says: "They did not at all understand the nature of time. This is a matter of course; for if the greatest philosophers became embarrassed when they investigated the nature of time, if some of them were altogether unable to comprehend what time really is, and if even Galen declared time to be something divine and incomprehensible, what can be expected of those who do not examine the nature of things?"[3] Yet it seems that there are people today to whom time is something quite clear and simple: "a dimension of space". That is all. Gone is the enigma. Einstein has solved it once and for all.

Is that really so?

I quote from Albert Einstein's essay "Physics and Reality". "An important property of our sense-experiences", Einstein writes, "is its time-like order. This kind of order leads to the mental conception of a subjective time, an ordinating scheme of our experience." But for science it was important to obtain "the notion of objective time for the happenings in the whole of space, by which notion alone the idea of local time is enlarged to the idea of time in physics". The necessity of introducing such a notion became obvious to Einstein when he examined the "time" of the propagation of light, the measurement of which presupposes an understanding of simultaneity. Prior to the enunciation of the theory of relativity, it was assumed "that from the point of view of experience, the meaning of simultaneity in relation to happenings distant in space, and consequently that the meaning of time in physics, is a priori clear".[4]

Einstein's problem, then, was to find a method by which it could be determined as accurately as possible which events at a distance from each other were simultaneous. He noticed, for example, that the hearing of the same sound by two people occurred at different times depending on the position of their bodies in physical space as well as on the position in time and space of the event producing the sound. And he concluded that the time-order of events separated by distance was, within certain limits, arbitrary.

The relativity of simultaneity of events separated by distance is particularly important for the astronomic observer who is engaged in determining the time-order of events separated by vast spatial intervals. He manages this by measuring the distance from the star to his position on the earth and dividing this figure by the velocity of light; in this way, he gets the time it took for the light to traverse the distance. To do this, however, he must know the velocity of light. But here we discover that the measurement of space depends on simultaneity. This principle is expressed mathematically by bringing together space and time into a four-dimensional structure, or space-time-manifold.

Following Minkowski, Einstein reduced space and time to a space-time continuum. Space and time are no longer considered different classes of physical object-concepts; the world is a four-dimensional manifold, and all physical events must be characterized by space-time coordinates. The theory of relativity reduces the content and form of all laws of nature to coincidences or meetings of points defined by these coordinates. The physical world of space-time is nothing but the system of such coordination. Hans Reichenbach makes this quite clear.[5]

Strangely enough, this procedure, which appears simple and harmless to the mathematician, has given cause for great surprise and for bewilderment to others. Many a reader of books on relativity thought that space was thereby transformed from a three-dimensional structure into a four-dimensional one; and he then attempted in vain to conceive the fourth dimension of space. He may have argued in this way: Imagine three sticks of wood meeting together at one point under right angles, like the length, width, and height of a room. These are three dimensions of space; is there any room for the fourth one? How is it possible to pass the fourth stick through the point, so that it would form right angles with the others? The author too cannot visualize how it would run; but the theory of relativity never asserted anything of the sort. It asserts merely that time should be added *as time,* to space; and this is something entirely different. We may imagine it this way: Three numbers are needed to determine a point in space. Suppose a lamp hangs in the room. How can we determine its place? We measure its distance from the floor, from the back-wall and from the side-wall; these three figures determine its position in space. The three numbers are called co-ordinates. The room is three-dimensional, because three figures are needed for statements of the kind described. If we want to determine not a point in space but an event, we require another figure, namely, the statement of time. Suppose that we switch on the light for a second and produce a flash of light; this is an event. It is completely determined if we know the three numbers defining the position of the lamp and in addition, the fourth number defining the time of the light-flash. Insofar as there are four figures, space and time together are called a four-dimensional manifoldness. This is the whole secret. Unfortunately, this simple circumstance is often depicted in a most obscure language.

It has been asserted that "thanks to Leibnitz, Planck, and Einstein, space and time are now recognized as virtually identical." This notion will surely come as a surprise to Einstein himself. The theory of relativity does not in the least eliminate the distinction between space and time, nor does it deprive time of its peculiar temporal character. Einstein himself has stated: "The non-divisibility of the four-dimensional continuum of events does not at all, however, involve the equivalence of space co-ordinates with the time co-ordinate. On the contrary, we must remember that the time co-ordinate is defined physically wholly differently from the space co-ordinates."[6]
The philosophical examination of the theory of relativity undertaken in the course of the past three decades has shown that time is something

even more profound than space. A. S. Eddington, the distinguished astronomer who so early recognized the importance of the theory of relativity, confesses himself baffled. "Time", he exclaims, "which is . . . Heaven knows what."

> Our knowledge of space-relations [he goes on to say] is indirect, like nearly all our knowledge of the external world—a matter of inference and interpretation of the impressions which reach us through our sense-organs. We have similar indirect knowledge of the time-relations existing between the events in the world outside us; but in addition, we have direct experience of the time-relations that we ourselves are traversing—a knowledge of time not coming through external sense-organs, but taking a short-cut into our consciousness. When I close my eyes and retreat into my inner mind, I feel myself *enduring,* I do not feel myself *extensive.* It is this feeling of time as affecting ourselves and not merely as existing in the relations of external events which is so peculiarly characteristic of it. Space on the other hand is always appreciated as something external.
>
> That is why time seems to us so much more mysterious than space. We know nothing about the intrinsic nature of space, and so it is quite easy to conceive it satisfactorily. We have intimate acquaintance with the nature of time and so it baffles our comprehension. It is the same paradox which makes us believe we understand the nature of an ordinary table whereas the nature of human personality is altogether mysterious. We never have that intimate contact with space and tables which would make us realize how mysterious they are; we have direct knowledge of time and of the human spirit which makes us reject as inadequate that merely symbolic conception of the world which is so often mistaken as an insight into its nature.[7]

There are concepts which are presupposed by science but are not subjected to analysis by any science. Among these is time as used by the physicists. What time means as a functioning concept in science is one thing, and what it means to the consciousness of man who reflects about his own vanishing existence is quite another. Indeed, "here is the point at which the ways of the physicist and of the philosopher definitely part, without their being thereby forced into conflict. What the physicist calls 'space' and 'time' is for him a concrete measurable manifold, which he gains as the result of coordination according to law of the particular points; for the philosopher, space and time signify the presuppositions of this coordination itself. They do not result for him from the coordination, but they are precisely this coordination and its fundamental directions . . . , coordination from the standpoint of coexistence and adjacency or from the standpoint of succession."[8]

To sum up, the theory of relativity is concerned with a mathematical and physical problem, namely, the measurement of events in time and space. The moment we leave the realm of physics, and change not merely the method but the very goal of knowledge, all concepts assume a different aspect and a different meaning. Space and time mean something totally different in philosophy and religion from what they mean in physics. "What space and time are as immediate contents of experience and as they offer themselves to our psychological and phenomenological analysis is unaffected in the use we make of them in the determination of the object, in the course of objective conceptual knowledge. The distance between these two types of consideration and conception is only augmented by the theory of relativity and thus only made known more distinctly but is not first produced by it."[9]

Simply to carry over a concept from physics, designed to measure physical events, into the realm of metaphysics is obviously naive. The heterogeneity of time and space has not lost its validity, and as every student of contemporary philosophy knows, it is a characteristic sign of modern thinking that it takes time seriously.

II

To the biblical man, the power of God was behind all phenomena.[10] and he was more concerned to know the will of God who governed nature than to know the order of nature itself. Important and impressive as nature was to him, God was vastly more so. That is why Psalm 104 is a hymn to God rather than an ode to the cosmos.

The idea of the cosmos as space is one of the outstanding contributions of Greek philosophy, and we can well understand why a similar conception did not emerge in Hebrew thinking. For the idea of a cosmos, of a totality of things, complete in itself, implies the concept of an immanent norm of nature, of an order which has its foundation in nature. Now the biblical man, of course, was conscious of an order of nature which could be relied upon in daily life. But that order was one which was invested in nature by the will of God and remained constantly dependent upon

Him. It was not an immanent law but a divine decree that dominated everything. God had given His decree to the sea; He had appointed the foundations of the earth (Prov. 8:29); and He continued to rule the world from without. Nature was the object of this perpetual care, but this very dependence of nature on divine care is an expression of its contingency. Biblical man did not take anything for granted, and to him the laws of nature were as much in need of derivation as the processes ruled by these laws. The continued existence of the world was guaranteed by God's faithfulness to this covenant. "Thus saith the Lord: if my covenant be not with day and night . . ." (Jer. 33:25). The world was not an ontological necessity. Indeed, heaven and earth may not last forever:

> Of old Thou didst lay the foundation of the earth:
> And the heavens are the work of Thy hands.
> They shall perish, but Thou shalt endure;
> Yea, all of them shall wax like a garment;
> As a vesture shalt Thou change them, and they shall pass away;
> But Thou art the selfsame,
> And Thy years shall have no end (Ps. 102:26–28).

The world was not the *all* to the Bible, and so the *all* could never come to denote the world. Biblical man was not enchanted by the given. He realized the alternative, namely the annihilation of the given. He was not enchanted by the order, because he had a vision of a new order. He was not lost to the here and now, nor to the beyond. He sensed the non-given with the given, the past and future with the present. He had been taught that "the mountains may depart, the hills be removed, but My kindness shall not depart from thee . . ." (Is. 54:10). The Hebrew conception has been rightly characterized by A. N. Whitehead as the doctrine of the *imposed* law, as contrasted with the doctrine of the *immanent* law developed in Greek philosophy. According to the doctrine of the *imposed* law, there is imposed on each existent the necessity of entering into relationships with the other constituents of nature. These imposed behavior patterns are the laws of nature. Newton, for example, clearly states that the correlated modes of behavior of the bodies forming the solar system require God for the imposition of the principles on which all depend.

The Greek philosophers were endeavoring to account for things in a way quite different from the manner of the Hebrews. They sought to find the causes of things within the phenomena themselves rather than in the will of some external power. They sought to know the mechanisms of nature rather than the will of the God who governs nature.

The doctrine of the imposed law leads to the monotheistic conception of God as essentially transcendent and only accidentally immanent; while the doctrine of the immanent law leads to the pantheistic doctrine of God as essentially immanent and in no way transcendent. "Subsequent speculation," Whitehead points out,[11] "wavers between these two extremes, seeking their reconciliation. In this, as in most other matters, the history of Western thought consists in the attempted fusion of ideas which in their origin are predominantly Hellenic, with ideas which in their origin are predominantly Semitic."

III

In ancient Israel, there was no single word to describe what is called in Indogermanic languages "world" or "universe", corresponding to the Greek *kosmos* or the Latin *mundus*.[12] When the biblical writers intended to refer to all of creation, they spoke of "heaven and earth" or "earth and heaven". *Kol* in Psalms 8:7; Isaiah 44:24, or *hakkol* in Ecclesiastes 3:11, is a sort of substitute for world, not a specific term. Even so late a book as Daniel has no other expression than *kol ar'a* to denote what we call the world (2:35, 39; 3:31; 4:8, 19). *Tebel* is not a word of wider meaning than *eretz;* it is frequently used in the sense of *oikoumene,* namely all the inhabitants of the earth (Is. 18:3; Ps. 33:8), but never in the sense of universe. Another synonym of *eretz, heled,* is related to the Arabic *khalada,* which is a time-concept and means to abide, to endure.

Now the word *'olam.* It is a truism that in the Bible it never means "world" (space), or the material universe; it always expresses a conception of time.[13] *'Olam* means distant time of the past[14], antiquity, such as "days of old" (Amos 9:11 calls the time of David *yeme 'olam*); ancient (*'am 'olam,* ancient people, Is. 44:7; *horbot 'olam,* a land which has long lain desolate, Is. 61:4). It is also used in the sense of remote, endless future; of indefinite future or forever (*'eved 'olam,* Deut. 15:17; *'olam ashirah,* "I will sing for ever", Ps. 89:2; "Let the king live for ever", Nehem. 2:3); of continuous existence (Eccl. 1:4; Ps. 78:69; Jer. 18:17).

'Olam is also used in the sense of everlastingness, as in *berit 'olam,* everlasting covenant (Gen. 9:16), and in *simhat 'olam* (Is. 35:10); or in the sense of eternity in regard to God, as *el 'olam* (Gen. 21:33), *elehe 'olam* (Is. 40:28), *melek 'olam* (Jer. 10:10).

It is only in the post-biblical literature that the word *'olam* came to denote also the world in the sense of space. In this sense, it occurs in the famous saying by Rabbi Simeon the Just (*ha-'olam,* M. Abot 1.2) and in the Jewish writings of the Hellenistic period.

In the Septuagint, the Greek translation of the Hebrew Bible, the word *kosmos* is never used for the world in the sense of space. It is in the writings of Jewish Hellenistic authors, such as the Wisdom of Solomon (9:3, 9; 11:17, 22), II Maccabees (7:9, 23; 8:18; 12:15; 13:14), and IV Maccabees, that we find the word *kosmos* in the sense which it acquired among the Greeks through philosophical usage, namely, as a word for the material universe.

IV

One of the unique features of the biblical record of creation is the complete absence of any concept of an eternal space which is characteristic of so many creation myths.

The Babylonian myth starts with the concept of a space in existence prior to the creation of the world. Thus we read in the opening words of the epic known among the Babylonians and Assyrians as *Enuma Elish*[15]:

When *above* the heaven had not [yet] been named,
[And] *below* the earth had not [yet] been called by a name.

The Babylonians could conceive of a state when there was neither heaven nor earth, but they could not conceive of a state when there was no space, no above or below. For them, matter, or the substance of which the world was formed, was eternal. But in the Book of Genesis, there is no mention of a primeval matter; the world is represented as created by the will of God rather than out of an eternal matter.

Pondering the origin of the universe, Hesiod proclaims: "In the beginning was chaos". What he meant was *space,* which is the final presupposition of all things and takes precedence over all things, because everything is somewhere.[16]

According to Plato, the cosmos is the work of a god, the *demiourgos*, who formed it after the pattern or idea of a perfect living being. The cosmos was not formed out of nothing but out of "matter", which to Plato meant space (*chora, topos*)[17]: "matter and space are the same".[18] The contrast with the Book of Genesis is apparent.

The biblical concept of creation does not start with chaos. On the contrary, it places chaos on earth after the latter had been created. And, significantly, the first word of the Bible signifying the act of creation denotes not a material but a temporal beginning *(reshit)*.

V

That God is beyond the category of space is a truism in Jewish literature. Saadia, for example, rejecting the view of those who identify God with space, stresses the non-spatiality of God and the inapplicability of the category of space to Him.[19] What is spiritual does not occupy space, asserts Ibn Gabirol.[20] The expression "God in heaven" is a mere metaphor, according to Jehudah Halevi.[21] Maimonides emphasizes the fact that the rabbis do not speak of God as "dwelling in" the sphere, which would have implied that "God occupies a place or is a power in the sphere, as was in fact believed by the Sabaeans who held that God was the soul of the sphere." By saying God is "dwelling over" the sphere, the rabbis indicated that He is separate from the universe, and is not a power comprehended within it.[22]

It was Spinoza who taught that space or extension was an attribute of God, in other words, that God was *not* immaterial. He knew well that in this he was breaking with the views of his predecessors and with the authoritative Jewish sources.[23]

Maqom ("place") is, indeed, an old synonym for God in ancient rabbinic literature. Its use was a puzzle to both the Amoraim and the medieval exegetes.

In a comment on Genesis 28:11, the question is asked in the name of R. Ammi: "Why do we give a changed name to the Holy One, blessed is He, and call Him 'The Place'? Because He is the Place of the world." "R. Jose ben Halafta said: We do not know whether God is the place of this world or whether the world is His place, but from the verse, *Behold, there is a place with Me* (Ex. 33:21), it follows that He is the place of His world, but His world is not His place . . . R. Abba ben Judan said: He is like a warrior riding a horse, his robes flowing over on both sides; the horse is subsidiary to the rider, but the rider is not subsidiary to the horse. Thus it says: *that Thou dost ride upon Thy horses, upon Thy chariots of victory* (Hab. 3:8)."[24] This explanation, far from implying an identification of God and space, asserts, on the contrary, the subordination of space to God.[25]

In the mainstream of Jewish tradition, the Presence of God in the world is not thought of as being static and permanently anchored to the world of space, but as being free, unfixed and conditioned on the attitude of man. "Why is He called *maqom?* Because wherever the *zaddikim* are, God is with them."[26] According to what man does, God's Presence is with or away from him. If he is steadily and regularly engaged in Torah and prayer, the Presence is with him steadily; if only occasionally he studies and prays, God's Presence will be with him only occasionally.[27]

The Presence of God is not to be understood in the sense of His being in a particular place. "He clings to us in a sort of spiritual air even if there is no sanctuary built of physical matter . . . everywhere . . . for the world is not His place; He is the place of the world. He is not limited by space, because He is immaterial". So writes one of the great Jewish theologians, Rabbi Samuel Edels.[28]

God has no geographical address nor a permanent residence. He is not in the world once and for all in that sense. He is in events, in acts, in time, in history, rather than in things. And when in things, He may be profaned and driven out, or kept by the power of our deeds: "If thou seek Him, He will be found of thee: if thou forsake Him, He will cast thee off forever" (I Chron. 28:9).

The original meaning of the term *maqom* may well have been that "of the omnipresence of God within a universe from which He is separated and which He transcends."[29] It may have also perhaps come into use as a metonym for "heaven", which is an ancient synonym for God;[30] or as a metonym for the sanctuary in Jerusalem, which was called *maqom*.[31]

VI

In biblical Hebrew, *hefetz* in its verbal form generally means "to take pleasure or delight in, to desire." As a noun, it means "delight", "pleasure", "longing", but never "thing". In Proverbs 3:15, Rashi explains it as meaning *hemdah*. According to the International Critical Commentary, it means literally "what is desired, desirable, precious". *The Bible: An American Translation* renders it "your heart's desire". Even in late biblical Hebrew, the word still retains its original meaning of a volitional act.[32] Only in mishnaic Hebrew does *hefetz* come to denote "thing" (M. Ned. 3.1; M. Git. 3.5; M. Baba Metzia 4.10).

VII

I have never maintained, as has been charged that "there is an eternal and unbridgeable dichotomy between time and space", nor have I ever undertaken to offer "proof of Judaism's disdain for space." In fact, I have said the very opposite. In my article, "The Architecture of Time", I state: "To disparage space and the blessings of things of space is to disparage the works of creation. . . . The world cannot be seen exclusively *sub specie temporis*. Time and space are interrelated. To overlook either of them is to be partially blind."[33] R. Simeon ben Yohai's condemnation of all worldly activities was rejected by a "heavenly voice". The Jewish "answer to the problem of civilization", I state, is "not to flee from the realm of space; [it is] to work with things of space, but to be in love with eternity".[34] This is my position.

Notes

1. *Confessions*, xi, 14.
2. *The Concept of Nature*, p. 73.
3. *The Guide for the Perplexed*, I, ch. 73, Third Proposition.
4. See *Out of My Later Years*, pp. 65 ff.
5. *From Copernicus to Einstein*, pp. 112f.
6. *The Meaning of Relativity* (3rd ed.), p. 31.
7. *The Nature of the Physical World*, pp. ix, 51–52.
8. Ernst Cassirer, *Substance and Function in Einstein's Theory of Relativity*, p. 417.
9. Cassirer, *op. cit.*, pp. 450f. On the differences between the method of metaphysics and the method of mathematics, see Samuel Alexander, *Space, Time and Deity*, vol. I, p. 175.

10. Every occurrence in nature was regarded as an act of divine providence; cp. Is. 40:26; Job 27: 4–6.

11. *Adventures of Ideas,* p. 154.

12. See, e.g., Alfred Bertholet, *A History of Hebrew Civilization,* p. 289; Gustaf Dalman, *Die Worte Jesu,* p. 132; Robert Gordis, *Koheleth: The Man and His World,* p. 221.

13. See Brown, Driver, Briggs, *Hebrew and English Lexicon,* p. 761; Gesenius, *Handwörterbuch über das Alte Testament* (17th ed.), p. 571.—The passage in Eccl. 3:11 is obscure.

14. "Einen Begriff, der da anfängt, wo unset Wahrnehmungsvermögen aufhört" (C. V. Orelli, *Die Hebräischen Synonyma der Zeit und Ewigkeit,* p. 70).

15. Alexander Heidel, *The Babylonian Genesis,* p. 18.

16. The term "chaos" has been variously interpreted. We follow here the interpretation given by Aristotle, *Physics,* IV, 1, 208 b; see also F. Lukas, *Die Grundbegriffe in den Kosmogenien der alten Voelker,* pp. 157f.

17. "And there is a third nature, which is space, and is eternal, and admits not of destruction, and provides a home for all created things, and is apprehended without the help of sense, by a kind of spurious reason, and is hardly real" (*Timaeus,* 52). See Eduard Zeller, *Grundriss der Geschichte der Griechischen Philosophie* (9th ed.), pp. 140f; F. Ueberweg-Karl Praechter, *Grundriss der Geschichte der Philosophie* (12th ed.), vol. I, p. 310. For a survey of the famous controversy about the meaning of matter in Plato, see Cl. Baeumker, *Das Problem der Materie,* pp. 151ff.

18. See Aristotle, *Physics,* IV, 1, 209 b.

19. *Emunot,* ch. ii, 9; see Jakob Guttmann, *Die Religionsphilosophie Saadias,* p. 116, n. 2.

20. "Omne simplex et spirituale locum non occupat" (*Fons Vitae,* III, 32, p. 153).

21. *Kuzari,* IV, 3.

22. *Guide for the Perplexed,* I, ch. 70.

23. *Ethics,* I, prop, 15; see Harry A. Wolfson, *Spinoza,* vol. I, pp. 222f.

24. Genesis rabba, ch. 68.

25. A. J. Heschel, *The Sabbath,* p. 117.

26. Midrash Tehillim, 90:1; Pirke de Rabbi Eliezer, ch. 35.

27. Tikkune Zohar (ed. Margolis), VI, p. 21a.

28. *Commentary on Bechorot,* 8f.

29. See Wolfson, *Crescas' Critique of Aristotle,* pp. 123, 201; Solomon S. Schechter, *Some Aspects of Rabbinic Theology,* p. 27, n. 1.

30. Dalman, *op. cit.,* pp. 189f.

31. See M. Maaser Sheni 3.10; M. Bikkurim 2.2; Tosafot Abodah Zarah 8b. W. Bacher (*Die Aggada der Tannaiten,* vol. I, p. 207) has called attention to a passage in Mekilta to 17:7, in which "the Great Court or Sanhedrin is called *maqom";* see Mekilta de R. Simeon (ed. Hoffmann), p. 81; Yalkut Shimoni, I, 62.

32. See Gordis, "The Translation Theory of Qohelet", *Jewish Quarterly Review*, vol. 40 (1949), p. 108.

33. *Judaism*, vol. I (1952), p. 46; *The Sabbath*, p. 6.

34. *The Sabbath*, p. 48.

Chapter 9

THE CONCEPT OF MAN IN JEWISH THOUGHT

I. *The Meaning of Existence*

Our theories will go away, will all throw dust into our eyes, unless we dare to confront not only the world but the soul as well, and begin to be amazed at our lack of amazement in being alive, at our taking life for granted.

Confronting the soul is an intellectual exposure that tears open the mind to incalculable questions, the answers to which are not easily earned. Modern man, therefore, believes that his security lies in refraining from raising such issues. Ultimate questions have become the object of his favorite unawareness. Since the dedication to tangible matters is highly rewarded, he does not care to pay attention to imponderable issues and prefers to erect a tower of Babel on the narrow basis of deeper unawareness.

Unawareness of the ultimate is a possible state of mind as long as man finds tranquility in his dedication to partial objectives. But when the tower begins to totter, when death wipes away that which seemed mighty and independent, when in evil days the delights of striving are replaced by the nightmare of futility, he becomes conscious of the peril of evasiveness, of the emptiness of small objectives. His apprehension lest in winning small prizes he did not gamble his life away, throws his soul open to questions he was trying to avoid.

But what is there at stake in human life that may be gambled away? It is the meaning of life. In all acts he performs, man raises a claim to meaning. The trees he plants, the tools he invents, are *answers to a need* or a purpose. In its very essence, consciousness is a dedication to design. Committed to the task of coalescing being with meaning, things with ideas, the mind is driven to ponder whether meaning is something it may invent and invest, something which ought to be attained, or whether there is meaning to existence as it is, to existence as existence, independent of what we may add to it. In other words, is there only meaning to what *man does,* but none to what *he is?* Becoming conscious of himself he does not stop at knowing: 'I am'; he is driven to know 'what' he is. Man may, indeed, be characterized as *a subject in quest of a predicate,* as a being in quest of a meaning of life, of all of life, not only of particular actions or single episodes which happen now and then.

Meaning denotes a condition that cannot be reduced to a material relation and grasped by the sense organs. Meaning is compatibility with an idea, it is, furthermore, that which a fact is for the sake of something else; the pregnancy of an object with value. Life is precious to man. But is it precious to him alone? Or is someone else in need of it?

Imbedded in the mind is a certainty that the state of existence and the state of meaning stand in a relation to each other, that life is assessable in terms of meaning. The will to meaning and the certainty of the legitimacy of our striving to ascertain it are as intrinsically human as the will to live and the certainty of being alive.

In spite of failures and frustrations, we continue to be haunted by that irrepressible quest. We can never accept the idea that life is hollow and incompatible with meaning.

If at the root of philosophy is not a self-contempt of the mind but the mind's concern for its ultimate surmise, then our aim is to examine in order to know. Seeking contentment in a brilliant subterfuge, we are often ready to embezzle the original surmise. But why should we even care to doubt, if we cease to surmise? Philosophy is what man dares to do with his ultimate surmise of the meaning of existence.

Animals are content when their needs are satisfied; man insists not only on being satisfied but also on being able to satisfy, on *being a need* not only on *having needs.* Personal needs come and go, but one anxiety remains: *Am I needed?* There is no man who has not been moved by that anxiety.

It is a most significant fact that man is not sufficient to himself, that life is not meaningful to him unless it is serving an end beyond itself, unless it is of value to someone else. The self may have the highest rate of exchange, yet men do not live by currency alone, but by the good attainable in expending it. To hoard the self is to grow a colossal sense for the futility of living.

Man is not an all-inclusive end to himself. The second maxim of Kant, never to use human beings merely as means but to regard them also as ends, only suggests how a person ought to be treated by other people, not how he ought to treat himself. For if a person thinks that he is an end to himself, then he will use others as means. Moreover, if the idea of man being an end is to be taken as a true estimate of his worth, he cannot be expected to sacrifice his life or his interests for the good of someone else or even of a group. He must treat himself the way he expects others to treat him. Why should even a group or a whole people be worth the sacrifice of one's life? To a person who regards himself as an absolute end a thousand lives will not be worth more than his own life.

Sophisticated thinking may enable man to feign his being sufficient to himself. Yet the way to insanity is paved with such illusions. The feeling of futility that comes with the sense of being useless, of not being needed in the world, is the most common cause of psycho-neurosis. The only way to avoid despair *is to be a need* rather than an end. *Happiness,* in fact, may be defined as the *certainty of being needed.* But *who* is in need of man?

The first answer that comes to mind is a social one—man's purpose is to serve society or mankind. The ultimate worth of a person would then be determined by his usefulness to others, by the efficiency of his social work. Yet, in spite of his instrumentalist attitude, man expects others to take him not for what he may mean to them but as a being valuable in himself. Even he who does not regard himself as an absolute end, rebels against being treated as a means to an end, as subservient to other men. The rich, the men of the world, want to be loved for their own sake, for their essence, whatever it may mean, not for their achievements or possessions. Nor do the old and sick expect help because of what they may give us in return. Who needs the old, the incurably sick, the maintenance of whom is a drain on the treasury of the state? It is, moreover, obvious that such service does not claim all of one's life and can therefore not be the ultimate answer to his quest of meaning for life as a whole. Man has more to give than what other men are able or willing to accept. To say that life could consist of care for others, of incessant service to the world, would be a vulgar boast. What we are able to bestow upon others is usually less and rarely more than a tithe.

There are alleys in the soul where man walks alone, ways that do not lead to society, a world of privacy that shrinks from the public eye. Life comprises not only arable, productive land, but also mountains of dreams, an underground of sorrow, towers of yearning, which can hardly be utilized to the last for the good of society, unless man be converted into a machine in which every screw must serve a function or be removed. It is a profiteering state which, trying to exploit the individual, asks all of man for itself.

And if society as embodied in the state should prove to be corrupt and my effort to cure its evil unavailing, would my life as an individual have been totally void of meaning? If society should decide to reject my services and even place me in solitary confinement, so that I will surely die without being able to bequeath any influence to the world I love, will I then feel compelled to end my life?

Human existence cannot derive its ultimate meaning from society, because society itself is in need of meaning. It is as legitimate to ask: Is mankind needed?—as it is to ask: Am I needed?

Humanity begins in the individual man, just as history takes its rise from a singular event. It is always one man at a time whom we keep in mind when we pledge: 'with malice toward none, with charity for all', or when trying to fulfil: 'Love thy neighbour as thyself'. The term 'mankind', which in biology denotes the human species, has an entirely different meaning in the realm of ethics and religion. Here mankind is not conceived as a species, as an abstract concept, stripped from its concrete reality, but as an abundance of specific individuals; as a community of persons rather than as a herd of a multitude of nondescripts.

While it is true that the good of all counts more than the good of one, it is the concrete individual who lends meaning to the human race. We do not think that a human being is valuable because he is a member of the race; it is rather the opposite: the human race is valuable because it is composed of human beings.

While dependent on society as well as on the air that sustains us, and while other men compose the system of relations in which the curve of our actions takes its course, it is as individuals that we are beset with desires, fears and hopes, challenged, called upon and endowed with the power of will and a spark of responsibility.

Of all phenomena which takes place in the soul, desires have the highest rate of mortality. Like aquatic plants, they grow and live in the waters of oblivion, impatiently eager to vanish. Inherent in desire is the intention to expire; it asserts itself in order to be quenched, and in attaining satisfaction it comes to an end, singing its own dirge.

Such suicidal intention is not vested in all human acts. Thoughts, concepts, laws, theories are born with the intent to endure. A problem, for example, does not cease to be relevant when its solution is achieved. Inherent in reason is the intention to endure, a striving to comprehend the valid, to form concepts the cogency of which goes on for ever. It is, therefore, not in pondering about ideas, but in surveying one's inner life and discovering the graveyard of needs and desires, once fervently cherished, that we become intimately aware of the temporality of existence.

Yet, there is a curious ambiguity in the way in which this awareness is entertained. For while there is nothing man is more intimately sure of than the temporality of existence, he is rarely resigned to the role of a mere undertaker of desires.

Walking upon a rock that is constantly crumbling away behind every step and anticipating the inevitable abruption which will end his walk, man cannot restrain his bitter yearning to know whether life is nothing but a series of momentary physiological and mental processes, actions and forms of behavior, a flow of vicissitudes, desires and sensations, running like grains through an hourglass, marking time only once and always vanishing.

He wonders whether, at the bottom, life is not like the face of the sundial, outliving all shadows that rotate upon its surface. Is life nothing but a medley of facts, unrelated to one another; chaos camouflaged by illusion?

There is not a soul on this earth which, however vaguely or rarely, has not realized that life is dismal if not mirrored in something which is lasting. We are all in search of a conviction that there is something which is worth the toil of living. There is not a soul which has not felt a craving to know of something that outlasts life, strife and agony.

Helpless and incongruous is man with all his craving, with his tiny candles in the mist. Is it his will to be good that would heal the wounds of his soul, his fright and frustration? It is too obvious that his will is a door to a house divided against itself, that his good intentions, after enduring for a while, touch the mud of vanity, like the horizon of his life which some day will touch the grave. Is there anything beyond the horizon of our good intentions?

Despair, the sense of futility of living, is an attitude, the reality of which no psychologist will question. But just as real is our fear of despair, our horror of futility. Human life and despair seem to be incompatible. Man is a being in search of ultimate meaning of existence. But where is ultimate meaning to be found?

Ultimate meaning implies not only that man is part of a whole, an adjunct to greatness, but an answer to a question, the satisfaction of a need; not only that man is tolerated but also needed, precious, indispensable. Life is precious to man. But is it precious to man alone?

2. A Need of God

The Bible is a book about man. It is not a theology from the point of view of man but rather an anthropology from the point of view of God. And it is man who is becoming the central issue of contemporary thinking. His physical and mental reality is beyond dispute; his meaning, his spiritual relevance, is a question that cries for an answer.

It is the uniqueness of man that puzzles our mind. All other beings seem to fit perfectly into a natural order and are determined by permanent principles. Man alone occupies a unique status. As a natural being he is determined by natural laws. As a human being he must frequently choose; confined in his existence, he is unrestrained in his will. His acts do not emanate from him like rays of energy from matter. Placed in the parting of the ways, he must time and again decide which direction to take. The course of his life is, accordingly, unpredictable; no one can write his autobiography in advance.

Is man, who occupies such a strange position in the great realm of being, an outcast of the universal order? an outlaw, a freak of nature? a shred of yarn dropped from nature's loom, which has since been strangely twisted by the way? Astronomy and geology have taught us to disdain the over-weening vanity of man. Compared with the infinite universe, man is, indeed, a most insignificant speck.

However, if man's value and position in the universe are to be defined as one divided by the infinite, the infinite designating the number of beings which populate the universe; if man $= \dfrac{1}{\infty}$, how should we account for the fact that infinitesimal man is obviously the only being on this planet capable of making such an equation?

An ant is never stricken with amazement, nor does a star consider itself a nonentity. Immense is the scope of astronomy and geology, yet what is astronomy without the astronomer? What is geology without the geologist?

If we had to characterize an individual like William Shakespeare in terms of a measuring rod, we would surely avail ourselves of Eddington's description of man's position within the universe and say that Shakespeare is almost precisely halfway in size between an atom and a star. To assess his vegetative existence, it is important to know, for example, that man consists of a hundred million cells. However, to assess the essence of man, which alone accounts for the fact of his being anxious to assess his existence, we must discern what is unique about him.

Reflecting about the infinite universe we could perhaps afford to resign ourselves to the trivial position of being a nonentity. However, pondering over our reflection, we discover that we are not only carried and surrounded by the universe of meaning. Man is a fountain of immense meaning, not only a drop in the ocean of being.

The human species is too powerful, too dangerous to be a mere toy or a freak of the Creator. He undoubtedly represents something unique in the great body of the universe: a growth, as it were, an abnormal mass of tissue, which not only began to interact with other parts but also, to some degree, was able to modify their very status. What is its nature and function? Is it malignant, a tumor, or is it supposed to serve as a brain of the universe?

The human species shows at times symptoms of being malignant and, if its growth remains unchecked, it may destroy the entire body for the sake of its expansion. In terms of astronomical time, our civilization is in its infancy. The expansion of human power has hardly begun, and what man is going to do with his power may either save or destroy our planet.

The earth may be of small significance within the infinite universe. But if it is of some significance, man holds the key to it. For one thing man certainly seems to own: a boundless, unpredictable capacity for the development of an inner universe. There is more potentiality in his soul than in any other being known to us. Look at an infant and try to imagine the multitude of events it is going to engender. One child called Bach was charged with power enough to hold generations of men in his spell. But is there any potentiality to acclaim or any surprise to expect in a calf or a colt? Indeed, the essence of man is not in what he is, but in what he is able to be.

Yet the darkness of potentiality is the hotbed of anxiety. There is always more than one path to go, and we are forced to be free—we are free against our will—and have the audacity to choose, rarely knowing how or why. Our failures glare like flashlights all the way, and what is right lies underground. We are in the minority in the real realm of being, and, with a genius for adjustment, we frequently seek to join the multitude. We are in the minority within our own nature, and in the agony and battle of passions we often choose to envy the beast. We behave as if the animal kingdom were our lost paradise, to which we are trying to return for moments of delight, believing that it is the animal state in which happiness consists. We have an endless craving to be like the beast, a nostalgic admiration for animal within us. According to a contemporary scientist: "Man's greatest tragedy occurred when he ceased to walk on all fours and cut himself off from the animal world by assuming an erect position. If man had continued to walk horizontally, and rabbits had learned to walk vertically, many of the world's ills would not exist."

Man is continuous both with the rest of organic nature and with the infinite outpouring of the spirit of God. A minority in the realm of being, he stands somewhere between God and the beasts. Unable to live alone, he must commune with either of the two.

Both Adam and the beasts were blessed by the Lord, but man was also charged with conquering the earth and dominating the beast. Man is always faced with the choice of listening either to God or to the snake. It is always easier to envy the beast, to worship a totem and be dominated by it, than to hearken to the Voice.

Our existence seesaws between animality and divinity, between that which is more and that which is less than humanity: below is evanescence, futility, and above is the open door of the divine exchequer where we lay up the sterling coin of piety and spirit, the immortal remains of our dying lives. We are constantly in the mills of death, but we are also the contemporaries of God.

Man is "a little lower than the Divine" (*Psalms* 8:5) and a little higher than the beasts. Like a pendulum he swings to and fro under the combined action of gravity and momentum, of the gravitation of selfishness and the momentum of the divine, of a vision beheld by God in the darkness of flesh and blood. We fail to understand the meaning of our existence when we disregard our commitments to that vision. Yet only eyes vigilant and fortified against the glaring and superficial can still perceive God's vision in the soul's horror-stricken night of human folly, falsehood, hatred and malice.

Because of his immense power, man is potentially the most wicked of beings. He often has a passion for cruel deeds that only fear of God can soothe, suffocating flushes of envy that only holiness can ventilate.

If man is not more than human, then he is less than human. Man is but a short, critical stage between the animal and the spiritual. His state is one of constant wavering, of soaring or descending. Undeviating humanity is non-existent. The emancipated man is yet to emerge.

Man is more than what he is to himself. In his reason he may be limited, in his will he may be wicked, yet he stands in a relation to God which he may betray but not sever and which constitutes the essential meaning of his life. He is the knot in which heaven and earth are interlaced.

When carried away by the joy of acting as we please, adopting any desire, accepting any opportunity for action if the body welcomes it, we feel perfectly satisfied to walk on all fours. Yet there are moments in everyone's life when he begins to wonder whether the pleasures of the body or the interests of the self should serve as the perspective from which all decisions should be made.

In spite of the delights that are within our reach, we refuse to barter our souls for selfish rewards and to live without a conscience on the proceeds. Even those who have forfeited the ability for compassion have not forfeited the ability to be horrified at their inability to feel compassion. The ceiling has collapsed, yet the souls still hang by a hair of horror. Time and again everyone of us tried to sit in judgment over his life. Even those who have gambled away the vision of virtue are not deprived of the horror of crime. Through disgust and dismay we struggle to know that to live on selfish needs is to kill what is still alive in our dismay. There is only one way to fumigate the obnoxious air of our world—to live beyond our own needs and interests. We are carnal, covetous, selfish, vain, and to live for the sake of unselfish needs means to live beyond our own means. How could we be more than what we are? How beyond our own means? How could we be more than what we are? How could we find resources that would give our souls a surplus that is not our own? To live beyond our needs means to be independent of selfish needs. Yet how would man succeed in breaking out of the circle of his self?

The possibility of eliminating self-regard ultimately depends on the nature of the self; it is a metaphysical rather than a psychological issue. If the self exists for its own sake, such independence would be neither possible nor desirable. It is only in assuming that the self is not the hub but a spoke, neither its own beginning nor its own end, that such possibility could be affirmed.

Man *is* meaning, but not his own meaning. He does not even know his own meaning, for a meaning does not know what it means. The self *is* a need, but not its own need.

All our experiences are needs, dissolving when the needs are fulfilled. But the truth is, our existence, too, is a need. We are such stuff as needs are made of, and our little life is rounded by a will. *Lasting* in our life is neither passion nor delight, neither joy nor pain, but the answer to a need. The lasting in us is not our will to live. There is a need for our lives, and in living we satisfy it. Lasting is not our desire, but our answer to that need, an agreement not an impulse. Our needs are temporal, while our being needed is lasting.

We have started our inquiry with the question of the individual man— what is the meaning of the individual man?—and established his unique-ness in his being pregnant with immense potentialities, of which he becomes aware in his experience of needs. We have also pointed out that he finds no happiness in utilizing his potentialities for the satisfaction of his own needs, that his destiny is to be a need.

But who is in need of man? Nature? Do the mountains stand in need of our poems? Would the stars fade away if astronomers ceased to exist? The earth can get along without the aid of the human species. Nature is replete with opportunity to satisfy all our needs except one—the need of being needed. Within its unbroken silence man is like the middle of a sentence and all his theories are like dots indicating his isolation within his own self.

Unlike all other needs, the need of being needed is a striving to give rather than to obtain satisfaction. It is a desire to satisfy a transcendent desire, a craving to satisfy a craving.

All needs are one-sided. When hungry we are in need of food, yet food is *not* in need of being consumed. Things of beauty attract our minds; we feel the need of perceiving them, yet they are not in need of being perceived by us. It is in such one-sidedness, that most of living is imprisoned. Examine an average mind, and you will find that it is dominated by an effort to cut reality to the measure of the ego, as if the world existed for the sake of pleasing one's ego. Everyone of us entertains more relations with things than with people, and even in dealings with people we behave toward them as if they were things, tools, means to be used for our own selfish ends. How rarely do we face a person as a person. We are all dominated by the desire to appropriate and to own. Only a free person knows that the true meaning of existence is experienced in giving, in endowing, in meeting a person face to face, in fulfilling other people's needs.

When realizing the surplus of what we see over what we feel, the mind is evasive, even the heart is incomplete. Why are we discontent with mere living for the sake of living? Who has made us thirsty for what is more than existence?

Everywhere we are surrounded by the ineffable, our familiarity with reality is a myth. To the innermost in our soul even beauty is an alloy mixed with the true metal of eternity. There is neither earth nor sky, neither spring nor autumn; there is only a question, God's eternal question of man: Where art Thou? Religion begins with the certainty that something is asked of us, that there are ends which are in need of us. Unlike all other values, moral and religious ends evoke in us a sense of obligation. They present themselves as tasks rather than as objects of perception. Thus, religious living consists in serving ends which are in need of us.

Man is not an innocent bystander in the cosmic drama. There is in us more kinship with the divine than we are able to believe. The souls of men are candles of the Lord, lit on the cosmic way, rather than fireworks produced by the combustion of nature's explosive compositions, and every soul is indispensable to Him. Man is needed, he is *a need of God.*

3. The Paradox of Divine Concern

There are many things about man which are hard to understand. What is his nature? What is his purpose? What is his place in the universe? What is his relation to God? None of these issues is central in Biblical thinking.

The problem that challenged the Biblical mind was not the obscurity of his nature but the paradox of his existence. The starting-point was not a question about man but the distinction of man; not the state of ignorance about the nature of man and the desire to find an answer to the question, What is man? but rather a state of amazement at what we know about man, namely: Why is man so significant in spite of his insignificance? Not the question, Why is man mortal? but the question, Why is he so distinguished?

The problem that challenged the Biblical mind was not man in and by himself. Man is never seen in isolation but always in relation to God who is the Creator, the King, and the Judge of all beings. The problem of man revolved around God's relation to man. Two passages may serve as an illustration.

> Lord,
> What is man,
> That thou takest knowledge of him?
> Or the son of man,
> That thou makest account of him?
> Man is like unto a breath;
> His days are as a shadow
> That passeth away.
>
> (*Psalms* 144:3–4)

> When I behold Thy heavens,
> The work of Thy fingers,
> The moon and the stars
> Which Thou hast established
> What is man
> That Thou shouldst be mindful of him?
> And the son of man
> That Thou shouldst think of him?
> And make him

But a little lower than the Divine,
And crown him with glory and honour,
And make him rule over the works of Thy hands?
Thou hast put all things under his feet:
Sheep and oxen, all of them,
Yes, and the beasts of the field;
The fowl of the air, and the fish of the sea,
That pass through the paths of the seas.

(Psalms 8:2–9)

What gives the Psalmist the certainty that God is mindful of man? Is it inference from the facts of human existence namely that man was made 'a little lower than the Divine', that he was crowned 'with glory and honour', and that he was made to rule over the works of God's creation? Perhaps it was not such an inference but rather an immediate insight, a fundamental awareness, that was the source of the Psalmist's certainty.

The power and intensity of God's concern are at times beyond the endurance of man.

Therefore I will not refrain my mouth;
I will speak in the anguish of my spirit;
I will complain in the bitterness of my soul.
Am I a sea, or a sea-monster,
That Thou settest a watch over me?
When I say; 'My bed shall comfort me,
My couch shall ease my complaint';
Then Thou scarest me with dreams,
And terrifiest me through visions;
So that my soul chooseth strangling,
And death rather than these my bones,
I loathe it; I shall not live always:
Let me alone; for my days are vanity.
What is man, that Thou shouldst magnify him,
And that Thou shouldst set Thy heart upon him,
And that Thou shouldst remember him every morning,
And try him every moment?
How long wilt Thou not look away from me,
Nor let me alone till I swallow down my spittle?
If I have sinned, what do I unto Thee,
   O Thou watcher of men?

Why hast Thou set me as a mark for Thee,
So that I am a burden to myself?
And why dost Thou not pardon my transgression,
And take away mine iniquity?
For now shall I lie down in the dust;
And Thou wilt seek me,
But I shall not be.

(*Job* 7:11–21)

Plants, stars, and beasts are expected to exist in conformity with the cosmic order, to continue to be what they are. Man, on the other hand, is expected to act in agreement with the will of the living God, to decide, to make a choice, to prevail. What man faces is not a principle but a living concern which expresses itself in God addressing man as well as in His guiding the history of man. God does not address the stars; He addresses man.

The insignificance of man compared with the grandeur of God underscores the paradox of God's concern for him. Neither Job nor the Psalmist offers an answer to the overwhelming enigma which thus remains the central mystery of human existence.

Yet the acceptance of that fact of Divine concern established the Biblical approach to the existence of man. It is from the perspective of that concern that the quest for an understanding of the meaning of man begins.

Nowhere in Plato's Socratic dialogues do we find a direct solution to the problem, 'What is man?' There is only an indirect answer, 'Man is declared to be that creature who is constantly in search of himself—a creature who in every moment of his existence must examine and scrutinize the conditions of his existence.'[1] The Biblical answer would not be that man is a creature who is constantly in search of himself, but rather that man is a creature God is constantly in search of.

The Greeks formulated the search of meaning as man in search of a thought; the Hebrews formulated the search of meaning as God's thought (or concern) in search of man. The meaning of existence is not naturally given; it is not an endowment but an art. It rather depends on whether we respond or refuse to respond to God who is in search of man; it is either fulfilled or missed.

The primary topic, then, of Biblical Thinking is not man's knowledge of God but rather man's being known by God, man's being an object of Divine knowledge and concern. This is why the great puzzle was: Why should God, The Creator of heaven and earth, be concerned with man? Why should the deeds of puny man be relevant enough to affect the life of God?

> Can a man be profitable unto God?
> Or can he that is wise be profitable unto Him?
> Is it any advantage to the Almighty, that thou art righteous?
> Or is it gain to Him, that thou makest thy ways blameless?
> (*Job* 22:2–3)

God takes man seriously. He enters a direct relationship with man, namely *a Covenant,* to which not only man but also God is committed. In his ultimate confrontation and crisis the Biblical man knows not only God's eternal mercy and justice but also *God's commitment to man.* Upon this sublime fact rests the meaning of history and the glory of human destiny.

There is only one way to define Jewish religion. It is the *awareness of God's interest in man,* the awareness of a *covenant,* of a responsibility that lies on Him as well as on us. Our task is to concur with His interest, to carry out His vision of our task. God is in need of man for the attainment of His ends, and religion, as Jewish tradition understands it, is a way of serving these ends, of which we are in need, even though we may not be aware of them, ends which we must learn to feel the need of.

Life is a *partnership* of God and man; God is not detached from or indifferent to our joys and griefs. Authentic vital needs of man's body and soul are a divine concern. This is why human life is holy. God is a partner and a partisan in man's struggle for justice, peace and holiness, and it is because of His being in need of man that He entered a *covenant* with him for all time, a mutual bond embracing God and man, a relationship to which God, not only man, is committed.

> This day you have avowed the Lord to be your God, promising to walk in His ways, to obey His rules and commandments, and to hearken to His voice;
> And this day the Lord has avowed you to be His very own people, as He has promised you, and to obey His commandments.
> (*Deuteronomy* 26:17–18)

Some people think that religion comes about as a perception of an answer to a prayer, while in truth it comes about in our knowing that God shared our prayer. The essence of Judaism is the awareness of the *reciprocity* of God and man, of man's *togetherness* with Him who abides in eternal otherness. For the task of living is His and ours, and so is the responsibility. We have rights, not only obligations; our ultimate commitment is our ultimate privilege.

In interpreting *Malachi* 3:18, Rabbi Aha ben Ada said: 'Then shall ye again discern between the righteous and the wicked,' meaning: 'between him who has faith and him who has no faith'; 'between him that serveth God and him that serveth Him not,' meaning: 'between him who serves God's *need* and him who does not serve God's *need*. One should not make of the Torah a spade with which to dig, a tool for personal use or a crown to magnify oneself.'[2]

His need is a self-imposed concern. God is now in need of man, because He freely made him a partner in His enterprise, 'a partner in the work of creation'. 'From the first day of creation the Holy one, blessed be He, longed to enter into *partnership* with the terrestrial world'[3] to dwell *with* His creatures within the terrestrial world. Expounding the verse in *Genesis* 17:1, the Midrash remarked: 'In the view of Rabbi Johanan we need His honour; in the view of Rabbi Simeon ben Lakish He needs our honour.'[4]

'When Israel performs the will of the Omnipresent, they add strength to the heavenly power; as it is said: "To God we render strength" (*Psalms* 60:14). When, however, Israel does not perform the will of the Omnipresent, they weaken—if it is possible to say so—the great power of Him who is above; as it is written, "Thou didst weaken the Rock that begot Thee".'[5]

Man's relationship to God is not one of passive reliance upon His Omnipotence but one of active assistance. 'The impious rely on their gods . . . the righteous are the support of God.'[6]

The Patriarchs are therefore called 'the chariot of the Lord'.[7]

> He glories in me, He delights in me;
> My crown of beauty He shall be.
> His glory rests on me, and mine on Him;
> He is near to me, when I call on Him.
>
> (The Hymn of Glory)

The extreme boldness of this paradox was expressed in a Tannaitic interpretation of *Isaiah* 43:12: 'Ye are my witnesses, saith the Lord, and I am God'—when you are my witnesses I am God, and when you are not my witnesses I am not God.[8]

The God of the philosophers is all indifference, too sublime to possess a heart or to cast a glance at our world. His wisdom consists in being conscious of Himself and oblivious to the world. In contrast, the God of the prophets is all concern, too merciful to remain aloof to His creation. He not only rules the world in the majesty of His might; He is personally concerned and even stirred by the conduct and fate of man. 'His mercy is upon all His work.'[9]

These are the two poles of prophetic thinking: The idea that God is one, holy, different and apart from all that exists, and the idea of the inexhaustible concern of God for man, at times brightened by His mercy, at times darkened by His anger. He is both transcendent, beyond human understanding, and full of love, compassion, grief or anger.

God does not judge the deeds of man impassively, in a spirit of cool detachment. His judgment is imbued with a feeling of intimate concern. He is the father of all men, not only a judge; He is a lover engaged to His people, not only a king. God stands in a passionate relationship to man. His love or anger, His mercy or disappointment is an expression of His profound participation in the history of Israel and all men.

Prophecy, then, consists in the proclamation of the divine *pathos*, expressed in the language of the prophets as love, mercy or anger. Behind the various manifestations of His pathos is one motive, one need: The divine need for human righteousness.

The pagan gods had animal passions, carnal desires, they were more fitful, licentious than men; the God of Israel has a passion for righteousness. The pagan gods had selfish needs, while the God of Israel is only in need of man's integrity. The need of Moloch was the death of man, the need of the Lord is the life of man. The divine pathos which the prophets tried to express in many ways was not a name for His essence but rather for the modes of His reaction to Israel's conduct which would change if Israel modified its ways.

The surge of divine pathos, which came to the souls of the prophets like a fierce passion, startling, shaking, burning, led them forth to the perilous defiance of people's self-assurance and contentment. Beneath all songs and sermons they held conference with God's concern for the people, with the well, out of which the tides of anger raged.[10]

The Bible is not a history of the Jewish people, but the story of God's quest of the righteous man. Because of the failure of the human species as a whole to follow in the path of righteousness, it is an individual—Noah, Abraham—a people; Israel—or a remnant of the people, on which the task is bestowed to satisfy that quest by making every man a righteous man.

There is an eternal cry in the world: God is beseeching man. Some are startled; others remain deaf. We are all looked for. An air of expectancy hovers over life. Something is asked of man, of all men.

4. Image and Likeness

The Biblical account of creation is couched in the language of mystery. Nothing is said about the intention or the plan that preceded the creation of heaven and earth. The Bible does not begin: And God said: let us create heaven and earth. All we hear about is the mystery of God's creative act, and not a word about intention or meaning. The same applies to the creation of all other beings. We only hear what He does, not what He thinks. 'And God said: Let there be.' The creation of man, however, is preceded by a forecast: 'And God said: Let us make man in our image, after our likeness.' The act of man's creation is preceded by an utterance of His intention, God's knowledge of man is to precede man's coming into being. God knows him before He creates him. Man's being is rooted in his being known about. It is the creation of man that opens a glimpse into the thought of God, into the meaning beyond the mystery.

'And God said: Let us make man in our image *(tselem),* after our likeness *(demuth).* . . . And God created man in His image, in the image of God created He him' *(Genesis* 1:26 f).

These words which are repeated in the opening words of the fifth chapter of *Genesis*—'This is the book of the generations of man. When God created man, He made him in the likeness *(demuth)* of God'—contain, according to Jewish tradition, the fundamental statement about the nature and meaning of man.

In many religions, man is regarded as an image of a god. Yet the meaning of such regard depends on the meaning of the god whom man resembles. If the god is regarded as a man magnified, if the gods are conceived of in the image of man, then such regard tells us little about the nature and destiny of man. Where God is one among many gods, where the word Divine is used as mere hyperbolic expression; where the difference between God and man is but a difference in degree, then an expression such as the Divine image of man is equal in meaning to the idea of the supreme in man. It is only in the light of what the Biblical man thinks of God, namely a Being who created heaven and earth, the God of absolute justice and compassion, the master of nature and history who transcends nature and history, that the idea of man having been created in the image of God refers to the supreme mystery of man, of his nature and existence.

Image and likeness of God. What these momentous words are trying to convey has never ceased to baffle the Biblical reader. In the Bible, *tselem,* the word for image, is nearly always used in a derogatory sense, denoting idolatrous images.[11] It is a cardinal sin to fashion an image of God. The same applies to *demuth,* the word for likeness.

'To whom will you liken God? Or what likeness *(demuth)* will ye compare to Him? (*Isaiah* 40:18). 'To whom will ye liken Me, and make Me equal, and compare Me, that we may be like?' (*Isaiah* 46:5) 'For who in the skies can be compared unto the Lord, who among the sons of might can be likened unto the Lord?' (*Psalms* 89:7).

God is Divine, and man is human. This contrast underlies all Biblical thinking. God is never human, and man is never Divine. 'I will not execute the fierceness of Mine anger, I will not return to destroy Ephraim; for I am God and not man.'[12] 'God is not a man, that he should lie; neither the son of man, that He should repent.'[13]

Thus, the likeness of God means the likeness of Him who is unlike man. The likeness of God means the likeness of Him, compared with whom all else is like nothing.

Indeed, the words 'image and likeness of God' conceal more than they reveal. They signify something which we can neither comprehend nor verify. For what is our image? What is our likeness? Is there anything about man that may be compared with God? Our eyes do not see it; our minds cannot grasp it. Taken literally, these words are absurd, if not blasphemous. And still they hold the most important truth about the meaning of man.

Obscure as the meaning of these terms is, they undoubtedly denote something *un-earthly,* something that belongs to the sphere of God. *Demuth* and *tselem* are of a *higher sort of being* than the things created in the six days. This, it seems, is what the verse intends to convey: Man partakes of an unearthly Divine sort of being.

An idea is relevant if it serves as an answer to a question. To understand the relevance of 'the Divine image and likeness', we must try to ascertain the question which it comes to answer.

Paradoxically, the problem of man arises more frequently as the problem of death than as the problem of life. It is an important fact, however, that in contrast with Babylonia and particularly Egypt, where the preoccupation with death was the central issue of religious thinking, the Bible hardly deals with death as a problem. Its central concern is not, as in the Gilgamesh epic, how to escape death, but rather how to sanctify life. And the Divine image and likeness does not serve man to attain immortality but to attain sanctity.

Man is man not because of what he has in common with the earth, but *because of what he has in common with God.* The Greek thinkers sought to understand man as *a part of the universe:* the Prophets sought to understand man as *a partner of God.*

It is a concern and a task that man has in common with God.

The intention is not to indentify 'the image and likeness' with a particular quality or attribute of man, such as reason, speech, power or skill. It does not refer to something which in later systems was called 'the best in man', 'the divine spark', 'the eternal spirit' or 'the immortal element' in man. It is the whole man and every man who was made in the image and likeness of God. It is both body and soul, sage and fool, saint and sinner, man in his joy and in his grief, in his righteousness and wickedness. The image is not in man; it is man.

The basic dignity of man is not made up of his achievements, virtues, or special talents. It is inherent in his very being. The commandment 'Love thy neighbour as thyself' (*Leviticus* 19:18) calls upon us to love not only the virtuous and the wise but also the vicious and the stupid man. The Rabbis have, indeed, interpreted the commandment to imply that even a criminal remains our neighbour.[14]

The image-love is a love of what God loves, an act of sympathy, of participation in God's love. It is unconditional and regardless of man's merits or distinctions.

According to many thinkers, love is induced by that which delights or commands admiration. Such a view would restrict love to those worthy of receiving it and condition it upon whether a person might invoke delight or admiration. It would exclude the criminal and the corrupt members of society. In contrast, to love man according to Judaism is not a response to any physical, intellectual, or moral value of a person. We must love man because he is made in the image of God. Said Rabbi Akiba: *'Love thy neighbour as thyself* is the supreme principle of the Torah. You must not say, since I have been put to shame (by a fellow man), let him be put to shame; since I have been slighted, let him be slighted. Said Rabbi Tanhuma: If you do so, know whom you put to shame, for in the likeness of God made He him.'[15]

Thus God loves Israel notwithstanding its backslidings.[16] His love is a gift rather than an earning.[17] 'The Lord did not set His love upon you, nor choose you, because ye were more in number than any people . . . for ye were the fewest of all peoples . . . but because the Lord loved you. . . .'[18]

Sparingly does the term 'image of God' occur in the Bible. Beyond the first chapter of *Genesis,* it comes forth in two instances: To remind us that every thing found on earth was placed under the dominion of man, except human life, and to remind us that the body of man, not only his soul, is endowed with Divine dignity.

The image of God is employed in stressing the criminality of murder. 'For your lifeblood I will surely require a reckoning; of every beast I will require it and of man; of every man's brother I will require the life of man. Whosoever sheds the blood of man, by man shall his blood be shed; for God made man in His own image.'[19]

The image of man is also referred to in urging respect for the body of a criminal following his execution. 'If a man has committed a crime punishable by death and he is put to death, and you hang him on a tree, his body shall not remain all night upon the tree, but you shall bury him the same day, for the dignity (or glory) of God is hanged (on the tree).'

The intention of the verse is stressed boldly by Rabbi Meir, an outstanding authority of the second century of the common era, in the form of a parable. 'To what may this be compared? To twin brothers who lived in one city; one was appointed king, and the other took to highway robbery. At the king's command they hanged him. But all who saw him exclaimed: The king is hanged! (For being twins their appearance was similar). Whereupon the king issued a command and he was taken down.'

Great, therefore, must be our esteem for every man. 'Let the honour of your disciple be as dear to you as your own, let the regard for your colleague be like the reverence due to your teacher, and let the reverence for your teacher be like the reverence for God.'[20] Thus, the esteem for man must be as great as the esteem for God. From this statement, a medieval authority concludes that our esteem for man must be as great as our esteem for God.[21]

(1) The observance of this law is apparently reflected in *Joshua* 10:26 f.

(2) Our translation assumes that *qelalah* is a euphemism for *kavod*. This assumption is implied in the Rabbinic interpretation of the verse and is similar in intention to Rashi's comment: 'It is a slight to the King, because man is made in the image of God.' *Qelalah* in the sense of reproach or insult is used in *Exodus* 21:17. A similar interpretation is found in *Pseudo-Jonathan*. Compare the rendering by Ariston of Pella: 'For he that is hanged is a reproach to God,' quoted by Jerome.[22] However, the *Septuagint* as well as the *Mishnah*[23] take the verse to mean 'for he is hanged because of a curse against God' . . . 'as if to say why was he hanged? because he cursed the name of God: and so (if his body be left hanging, thus reminding man of his blasphemy) the name of God is profaned.'

The divine likeness of man is an idea known in many religions. It is the contribution of Judaism to have taught the tremendous implication of that idea: the metaphysical dignity of man, the divine preciousness of human life. Man is not valued in physical terms; his value is infinite. To our common sense, one human being is less than two human beings. Jewish tradition tries to teach us that he who has caused a single soul to perish, it is as though he had caused a whole world to perish; and that he who has saved a single soul, it is as though he has saved a whole world. This thought was conveyed in the solemn admonition to witnesses, not by false testimony to be the cause of the death of an innocent man.[24]

No person may be sacrificed to save others. If an enemy said to a group of women, 'Give us one from among you that we may defile her, and if not we will defile you all, let the enemy defile them all, but let them not betray to them one single soul.'[25]

The metaphysical dignity of man implies not only inalienable rights but also infinite responsibilities. Stressing the idea that one man came to be the father of all men, the *Mishnah* avers: 'Therefore every man is bound to say, On account of *me* the world was created.'[26] That is, every man is to regard himself as precious as a whole world, too precious to be wasted by sin.[27]

In several ways man is set apart from all beings created in the six days. The Bible does not say, God created the plant or the animal; it says, He created different kinds of plants and different kinds of animals. In striking contrast, it does not say that God created different kinds of man, men of different colours and races; it says, He created one single man. From one single man all men are descended.

When the Roman government issued a decree that the Jews of Palestine should not study the *Torah,* should not circumcise their sons and should profane the Sabbath, the Jewish leaders went to Rome and marched through streets at night-time, proclaiming: 'Alas, in heaven's name, are we not your brothers, are we not the sons of one father and the sons of one mother? Why are we different from every nation and tongue that you issue such harsh decrees against us?'[28]

'Why was only a single man created? To teach you that he who destroys one man, it is regarded as if he had destroyed all men, and that he who saves one man, it is regarded as though he had saved all men. Furthermore, it was for the sake of peace, so that man might not say to his fellow-man, "My father was greater than thy father".'[29]

The awareness of divine dignity must determine even man's relation to his own self. His soul as well as his body constitute an image of God. This is why one is under obligation to keep his body clean. 'One must wash his face, hands, and feet daily in his Maker's honour.'[30] Hillel, it is said, explained this obligation by a parable. Those who are in charge of the icons of kings which are set up in their theatres and circuses scour and wash them off, and are rewarded and honoured for so doing; how much more, who was created in the image and likeness of God.[31]

Indeed, Jewish piety may be expressed in the form of a supreme imperative: *Treat thyself as an image of God.* It is in the light of this imperative that we can understand the meaning of the astonishing commandment: Ye shall be holy, for I the Lord your God am holy (*Leviticus* 19:2). Holiness, an essential attribute of God, may become a quality of man. The human can become holy.

5. *Man the Symbol of God*

From time immemorial man has been concerned with the question
how to create a symbol of the Deity, a visible object in which its presence
would be enshrined, wherein it could be met and wherein its power
would be felt at all times.

That religious eagerness found an ally in one of man's finest skills: the
skill to design, to fashion, and to paint in material form what mind and
imagination conceive. They became wedded to each other, *Art* became
the helpmate of *religion,* and rich was the offspring of that intimate
union. It is alone through religion and cult that the consciousness of
higher laws could mature and be imposed 'upon the individual artist,
who would otherwise have given free rein to his imagination, *style.'*
'There, in the sanctuary, they took their first step toward the sublime.
They learned to eliminate the contingent from form. Types came into
being; ultimately the first ideals.'[32] Religion and cult inspired the artist to
bring forth images of majesty, magnificent temples and awe-inspiring
altars, which in turn stirred the heart of the worshipper to greater
devotion. What would art have been without the religious sense of
mystery and sovereignty, and how dreary would have been religion
without the incessant venture of the artist to embody the invisible in
visible forms, to bring his vision out of the darkness of the heart, and to
fill the immense absence of the Deity with the light of human genius?
The right hand of the artist withers when he forgets the sovereignty of
God, and the heart of the religious man has often become dreary without
the daring skill of the artist. Art seemed to be the only revelation in the
face of the Deity's vast silence.

One is overwhelmed by the sight of the great works of art. They
represent in a deep sense man's attempt to celebrate the works of God.
God created heaven and earth, and man creates symbols of heaven and
symbols of earth. Yet man is not satisfied with the attempt to praise the
work of God; he even dares to express the essence of God. God created
man, and man creates images of God.

A distinction ought to be made here between *real* and *conventional*
symbols. *A real symbol* is a visible object that represents something
invisible; something present representing something absent. A real symbol represents, e.g. the Divine because it is assumed that the Divine
resides in it or that the symbol partakes to some degree of the reality of

the Divine. A *conventional symbol* represents to the mind an entity which is not shown, not because its substance is endowed with something of that entity but because it suggests that entity, by reason of relationship, association, or convention, e.g. a flag.

An image is a real symbol. The god and his image are almost identified. They are cherished as the representatives of the gods: he who has the image, has the god. It is believed that the god resides in the image or that the image partakes to some degree of the power and reality of the god. A victor nation would carry off the god-image of the conquered nation, in order to deprive it of the presence and aid of its god. In the fifteenth century before the common era, a statue of the goddess Ishtar of Nineveh was carried with great pomp and ceremony from Mesopotamia to Egypt, obviously for the purpose of letting Egypt enjoy the blessings which the goddess by her presence would bestow upon the land.[33] As Durkheim remarked, the images of a totem-creature are more sacred than the totem-creature itself. The image may replace the Deity.

What was the attitude of the prophets toward that grand alliance of religion and art? What is the attitude of the Bible toward the happy union of priest and artist? Did Israel contribute toward cementing that matrimony? Did it use its talents to create worthy symbols of the One God it proclaimed by inspiring its artists to embody in stone the Creator of heaven and earth? Indeed, if a religion is to be judged by the degree to which it contributes to the human need for symbolism, the Decalogue should have contained a commandment, saying: Thou shalt make unto thee a symbol, a graven image or some manner of likeness. . . . Instead, the making and worshiping of images was considered an abomination, vehemently condemned in the Bible.[34] If symbolism is the standard, then Moses will have to be accused of having had a retarding influence on the development of man. It is not with a sense of pride that we recall the making of the Golden Calf, nor do we condemn as an act of vandalism the role of Moses in beating it into pieces and grinding it very small, 'until it was as fine as dust,' and casting 'the dust thereof into the brook that descended out of the mount.'

It is perhaps significant that the Hebrew word that came to denote symbol, *semel,* occurs in the Bible five times, but always in a derogatory sense, denoting an idolatrous object.[35]

Nothing is more alien to the spirit of Judaism than the veneration of images. According to an ancient belief, the prophet Elijah, 'the angel of the covenant,' is present whenever the act of circumcision is performed. To concretize that belief, a vacant chair, called 'Elijah's chair,' is placed near the seat of the *sandek* (god-father).[36] This is the limit of representation: a vacant chair. To place a picture or statue of the prophet on it, would have been considered absurd as well as blasphemous. To Jewish faith there are no physical embodiments of the supreme mysteries. All we have are signs, reminders.

The Second Commandment implies more than the prohibition of images; it implies the rejection of all visible symbols for God; not only of images fashioned by man but also of 'any manner of likeness, of any thing that is in heaven above, or that is in the earth beneath, or that is in the water under the earth'. The significance of that attitude will become apparent when contrasted with its opposite view.

It would be alien to the spirit of the Bible to assert that the world is a symbol of God. In contrast, the symbolists exhort us: 'Neither say that thou hast now no Symbol of the Godlike. Is not God's Universe a Symbol of the Godlike; is not Immensity a Temple . . .?'[37]

What is the reason for that sharp divergence? To the symbolists 'All visible things are emblems. . . . Matter exists only spiritually, and to represent some Idea and *body* it forth'.[38] The universe is 'a mechanism of self-expression for the infinite'. The symbol is but the bodying forth of the infinite, and it is the very life of the infinite to be bodied forth.[39]

Now, the Bible does not regard the universe as a mechanism of the self-expression of God, for the world did not come into being in an act of self-expression but in an act of creation. The world is not of the essence of God, and its expression is not His. The world speaks to God, but that speech is not God speaking to Himself. It would be alien to the spirit of the Bible to say that it is the very life of God to be bodied forth. The world is neither His continuation nor His emanation but His creation and possession.

The fundamental insight that God is not and cannot be localized in a thing[40] was emphatically expressed at the very moment in which it could have been most easily forgotten, at the inauguration of the Temple in Jerusalem. At that moment Solomon exclaims:

> But will God in very truth dwell on earth? Behold, heaven and the heaven of heavens cannot contain Thee; how much less this house that I have built!
>
> (*I Kings* 8:27)

God manifests Himself in *events* rather than in *things,* and these events can never be captured or localized in things.

How significant is the fact that Mount Sinai, the place on which the supreme revelation occurred, did not retain any degree of holiness! It did not become a shrine, a place of pilgrimage.

The realization that the world and God are not of the same essence is responsible for one of the great revolutions in the spiritual history of man. Things may be *instruments,* never *objects of worship. Matza,* the *shofar,* the *lujav* are not things to be looked at, to be saluted, to be paid homage to, but things to be used. Being instruments they have symbolic meaning but, they are not primarily regarded as symbols in themselves. A symbol—because of its inherent symbolic quality—is an object of contemplation and adoration.

To a reverent Catholic the cross is a sacred symbol. Gazing at its shape, his mind is drawn into contemplation of the very essence of the Christian faith.

Thomas Aquinas taught that the cross was to be adored with *Latria,* i.e. supreme worship, and argued that one might regard a cross or an image in two ways: (1) in itself, as a piece of wood or the like, and so no reverence should be given to a cross or to an image of Jesus; (2) as representing something else, and in this way one might give to the Cross *relatively,* i.e. to the cross as carrying one's mind to Jesus—the same honour given to Jesus *absolutely,* i.e. in Himself. Adoration is also given to the Sacred Heart, as well as to images and relics of the saints.[41] In contrast, the image and shape of the scrolls, of a *shofar* or a *lulav* do not convey to us any inspiration beyond reminding us of its function and our obligation.

The spirit of Christian symbolism has shaped the character of church architecture, 'a noble church structure may be "a sermon in stone" '. According to Germanos, the Patriarch of Constantinople (715–730), the church is heaven on earth, the symbol of The Crucifixion, the Entombment, and Resurrection. From the fifth century, symbolism permeated the architecture of the Byzantine church building in all its details. 'The sanctuary, the nave and aisles were the sensible world, the upper parts of the church the intelligible cosmos, the vaults the mystical heaven.'[42] A similar spirit is to be found in Western Christianity, where, for example, the shape of church building is that of a cross, embodying the basic symbol of Christianity. The altar is often raised three or seven steps, signifying the Trinity or the seven gifts of the Holy Spirit.

In Jewish law, which prescribes countless rules for daily living, no directions are given for the shape of synagogue building.[43]

Any form of architecture is legally admissible. The synagogue is not an abode of the Deity but a house of prayer, a gathering place for the people. Entering a synagogue, we encounter no objects designed to impart any particular idea to us. Judaism has rejected the picture as a means of representing ideas; it is opposed to pictographic symbols. The only indispensable object is a Scroll to be read, not to be gazed at.

There is no *inherent* sanctity in Jewish ritual objects. The candelabrum in the synagogue does not represent another candelabrum either in Jerusalem or in heaven. It is not more than you see. It has no symbolic content. According to Jewish law, it is prohibited to imitate the seven-branched candelabrum as well as other features of the Temple in Jerusalem for ritual purposes. 'A man may not make a house in the form of the Temple, or an exedra in the form of the Temple hall, or a court corresponding to the Temple court, or a table corresponding to the table (in the Temple) or a candlestick corresponding to the candlestick (in the Temple), but he may make one with five or six or eight lamps, but with seven he should not make, even of other metals (than gold) . . . or even of wood.'[44] The anointing oil must not be produced in the same composition to be used outside the Sanctuary. 'It is holy and shall be holy unto you' (*Exodus* 30:32).

The purpose of ritual art objects in Judaism is not to inspire love of God but to enhance our love of doing a *mitsvah,* to add pleasure to obedience, delight to fulfillment. Thus the purpose is achieved not in direct contemplation but in combining it with a ritual act; the art objects have a religious function but no religious substance.

Jewish artists often embellished manuscripts and title pages with pictures of Moses and Aaron. Yet such decorations were regarded as ornaments rather than symbols.

And yet there is something in the world that the Bible does regard as a symbol of God. It is not a temple nor a tree, it is not a statue nor a star. The one symbol of God is *man, every man.* God Himself created man in His image, or, to use the biblical terms, in His *tselem* and *demuth.* How significant is the fact that the term, *tselem,* which is frequently used in a damnatory sense for a man-made image of God, as well as the term, *demuth*—of which Isaiah claims (40:18) no *demuth* can be applied to God—is employed in denoting man as an image and likeness of God!

Human life is holy, holier even than the Scrolls of the *Torah*. Its holiness is not man's achievement; it is a gift of God rather than something attained through merit. Man must therefore be treated with honour due to a likeness representing the King of kings.

Not that the Bible was unaware of man's frailty and wickedness. The Divine in man is not by virtue of what he does, but by virtue of what he is. With supreme frankness the failures and shortcomings of kings and prophets, of men such as Moses or David, are recorded. And yet, Jewish tradition insisted that not only man's soul but also his body is symbolic of God. This is why even the body of a criminal condemned to death must be treated with reverence, according to the book of *Deuteronomy* (21:23). 'He who sheds the blood of a human being, it is accounted to him as though he diminished (or destroyed) the Divine image.'[45] And in this sense, Hillel characterized the body as an 'icon' of God,[46] as it were, and considered keeping clean one's own body as an act of reverence for its Creator.[47]

As not one man or one particular nation but all men and all nations are endowed with the likeness of God, there is no danger of ever worshipping man, because only that which is extraordinary and different may become an object of worship. But the Divine likeness is something all men share.

This is a conception of far-reaching importance to Biblical piety. What it implies can hardly be summarized. Reverence for God is shown in our reverence for man. The fear you must feel of offending or hurting a human being must be as ultimate as your fear of God. An act of violence is an act of desecration. To be arrogant toward man is to be blasphemous toward God.

> He who oppresses the poor blasphemes his Maker,
> He who is gracious to the needy honours Him.
>
> (*Proverbs* 14:31)

Rabbi Joshua ben Levi said: 'A procession of angels pass before man wherever he goes, proclaiming: *Make way for the image (eikonion) of God*'.[48]

It is often claimed that 'Hebrew monotheism has ended by raising the

Deity too far above the earth and placing Him too far above man'.[49] This is a half-truth. God is indeed very much above man, but at the same time man is very much a reflection of God. The craving to keep that reflection pure, to guard God's likeness on earth, is indeed the motivating force of Jewish piety.

The *tselem* or God's image is what distinguishes man from the animal, and it is only because of it that he is entitled to exercise power in the world of nature. If he retains his likeness he has dominion over the beast; if he forfeits his likeness he descends, losing his position of eminence in nature.[50]

The idea of man's divine likeness is, according to one opinion in the *Talmud,* the reason for the prohibition to produce the human figure. The statement in *Exodus* 20:20, 'You shall not make with Me *(itti)* gods of silver, or gods of gold,' should be rendered as if it were written, 'You shall not make My symbol *(otti; ot* means symbol), namely, man, gods of silver, or gods of gold'.[51]

What is necessary is not to *have a symbol but to be a symbol.* In this spirit, all objects and all actions are not symbols in themselves but ways and means of enhancing the living symbolism of man.

The divine symbolism of man is not in what he *has*—such as reason or the power of speech—but in what he *is* potentially: he is able to be holy as God is holy. To imitate God, to act as He acts in mercy and love, is the way of enhancing our likeness. Man becomes what he worships. 'Says the Holy One, blessed be He: He who acts like Me shall be like Me.'[52] Says Rabbi Levi ben Hama: 'Idolators resemble their idols (*Psalms* 115:8); now how much more must the servants of the Lord resemble Him'.[53]

And yet that likeness may be defiled, distorted, and forfeited. It is from the context of this problem that the entire issue of Jewish symbolism must be considered. The goal of man is to recognize and preserve His likeness or at least to prevent its distortion.

But man has failed. And what is the consequence? 'I have placed the likeness of My image on them and through their sins I have upset it', is the dictum of God.[54]

The likeness is all but gone. Today, nothing is more remote and less plausible than the idea: man is a symbol of God. Man forgot Whom he represents or *that* he represents.

There is one hope. The *Midrash* interprets the verse *Deuteronomy* 1:10, as if it were written: 'Lo, today you are like the stars in heaven, but in the future you will resemble the Master'.[55]

6. Image and Dust

There are two ways in which the Bible speaks of the creation of man. In the first chapter of the book of *Genesis* which is devoted to the creation of the physical universe, man is described as having been created in the image and likeness of God. In the second chapter which tells us of the commandment not to eat of the fruit of the tree of knowledge, man is described as having been formed out of the dust of the earth. Together, image and dust express the polarity of the nature of man. He is formed of the most inferior stuff in the most superior image. The polarity of man may not imply an eternal contradiction. There is dignity to dust which, just as heaven, was created by God. There is, indeed, meaning and blessing in having been formed of the dust of the earth, for it is only because he is formed of the dust of the earth that he can fulfil his destiny to cultivate the earth. Yet while the duality of human nature may not imply an eternal tension, it does imply a duality of grandeur and insignificance, a relatedness to earth and an affinity with God.

The duality is not based on the contrast of soul and body and the principles of good and evil. Unlike the Pythagoreans, the Bible does not regard the body as the sepulchre and prisonhouse of the soul or even as the seat and source of sin. The contradiction is in what man does with his soul and body. The contradiction lies in his acts rather than in his substance. As nature is not the counterwork of God but His creation and instrument, dust is not the contradiction of the image but its foil and complement. Man's sin is in his failure to live what he is. Being the master of the earth, man forgets that he is servant of God.

> *Man is Dust*
> *Dust thou art, and unto dust thou shalt return*
> (*Genesis* 3:19)

These words with which the Lord addressed Adam after he sinned convey a basic part of the Biblical understanding of man. The fact of man having been created 'in the image and likeness of God' is mentioned as a Divine secret and uttered in a Divine monologue, while the fact of being dust is conveyed to man in God's dialogue with Adam. Nowhere in the Bible does man, standing before God, say, I am thy image and likeness. Abraham, pleading with God to save the city of Sodom, knows: 'Behold now, I have taken upon me to speak unto the Lord, who am but *dust and ashes' (Genesis* 18:27). Job prays: 'Remember, I beseech Thee, that Thou hast fashioned me as clay' (10:9). And his last words are: 'I abhor my words, and repent, seeing I am dust and ashes' (42:6; see 30:19). In this spirit, the Psalmist describes men as beings 'that go down to the dust' *(Psalms* 22:30). This miserable fact, however, is also a comfort to him who discovers his failures, his spiritual feebleness. The Psalmist is consoled in the knowledge that God understands our nature; He remembers that we are dust *(Psalms* 103:14).

God created man out of dust,
    And turned him back thereunto.
He granted them a (fixed) number of days,
    And gave them authority over all things on the earth.
He clothed them with strength like unto Himself,
    And made them according to His own image.
He put the fear of them upon all flesh,
    And caused them to have power over beasts and birds.
With insight and understanding He filled their heart,
    And taught them good and evil.
He created for them tongue, and eyes, and ears,
    And he gave them a heart to understand,
To show them the majesty of His works,
    And that they might glory in His wondrous acts;
That they might evermore declare His glorious works,
    And praise His holy name.
He set before them the covenant;
    The law of life He gave them for a heritage.
He made an everlasting covenant with them,
    And showed them His judgments,
Their eyes beheld His glorious majesty,
    And their ear heard His glorious voice;
And he said unto them, Beware of all unrighteousness;
    And he gave them commandment, to each man concerning his
    neighbour.

Their ways are ever before Him,
   They are not hid from His eyes.
For every nation He appointed a ruler,
   But Israel is the Lord's portion.
All their works are (clear) as the sun before Him,
   And His eyes are continually upon their ways.
Their iniquities are not hid from Him,
   And all their sins are (inscribed) before the Lord.
The righteousness of men is to Him as a signet,
   And the mercy of man He preserveth as the apple of an eye.
Afterwards He will rise up and recompense them,
   And will visit their deeds upon their own head.
Nevertheless to them that repent doth He grant a return,
   And comforteth them that lose hope.

                             (*Sirach* 17:1–24)

Man is an artifact

That the end of man is dust is an indisputable fact. But so is the end of the beast. And yet, the Bible emphasizes an absolute difference between man and all other creatures. According to the first chapter of *Genesis*, plants and animals were brought forth by the earth, by the waters (*Genesis* 1:11, 20, 24); they emerged from 'nature' and became an 'organic' part of nature. Man, on the other hand, is an artifact, formed in a special act, created in 'an image', 'according to a likeness' (*Genesis* 1:26). In the language of the second chapter of *Genesis*, every beast of the field, and every fowl of the air, was formed of the ground. Man, however, was made not of the ground which is the source of all vegetation and animal life, nor out of water which is a symbol for refreshment, blessing, and wisdom. He was made of arid dust, the stuff of the desert which is both abundant and worthless.[56]

Thus, the statement that man was made of dust stresses not only his fragility but also his nobility. He owes his existence not to the forces of nature but to the Creator of all. He is set apart from both the plants and the beasts. The earth is not his mother. Man has only a father.

Other expressions of the uniqueness and magnificence of man come to us from the prophets. Isaiah proclaims:

    Thus saith God the Lord,
    He that created the heavens

> And stretched them out,
> He that spread forth the earth
> And that which cometh out of it,
> He that giveth breath unto the people upon it,
> And spirit to them that walk therein (42:5).

In the same way, Sechariah speaks of the Lord who stretched out the heavens and founded the earth and formed the *spirit of man* within him (21:1).

What is stressed about man in these passages is the forming of the spirit, the grandeur of which is made manifest by its juxtaposition with heaven and earth. The spirit in man is as much a creation of God as heaven and earth. What is the source of human understanding? 'It is a spirit in man, and the breath of the Almighty that giveth them understanding' (*Job* 32:8). The parallelism seems to imply that the spirit in man is a spirit of the Almighty. 'The spirit of God hath made me, and the breath of the Almighty giveth me life,' we read in the same speech (*Job* 33:4).

The word spirit in the Bible has more than one meaning. Of Bezalel it is said that he is filled with the spirit of God 'in wisdom, in knowledge, understanding, and in all manner of workmanship' (*Exodus* 31:4). Of the prophets we hear that the spirit of God comes upon them (*Isaiah* 61:1; *Ezekiel* 11:5). Of the Messiah we are told that 'the spirit of God shall rest upon him, the spirit of wisdom and understanding, the spirit of counsel and might, the spirit of knowledge and of the fear of the Lord' (*Isaiah* 11:2). The spirit in these passages denotes an endowment of chosen men. But, as we have seen, it is also an endowment of all men; it is that which gives them understanding.

Man holds within himself a breath of God. 'The Lord formed man of the dust of the ground, and breathed into his nostrils a breath of life; and man became living soul' (*Genesis* 2:7). It probably is this non-earthly aspect of human nature, the breath of God, that served as a basis for the belief in an after-life.

'And the dust returneth to the earth as it was, and the spirit returneth unto God who gave it' (*Ecclesiastes* 12:7).

7. *The Self and the Deed*

Many modern theologians have consistently maintained that the Bible stands for optimism, that pessimism is alien to its spirit.[57] There is, however, very little evidence to support such a view. With the exception of the first chapter of the *Book of Genesis,* the rest of the Bible does not cease to refer to the sorrow, sins, and evil of this world. As Maimonides pointed out (in a different context and order), the ideas that apply to the world in the state of its coming into being do not apply to the world that is in being. The design of the Creator was for a world that was to be good, very good; but then something mysterious happened, to which Jewish tradition alludes in many ways, and the picture of the world profoundly changed. When the prophets look at the world, they behold 'distress and darkness, the gloom of anguish' (*Isaiah* 8:22). When they look at the land, they find it 'full of guilt against the Holy One of Israel' (*Jeremiah* 51:5). 'O Lord, how long shall I cry for help, and Thou wilt not hear? Or cry to Thee "violence!", and Thou wilt not save? Why dost Thou make me see wrongs and look upon trouble? Destruction and violence are before me; strife and contention arise. So the law is slacked and justice never goes forth. For the wicked surround the righteous, so justice goes forth perverted' (*Habakkuk* 1:2–4). This is a world in which the way of the wicked prosper and 'all who are treacherous thrive' (*Jeremiah* 12:1); a world which made it possible for some people to maintain that 'Everyone who does evil is good in the sight of the Lord, and He delights in them', and for others to ask, 'Where is the God of justice?' (*Malachi* 2:17).

The Psalmist did not feel that this was a happy world when he prayed: 'O God, do not keep silence; do not hold peace or be still, O God. For, lo, Thy enemies are in uproar; those who hate thee have raised their heads' (*Psalms* 83:2–3).

The terror and anguish that came upon the Psalmist were not caused by calamities in nature but by the wickedness of man, by the evil in history.

> Fearfulness and trembling come upon me,
> Horror has overwhelmed me.
> And I said, Oh that I had wings like a dove!
> Then would I fly away, and be at rest.
> *Psalms* 55:6–7.

These are the words of Moses in his last days: 'I know how rebellious and stubborn you are. . . . I know after my death you will surely act corruptly, and turn aside from the way which I have commanded you; and in the days to come evil will befall you, because you will do what is evil in the sight of the Lord' (*Deuteronomy* 31:27–29). It is not a sweet picture of man that Isaiah paints, saying: 'You have never heard, you have never known, from of old your ear has not been opened. For I knew that you would deal very treacherously, and that from birth you were called a rebel' (*Isaiah* 48:8).

There is one line that expresses the mood of the Jewish man throughout the ages: *'The earth is given into the hand of the wicked"* (*Job* 9:24).[58]

How does the world look in the eyes of God? Are we ever told that the Lord saw that the righteousness of man was great in the earth, and that He was glad to have made man on the earth? The general tone of the Biblical view of history is set after the first ten generations: 'The Lord saw the wickedness of man was great in the earth and that every imagination of the thoughts of his heart was only evil continually. And the Lord was sorry that he made man on the earth, and it grieved Him to His heart' (*Genesis* 6:5; *cf.* 8:21). One great cry resounds throughout the Bible:

> The wickedness of man is great on the earth. It is voiced by the prophets; it is echoed by the Psalmist.

Sentimentality and unreality have often been considered a distinctly Biblical attitude, while in truth the Bible constantly reminds us of man's frailty and unreliability. 'All flesh is grass, and all the strength thereof is as the flower of the field. The grass withers, the flower fades . . . surely the people is grass' (*Isaiah* 40:6–7). 'Put not your trust in princes, nor in the son of man, in whom there is no help' (*Psalms* 146:3). Isaiah calls upon us not to trust the world; the Psalmist tells us not to rely on man.

What the rabbis thought about the nature of man may be shown in the following comment. We read in *Habakkuk* 1:14, *And Thou makest man as the fishes of the sea, and as the creeping things, that have no ruler over them?* 'Why is man here compared to the fishes of the sea? . . . Just as among fishes of the sea, the greater swallow up the smaller ones, so with men, were it not for fear of government, man would swallow each other alive. This is just what we have learned: Rabbi Hanina, the Deputy High Priest, said, "Pray for the welfare of the government, for were it not for fear thereof, men would swallow each other alive".'[59]

According to Rabbi Jacob, 'This world is like a vestibule before the world to come; prepare yourself in the vestibule, so that you may enter the banquet hall'.[60] There is no reward for good deeds in this world.[61] The time for reward promised in the Bible is the life to come.[62] According to the *Rav,* 'The world was created for the extremely pious or the extremely wicked, for men like Rabbi Hanina ben Dosa (a saint who lived in the first century of the common era) or for men like King Ahab; this world was created for the extremely wicked, the world to come was created for the extremely pious'.[63] 'In this world war and suffering, evil inclination, Satan, and the angel of death hold sway.'[64]

In the Jewish mystical literature of the thirteenth century the doctrine is advanced that world history consists of seven periods *(shemitah),* each lasting seven thousand years, which in the Jubilee, the fifty thousandth year, will reach its culmination. The current period is one which is dominated by the divine quality of 'stern judgment'. In it the evil urge, licentiousness, arrogance, forgetfulness, and unholiness prevail.[65]

According to Rabbi Shneur Zalman of Ladi: Anything that refuses to regard itself as nothing beside God but, on the contrary, asserts itself as an entity separate from God does not receive the light of its vitality, so to speak, from the 'hind-part' of his holiness, and only after it has gone through myriad channels of emanation and has been so obscured and contracted that it is capable of living 'in exile', apart from God. And that is why this material world is called a *'world of shells' (kelipoth) 'the other side' (sitra abra).* And this is why all the things that happen in this world are harsh and evil, and this is why the wicked prevail.[66]

The pious Jews put no trust in the secular world. 'They realized quite well that the world was full of ordeals and dangers, that it contained Cain's jealousy of Abel, the cold malevolence of Sodom, and the hatred of Esau, but they also knew that there was in it the charity of Abraham and the tenderness of Rachel. Harassed and oppressed, they carried deep within their hearts a contempt for the world, with its power and pomp, with its bustling and boasting. . . . They knew that the Jews were in exile, that the world was unredeemed.'[67] Dazzled by the splendour of Western civilization, the modern Jew has been prone to forget that the world is unredeemed, and that God is in exile. The present generation which has witnessed the most unspeakable horrors committed by man and sponsored by an extremely civilized nation is beginning to realize how monstrous an illusion it was to substitute faith in man for faith in God.

We do not feel 'at home' in the world. With the Psalmist we pray, 'I am a stranger on earth, hide not Thy commandments from me' (119:19). Indeed, if not for our endless power to forget and our great ability to disregard, who could be at ease even for one moment in a lifetime? In the face of so much evil and suffering, of countless examples of failure to live up to the will of God, in a world where His will is defied, where His kingship is denied, who can fail to see the discrepancy between the world and the will of God?

And yet, just because of the realization of the power of evil, life in this world assumed unique significance and worth. Evil is not only a threat; it is also a challenge. It is precisely because of the task of fighting evil that life in this world is so preciously significant. True, there is no reward for good deeds in this world; yet this does not mean that the world is a prison. It is rather a prelude, a vestibule, a place of preparation, of initiation, of apprenticeship to a future life, where the guests prepare to enter *tricilinium,* or the banquet hall.[68] Life in this world is a time for action, for good works, for worship and sanctification, as eternity is a time for retribution. It is eve of the Sabbath, on which the repast is prepared for the Lord's day; it is the season of duty and submission, as the morrow shall be that of freedom from every law. More precious, therefore, than all of life to come is a single hour of life on earth—an hour of repentance and good deeds. Eternity gives only in the degree that it receives. This is why the book of *Ecclesiastes* pronounced the dead lion less happy than the living dog.[69]

More frustrating than the fact that evil is real, mighty, and tempting is the fact that it thrives so well in the disguise of the good, and that it can draw its nutriment from the life of the holy. In this world, it seems, the holy and the unholy do not exist apart but are mixed, interrelated, and confounded; it is a world where idols are at home, and where even the worship of God may be alloyed with the worship of idols.

In Jewish mysticism we often come upon the view that in this world neither good nor evil exists in purity, and that there is no good without the admixture of evil nor evil without the admixture of good. The confusion of good and evil is the central problem of history and the ultimate issue of redemption. The confusion goes back to the very process of creation.

'When God came to create the world and reveal what was hidden in
the depths and disclose light out of darkness, they were all wrapped in
one another, and therefore light emerged from darkness and from the
impenetrable came forth the profound. So, too, from good issues evil
and from mercy issues judgment, and all are intertwined, the good
impulse and the evil impulse.'[70]

Ezekiel saw in his great vision that 'a stormy wind came out of the
north, and a great cloud, with brightness *(nogah)* round about it, and
fire flashing forth continually' (1:4). He first beheld the powers of
unholiness. A *great cloud* represents 'the power of destruction'; it is called
great, on account of its darkness, which is so intense that it hides and
makes invisible all the sources of light, thus overshadowing the whole
world. The *fire flashing forth* indicates the fire rigorous of judgment that
never departs from it. *With brightness round about it . . .* that is, although
it is the very region of defilement, yet it is surrounded by a certain
brightness . . . it possesses an aspect of holiness, and hence should not
be treated with contempt, but should be allowed a part in the side of
holiness.'[71] Even Satan contains a particle of sanctity. In doing his ugly
work as the seducer of man, his intention is 'for the sake of heaven', for
it is for a purpose such as this that he was created.[72]

The great saint Rabbi Hrish of Zydatschov once remarked to his
disciple and nephew: 'Even after I had reached the age of forty—the age
of understanding—I was not sure whether my life was not immersed in
that mire and confusion of good and evil *(nogah)*. . . . My son, every
moment of my life I fear lest I am caught in that confusion'.[73]

All of history is a sphere where good is mixed with evil. The supreme
task of man, his share in redeeming the work of creation, consists in an
effort to separate good from evil, and evil from good. Since evil can only
exist parasitically on good, it will cease to be when that separation will
be accomplished. Redemption, therefore, is contingent upon the *separation* of good and evil.

Judaism is also aware of the danger of evil's intrusion into the instrument of good. Therefore, at the great ritual on the Day of Atonement
the high priest would cast lots upon the two goats: one lot for the Lord
and the other lot for Azazel. He would lay both his hands upon the head
of the goat, on which the lot fell for Azazel, 'and confess over him all
the iniquities of the children of Israel, all their transgressions, all their
sins'. While the purpose of the goat upon which the lot fell for the Lord

was 'to make atonement *for the holy place,* because of the uncleannesses of the children of Israel, and because of their transgressions, even all their sins; and so shall he do for the tent of meeting, that dwells with them in the midst of their uncleannesses'.[74] At the most sacred day of the year the supreme task was to atone for the holy. It preceded the sacrifice, the purpose of which was to atone for the sins.

The ambiguity of human virtue has been a central issue in the lives of many Jewish thinkers, particularly in the history of Hasidism.

'God asks for the heart.'[75] Yet our greatest failure is in the heart. 'The heart is deceitful above all things, it is exceedingly weak—who can know it?' (*Jeremiah* 17:9). The regard for the ego permeates all our thinking. Is it ever possible to disentangle oneself from the intricate plexus of self-interests? Indeed, the demand to serve God in purity, selflessly, 'For His sake', on the one hand, and the realization of our inability to detach ourselves from vested interests, represent the tragic tension in the life of piety.[76] In this sense, not only our evil deeds, but even our good deeds precipitate a problem.

What is our situation in trying to carry out the will of God? In addition to our being uncertain of whether our motivation—*prior to the act*—is pure, we are continually embarrassed *during the act* with 'alien thoughts' which taint our consciousness with selfish intentions. And even following the act there is the danger of self-righteousness, vanity, and the sense of superiority, derived from what are supposed to be acts of dedication to God.

It is easier to discipline the body than to control the soul. The pious man knows that his inner life is full of pitfalls. The ego, the evil inclinations, is constantly trying to enchant him. The temptations are fierce, yet his resistance is unyielding. And so he proves his spiritual strength and stands victorious, unconquerable. Does not his situation look glorious? But then the evil inclination employs a more subtle device, approaching him with congratulations: What a pious man you are! He begins to feel proud of himself. And there he is caught in the trap (Rabbi Raphel of Bersht).

'For there is not a righteous man upon this earth, that does good and sins not' (*Ecclesiastes* 7:20). The commentators take this verse to mean that even a righteous man sins on occasion, suggesting that his life is a mosaic of perfect deeds with a few sins strewn about. The *Baal Shem,* however, reads the verse: *For there is not a righteous man upon earth that does good and there is no sin in the good.* 'It is impossible that the good should be free of self-interest.'[77] Empirically, our spiritual situation looks hopeless: 'We are all as an unclean thing, and all our deeds of righteousness are as filthy rags' (*Isaiah* 64:5).

'Even the good deeds we do are not pleasing but instead revolting. For we perform them out of the desire of self-aggrandizement and for pride, and in order to impress our neighbours.'[78]

Who can be trustful of his good intention, knowing that under the cloak of *kavanah* there may hide a streak of vanity? Who can claim to have fulfilled even one *mitsvah* with perfect devotion? Said Rabbi Elimelech of Lizhensk to one of his disciples, 'I am sixty years old, and I have not fulfilled one *mitsvah*'.[79] *There is not a single mitsvah which we fulfil perfectly* . . . except circumcision and the *Torah* that we study in our childhood,[80] for these two acts are not infringed upon by 'alien thoughts' or impure motivations.

The mind is never immune to alien intentions, and there seems to be no way of ever weeding them out completely. A Hassidic Rabbi was asked by his disciples, in the last hours of his life, whom they should choose as their master after his passing away. He said, 'If someone should give you the way to eradicate "alien thoughts", know he is not your master'.

We do not know with what we must serve until we arrive there (Exodus 10:26). 'All our service, all the good deeds we are doing in this world, we do not know whether they are of any value, whether they are really pure, honest or done for the sake of heaven—until we arrive there—in the world to come, only there shall we learn what our service was here.'[81]

The human will cannot circumvent the snare of the ego nor can the mind disentangle itself from the confusion of bias in which it is trapped. It often looks as if God's search for the righteous man will end in a cul-de-sac.[82]

Should we, then, despair because of our being unable to attain perfect purity? We should if perfection were our goal. Yet we are not obliged to be perfect once for all, but only to rise again and again. Perfection is divine, and to make it a goal of man is to call on man to be divine. All we can do is to try to wring our hearts clean in contrition. Contrition begins with a feeling of shame at our being incapable of disentanglement from the self. To be contrite at our failures is holier than to be complacent in perfection.

It is a problem of supreme gravity. If an act to be good must be done exclusively for the sake of God, are we ever able to do the good? Rabbi Nahman of Kossov gave an answer in the form of a parable. A stork fell into the mud and was unable to pull out his legs until an idea occurred to him. Does he not have a long beak? So he stuck his beak into the mud, leaned upon it, and pulled out his legs. But what was the use? His legs were out, but his beak was stuck. So another idea occurred to him. He stuck his legs into the mud and pulled out his beak. But what was the use? The legs were stuck in the mud. . . .

Such is exactly the condition of man. Succeeding in one way, he fails in another. We must constantly remember: We spoil, and God restores. How ugly is the way in which we spoil, and how good and how beautiful is the way in which he restores!

And yet, Judaism insists upon the deed and hopes for the intention. Every morning a Jew prays, 'Lord our God, make the words of Thy *Torah* pleasant in our mouth . . . so that we study Thy *Torah* for its own sake.'

While constantly keeping the goal in mind, we are taught that for pedagogic reasons one must continue to observe the law even when one is not ready to fulfil it 'for the sake of God'. For the good, even though it is not done for its own sake, will teach us at the end how to act for the sake of God. We must continue to perform the sacred deeds even though we may be compelled to bribe the self with human incentives. Purity of motivation is the goal; constancy of action is the way.

The ego is redeemed by the absorbing power and the inexorable provocativeness of a just task which we face. It is the deed that carries us away, that transports the soul, proving to us that the greatest beauty grows at the greatest distance from the centre of the ego.

Deeds that are set upon ideal goals, that are not performed with careless ease and routine but in exertion and submission to their ends, are stronger than the surprise and attack of caprice. Serving sacred goals may eventually change mean motives. For such deeds are exacting. Whatever our motive may be in beginning such an act, the act itself demands an undivided attention. Thus the desire for reward is not the driving force of the poet in his creative moments, and the pursuit of pleasure or profit is not the essence of a religious or moral act.

At the moment in which an artist is absorbed in playing a concerto, the thought of applause, fame, or remuneration is far from his mind.

The complete attention of the artist, his whole being, is involved in the music. Should any extraneous thought enter his mind, it would arrest his concentration and mar the purity of his playing. The reward may have been on his mind when he negotiated with his agent, but during the performance it is only the music that claims his complete concentration.

Similar may be man's situation in carrying out a religious or moral act. Left alone the soul is subject to caprice. Yet there is a power in the deed that purifies desires. It is the act, life itself, that educates the will. The good motive comes into being while doing the good.

If the antecedent motive is sure of itself, the act will continue to unfold, and obtrusive intentions could even serve to invigorate the initial motive which may absorb the vigour of the intruder into its own strength. Man may be replete with ugly motives, but a deed and God are stronger than ugly motives. The redemptive power discharged in carrying out the good purifies the mind. The deed is wiser than the heart.

This, then, seems to be the attitude of Judaism. Though deeply aware of how impure and imperfect all our deeds are, the fact of our doing is cherished as the highest privilege, as a source of joy, as that which endows life with ultimate preciousness. We believe that moments lived in fellowship with God, acts fulfilled in imitation of God's will, never perish; the validity of the good remains regardless of all impurity.

Biblical history bears witness to the constant corruption of man; *it does not, however, teach the inevitable corruptibility of the ultimate in the temporal process.* The holiness of Abraham, Isaac, and Jacob, and the humility of Moses are the rock on which they rely. *There are good moments in history that no subsequent evil may obliterate.* The Lord himself testified to it. The integrity of Job proved it. Abraham could not find ten righteous men in Sodom by whose merit the city would have been saved. Yet there is not a moment in history without thirty-six righteous men, unknown and hidden, by whose merit the world survives. We believe that there are corners full of light in a vastness that is dark, that unalloyed good moments are possible. It is, therefore, difficult from the point of view of Biblical theology to sustain Nieburh's view, *plausible and profound as it is.*

If the nature of man were all we had, then surely there would be no hope for us left. But we also have the word of God, the commandment, the *mitsvah.* The central Biblical fact is *Sinai,* the covenant, the word of God. *Sinai* was superimposed on the failure of Adam. Is not the fact that we were given the knowledge of His will a sign of some ability to carry out His will? Does the word of God always remain a challenge, a gadfly? Is not the voice of God powerful enough to shake the wilderness of the soul, to strip the ego bare, to flash forth His will like fire, so that we all cry 'Glory'?

To the Jew, Sinai is at stake in every act of man, and the supreme problem is not good and evil but God, and His commandment to love good and to hate evil. The central issue is not the sinfulness but the obligations of men.

While insisting upon the contrast between God's power and man's power, God's grace and human failure, Judaism stresses a third aspect, the *mitsvah*. It is a *mitsvah* that gives meaning to our existence. The *mitsvah,* the carrying out of a sacred deed, is given to us as a constant opportunity. Thus there are two poles of piety; the right and the wrong deed; *mitsvah* and sin. The overemphasis upon sin may lead to a depre-cation of 'works'; the overemphasis upon *mitsvah* may lead to self-righteousness. The first may result in a denial of the relevance of history and in an overtly eschatological view; the second in a denial of messia-nism and a secular optimism. Against both dangers Judaism warns repeatedly.

We must never forget that we are always exposed to sin. 'Be not sure of yourself till the day of your death,' said Hillel.[83] We have been taught that one may be impregnated with the spirit of the holy all the days of his life, yet one moment of carelessness is sufficient to plunge into the abyss. *There is but one step between me and death* (I Samuel 20:3). On the other hand, we are taught to remember that we are always given the opportunity to serve Him. Significantly, Jewish tradition, while con-scious of the possibilities of evil in the good, stresses the *possibilities of further good in the good*. Ben Azzai said, 'Be eager to do a minor *mitsvah* and flee from transgression; for one *mitsvah* leads to (brings on) another *mitsvah,* and one transgression leads to another transgression; for the reward of a *mitsvah* is a *mitsvah,* and the reward of a transgression is a transgression.'[84]

Judaism, in stressing the fundamental importance of the *mitsvah,* assumes that man is endowed with the ability to fulfil what God demands, at least to some degree. This may, indeed, be an article of prophetic faith: the belief in our ability to do His will. 'For this com-mandment *(mitsvah)* which I command thee this day, it is not too hard for thee, neither is it far off. It is not in heaven, that thou shouldest say, Who shall go up for us to heaven and bring it unto us and make us hear it, that we may do it? Neither is it beyond the sea that thou shouldest say, Who shall go over the sea for us, and bring it unto us, and make us hear it, that we may do it? But the word is very nigh unto thee, in thy mouth and in thy heart, that thou mayest do it' (*Deuteronomy* 30:11–14). Man's actual failures rather than his essential inability to do the good are constantly stressed by Jewish tradition, which claims that man is able to acquire 'merit' before God. The doctrine of merits implies the certainty that for all imperfection the worth of good deeds remains in all eternity.

It is true that the law of love, the demand for the impossible, and our constant failures and transgression create in us grief and a tension that may drive us to despair. Yet, is not the reality of God's love greater than the law of love? Will He not accept us in all our frailty and weakness? 'For He knows our nature *(Yetsen);* He remembers that we are dust' (*Psalms* 103:14).

Judaism would reject the axiom, 'I ought, therefore, I can'; it would claim, instead, 'Thou art commanded, therefore thou canst.' It claims, as I have said, that man has the resources to fulfil what God commands, at least to some degree. On the other hand, we are continually warned lest we rely on man's own power and believe that the 'indeterminate extension of human capacities would eventually alter the human situation.' Our tradition does not believe that the good deeds alone will redeem history; it is the obedience to God that will make us worthy of being redeemed by God.

If Judaism had relied on the human resources for the good, on man's ability to fulfil what God demands, on man's power to achieve redemption, why did it insist upon the promise of messianic redemption? Indeed, messianism implies that any course of living, even the supreme human efforts, must fail in redeeming the world. In other words, history is not sufficient to itself.

Yet the Hebraic tradition insists upon the *mitsvah* as the instrument in dealing with evil. At the end of days, evil will be conquered all at once; in historic times evils must be conquered one by one.

Notes

1. E. Cassirer, *An Essay on Man,* New Haven, 1944, p. 5.
2. *Midrash Tehillim,* ed. Buber, p. 240.

3. *Numbers Rabba,* ch. 13, 6; compare *Genesis Rabba,* ch. 3, 9.
4. *Genesis Rabba,* ch. 30; unlike *Theodor,* p. 277.
5. *Pesikta,* ed. Buber, XXVI, 166b; (compare the two versions).
6. *Genesis Rabba,* ch. 69, 3.
7. *Genesis Rabba,* ch. 47, 6; 83, 6.
8. *Sifre Deuteronomy,* 346; (compare the interpretation of *Psalms* 123:1).
9. *Psalms* 145:9.
10. See A. Heschel, *Die Prophetic,* Cracow, 1936, pp. 56–87; 127–180.
11. *Numbers* 33:52; *I Samuel* 6:5, 6, 11; *II Kings* 11:18; *Ezekiel* 7:20; 16:17; 23:14; *II Chronicles* 23:17.
12. *Hosea* 11:9.
13. *Numbers* 23:19.
14. *Pesahim,* 75a.
15. *Genesis Rabba,* 24, 8.
16. *Hosea* 11:1 f.
17. *Hosea* 14:5.
18. *Deuteronomy* 7:7–8.
19. *Genesis* 9:5 f. It is not clear, however, whether the last words of this sentence contain a condemnation of murder or a justification of man and the right to pronounce the death penalty for murder.
20. *Aboth,* 4, 15.
21. Rabbi Meir de Todros Halevi Abulafia (1180–1244), quoted by Rabbi Samuel da Uceda, *Midrash Shemuel,* Venice, 1579, *ad locum.*
22. Driver, *Deuteronomy* (International Critical Commentary), Edinburgh, 1895, p. 248 f. 'For man was made in the image of God,' Rashi.
23. *Sanhedrin,* 6, 4, *Sanhedrin,* 46b; *Tosefta Sanhedrin,* 9, 7.
24. *Mishnah Sanhedrin,* 4, 5.
25. *Mishnah Terumoth,* 8, 12.
26. *Mishnah Sanhedrin,* 37a.
27. *Rashi, Sanhedrin,* 37a.
28. *Rosh Hashanah,* 19b.
29. *Mishnah, Sanhedrin,* IVm, 5.
30. *Shabbath* 50b, and Rashi *ad locum.*
31. *Leviticus,* Rabba 34, 3; see *Aboth de Rabbi Nathan,* Version B, ch. 30, ed., Schechter, p. 66; *Midrash Tehillim,* 103; *Sheeltoth,* 1.
32. Jacob Burckhardt, *Force and Freedom,* New York, Pantheon Books, Inc., 1943, pp. 191, 318.
33. Hugo Winckler, *The Tell-el-Amarna Letters,* Berlin, Reuther & Reichard, 1896, pp. 48 f.
J. A. Knudtzon, *Die El-Amarna-Tafeln, Vorderasiatische Bibliothek,* Leipzig, 1915, pp. 178 f, (no. 23) 1050 f.
34. *Cf.* for example, *Deuteronomy* 27:15; *Leviticus* 4:15.
35. *Deuteronomy* 4:16; *Ezeckiel* 8:3; 5:2; *Chronicles* 33:7, 15. However, by means of a metathesis, Ibn. Exra finds the word *selem* in *sulam* (ladder); *cf.* his interpretation of Jacob's ladder in his *Commentary* on *Genesis* 28:11.

36. See A. T. Glassberg, *Zikron Berith la-Rishonim,* Berlin, 1892, pp. 176 ff., 231 ff.

37. Thomas Carlyle, *Sartor Resartus,* New York: Doubleday, Doran & Company, Inc., 1937, Book III, Chapter 7, pp. 253–254.

38. *Ibid.,* Book I, Chapter 11, p. 72.

39. H. F. Dunbar, *Symbolism in Mediaeval Thought and Its Consummation in the Divine Comedy,* New Haven: Yale University Press, 1929, pp. 15 f.

40. See my, *The Sabbath, Its Meaning to Modern Man,* New York: Farrar, Strauss & Young, 1951, pp. 4 ff; 'Space, Time and Reality,' *Judaism,* 1, 3, July, 1952, pp. 268 f.

41. William Edward Addis and T. Arnold, 'Latria,' *Catholic Dictionary,* Catholic Publication Society Company, London: Kegan Paul, Trench & Company, 1884, p. 505.

42. Charles R. Morey, *Mediaeval Art,* New York: W. W. Norton Company, 1942, pp. 104 f.

43. Rabbi Yeheskel Landau, *Noda be-Yehudah,* Second Series, *Orah Havim,* responsum 19.

44. Rosh Hashnah, 242; *Avodah Zarah,* 43a.

45. *Mekilta to Exodus,* 20:16.

46. *Tselem elohim in Genesis,* 1:27 is translated in the Septuagint *kat' eikona theou.*

47. *Leviticus Rabba,* 34, 3; see above (manuscript p. 41). Significant are the statements in *Jer, Berachoth III,* 8a, and *Moed Katan,* 83a.

48. *Deuteronomy Rabba,* 4, 4; see *Midrash Tehillim,* chapter 17. That one lives in the company of angels, 'ministers of the Supreme', was something one is expected by *Jewish law* to be always conscious of. This is evidenced by the prayer *hithhabdu, Berachoth* 60b and *Mishne Torah, Tefillah,* 7, 4. The general belief, based on *Psalms* 91:11, is clearly stated in *Tacanith* 11a. According to *Exodus Rabba,* 32, 6, and *Tanhuma, Mishpatim,* end, angels are assigned to a person according to the good deeds he performs; *Seder Eliahu Rabba,* chapter XVIII, edition Friedmann, p. 100. Compare also the statement of the two 'ministering angels' that accompany a person on Sabbath eve on his way from the synagogue to his home, *Shabbath* 119b. 'Rabbi Simeon said: When a man rises at midnight and gets up and studies the Torah till daylight, and when the daylight comes he puts the phylacteries with the holy impress on his head and his arm, and covers himself with his fringed robe, and as he issues from the door of his house he passes the *mezusah* containing the imprint of the Holy Name on the post of his door, then four holy angels join him and issue with him from the door of his house and accompany him to the synagogue and proclaim before him: Give honour to the image of the Holy King, give honour to the son of the King, to the precious countenance of the King.' *Zohar,* III, p. 265a.

49. 'It was left for the Christian religion to call down its god from the heights of heaven to earth, and to represent this god by means of art.' (A. D. Seta, *Religion and Art,* New York: Charles Scribner's Sons, 1914, p. 148). Indeed, this

was not the way of Judaism which insisted upon its worship being independent of art. It is life itself that must represent the God of Israel.

50. *Genesis Rabba*, 8, 12.

51. *Abodah Zarah*, 43b.

52. *Deuteronomy Rabba*, 1, 10.

53. See *Deuteronomy Rabba*, 5, 9.

54. *Moed Kattan*, 15b.

55. *Deuteronomy*, Rabba 1, 10.

56. *Zephania* 1:17; *Zacharia* 9:3; *Job* 22:24.

57. It was Schopenhauer who claimed that the Hebrew spirit was characteristically optimistic, whereas Christianity was pessimistic. *Die Welt als Wille und Vorstellung*, II, chap. 48; *Parerga and Paralipomena*, Gusbach ed., II, 397. *Samtliche Werke*, Franenstadt ed., III, 712 f.

58. Raba, in *Baba Bathra* 9a, referred to the end of the verse as denying Divine Providence.

59. *Abodah Zarah*, 3b–4a; see also *Aboth*, III, 2.

60. *Aboth*, 4:21.

61. *Erubin*, 22a.

62. *Kiddushin*, 39b.

63. *Berachoth*, 61b. This world is often compared to 'night'; it is even called 'the world of falsehood'.

64. *Midrash Vayosha, Beth Hamidrash,* ed. Jellinek, 2nd ed., Jerusalem, 1938, 1, 55.

65. *Temunah* (Koretz, 1784), p. 39b.

66. Rabbi Shneur Zalman of Ladi, *Tanya*, p. 10b.

67. A. J. Heschel, *The Earth Is the Lord's* (New York, 1950), p. 96.

68. *Aboth* 4:22.

69. *Shabbat*, 30a.

70. *Sohar*, III, 80b; see also 1, 156a.

71. *Ibid.*, II, 203a–203b; see pp. 69a–69b. The *kelipoth*, or the forces of the unholy, are unclean and harmful from the aspect of man. However, from the aspect of the holy, they exist because of the will of the Creator and for His sake. A spark of holiness abides in them and maintains them. Rabbi Abraham Azulai, *Or Hahamah* (Przemysl, 1897), II, 218a.

72. *Baba Bathra*, 16a.

73. Rabbi Eisik Safran, *Zohar Hai*, 1.

74. Leviticus 16:16.

75. *Sanhedrin*, 106b.

76. The essence of idolatry is to regard something as a thing in itself, separated from the holiness of God. In other words, to worship an idol does not mean to deny God; it means not to deny the self. This is why pride is idolatry. *Tanya*, 28b.

77. Rabbi Yaakob Yosel of Plynoye, *Toldoth Yankov Yosel* (Lemburg, 1863), p. 150d.

78. Rabbi David Kimhi, *Commentary on Isaiah,* ad locum. Similarly, S. D. Luzatto in his commentary. *Cf.* N. J. Berlin, *Commentary on Sheeltoth,* sec. 64, p. 420. According to *Sheeltoth* the meaning of the verse is that our deeds of righteousness are as a cloth put together in patches, not woven together properly.

79. Rabbi Yaakob Aaron of Zalshin, *Beth Yaakov* (Pietrkov, 1899), p. 144; Aboth 2:20.

80. *Midrash Tehillim,* 6, 1.

81. Rabbi Isaac Meir of Ger.

82. Moments of despair were known to the prophets. Elijah, fleeing from Jezebel, fled to the wilderness, and there he sat down under a broom-tree and said, 'It is enough; now, O Lord, take away my life, for I am not better than my fathers' (*I Kings* 19:4). Jeremiah exclaims, 'Cursed be the day wherein I was born' (20:14). *Cf.,* also *Psalms* 22, 39, 88; *Job* 9:21, 10:20 f; 14:6 f; *Ecclesiastes* 4:2.

83. *Aboth* 2:5.

84. *Ibid.,* 4:3.

Chapter 10

THE RELIGIOUS MESSAGE

I

Little does religion ask of contemporary man. It is ready to offer comfort; it has no courage to challenge. It is ready to offer edification; it has no courage to break the idols, to shatter the callousness. The trouble is that religion has become "religion"—institution, dogma, securities. It is not an event anymore. Its acceptance involves neither risk nor strain. Religion has achieved respectability by the grace of society, and its representatives publish as a frontispiece that *nihil obstat* signed by social scientists.

There is no substitute for faith, no alternative for revelation, no surrogate for commitment. This we must remember in order to save our thought from confusion. And confusion is not a rare disease. We are guilty of committing the fallacy of misplacement. We define self-reliance and call it faith, shrewdness and call it wisdom, anthropology and call it ethics, literature and call it Bible, inner security and call it religion, conscience and call it God. However, nothing counterfeit can endure forever.

It is customary to blame secular science and anti-religious philosophy for the eclipse of religion in modern society. It would be more honest to blame religion for its own defeats. Religion declined not because it was refuted, but because it became irrelevant, dull, oppressive, insipid. When faith is completely replaced by creed, worship by discipline, love by habit; when the crisis of today is ignored because of the splendor of the past; when faith becomes an heirloom rather than a living fountain; when religion speaks only in the name of authority rather than with the voice of compassion, its message becomes meaningless.

Religion is an answer to ultimate questions. The moment we become oblivious to ultimate questions, religion becomes irrelevant, and its crisis sets in. The primary task of religious thinking is to rediscover the questions to which religion is an answer, to develop a degree of sensitivity to the ultimate questions which its ideas and acts are trying to answer.

Religious thinking is an intellectual endeavor out of the depths of reason. It is a source of cognitive insight into the ultimate issues of human existence. Religion is more than a mood or a feeling. Judaism, for example, is a way of thinking, not only a way of living. Unless we understand its categories, its mode of apprehension and evaluation, its teachings remain unintelligible.

It is not enough to call for good will. We are in desperate need of good thinking.

Our theme is religion and its relation to the free society. Such a relation can only be established if we succeed in rediscovering the intellectual relevance of the Bible.

Now the most serious obstacle which modern men encounter in entering a discussion about the ideas of the Bible, is the absence of the problem to which the Bible refers. This, indeed, is the status of the Bible in modern society: it is a sublime answer, but we no longer know the question to which it responds. Unless we recover the question, there is no hope of understanding the Bible.

The Bible is an answer to the question, What does God require of Man? But to modern man, this question is suppressed by another one, namely, What does man demand of God? Modern man continues to ponder: What will I get out of life? What escapes his attention is the fundamental, yet forgotten question: What will life get out of me?

The alarming fact is that man is becoming "a fighter for needs" rather than "a fighter for ends," as defined by William James.

Absorbed in the struggle for the emancipation of the individual we have concentrated our attention upon the idea of human rights and overlooked the importance of human obligations. More and more the sense of commitment, which is so essential a component of human existence, was lost in the melting pot of conceit and sophistication. Oblivious to the fact of his receiving infinitely more than he is able to return, man began to consider his self as the only end. Caring only for his needs rather than for his being needed, he is hardly able to realize that rights are anything more than legalized interests.

Needs are looked upon today as if they were holy, as if they contained the totality of existence. Needs are our gods, and we toil and spare no effort to gratify them. Suppression of a desire is considered a sacrilege that must inevitably avenge itself in the form of some mental disorder. We worship not one but a whole pantheon of needs and have come to look upon moral and spiritual norms as nothing but personal desires in disguise.

Specifically, need denotes the absence or shortage of something indispensable to the well-being of a person, evoking the urgent desire for satisfaction. The term "need" is generally used in two ways: one denoting the actual lack, an objective condition, and the other denoting the awareness of such a lack. It is in the second sense, in which need is synonymous with interest, namely "an unsatisfied capacity corresponding to an unrealized condition" that the term is used here.

Every human being is a cluster of needs, yet these needs are not the same in all men or unalterable in any one man. There is a fixed minimum of needs for all men, but no fixed maximum for any man. Unlike animals, man is the playground for the unpredictable emergence and multiplication of needs and interests, some of which are indigenous to his nature, while others are induced by advertisement, fashion, envy, or come about as miscarriages of authentic needs. We usually fail to discern between authentic and artificial needs and, misjudging a whim for an aspiration, we are thrown into ugly tension. Most obsessions are the perpetuation of such misjudgments. In fact, more people die in the epidemics of needs than in the epidemics of disease. To stem the expansion of man's needs, which in turn is brought about by technological and social advancement, would mean to halt the stream on which civilization is riding. Yet the stream unchecked may sweep away civilization itself, since the pressure of needs turned into aggressive interests is the constant cause of wars and increases in direct proportion to technological progress.

We cannot make our judgments, decisions and directions for action dependent upon our needs. The fact is that man who has found out so much about so many things knows neither his own heart nor his own voice. Many of the interests and needs we cherish are imposed on us by the conventions of society; they are not indigenous to our essence. While some of them are necessities, others, as I said before, are fictitious, and adopted as a result of convention, advertisement or sheer envy.

The contemporary man believes he has found the philosopher's stone in the concept of needs. But who knows his true needs? How are we going to discern authentic from fictitious needs, necessities from make-believes?

Having absorbed an enormous amount of needs and having been taught to cherish the high values, such as justice, liberty, faith, as private or national interests, we are beginning to wonder whether needs and interests should be relied upon. While it is true that there are interests which all men have in common, most of our private and national interests, as asserted in daily living, divide and antagonize rather than unite us.

Interest is a subjective, dividing principle. It is the excitement of feeling, accompanying special attention paid to some object. But do we pay sufficient attention to the demands for universal justice? In fact, the interest in universal welfare is usually blocked by the interest in personal welfare, particularly when it is to be achieved at the price of renouncing one's vested interests. It is just because the power of interests is tyranniz-ing our lives, determining our views and actions, that we lose sight of the values that count most.

Short is the way from need to greed. Evil conditions make us seethe with evil needs, with mad dreams. Can we afford to pursue all our innate needs, even our will for power?

In the tragic confusion of interests, in which every one of us is caught, no distinction seems to be as indispensable as the distinction between right and wrong interests. Yet the concepts of right and wrong, to be standards in our dealing with interests, cannot themselves be interests. Determined as they are by temperament, bias, background and environ-ment of every individual and group, needs are our problems rather than our norms. They are in need of, rather than the origins of, standards.

He who sets out to employ the realities of life as means for satisfying his own desires will soon forfeit his freedom and be degraded to a mere tool. Acquiring things, he becomes enslaved to them; in subduing others, he loses his own soul. It is as if unchecked covetousness were double-faced; a sneer and subtle vengeance behind a captivating smile. We can ill afford to set up needs, an unknown, variable, vacillating and eventually degrading factor, as a universal standard, as a supreme, abiding rule or pattern for living.

We feel jailed in the confinement of personal needs. The more we indulge in satisfactions, the deeper is our feeling of oppressiveness. To be an iconoclast of idolized needs, to defy our own immoral interests, though they seem to be vital and have long been cherished, we must be able to say *no* to ourselves in the name of a higher *yes*. Yet our minds are late, slow and erratic. What can give us the power to curb the deference to wrong needs, to detect spiritual fallacies, to ward off false ideals and to wrestle with inattentiveness to the unseemly and holy?

This, indeed, is the purpose of our religious traditions: to keep alive the higher "yes" as well as the power of man to say "Here I am"; to teach our minds to understand the true demand and to teach our conscience to be present. Too often, we misunderstand the demand; too often the call goes forth, and history records our conscience as absent.

Religion has adjusted itself to the modern temper by proclaiming that it too is the satisfaction of a need. This conception, which is surely diametrically opposed to the prophetic attitude, has richly contributed to the misunderstanding and sterilization of religious thinking. To define religion primarily as a quest for personal satisfaction, as the satisfaction of a human need, is to make of it a refined sort of magic. Did the thunderous voice at Sinai proclaim the ten Words in order to satisfy a need? The people felt a need for a graven image, but that need was condemned. The people were homesick for the fleshpots of Egypt. They asked: Give us flesh. And the Lord gave them spirit, not only flesh.

The Bible does not begin with man, or the history of religion, or man's need for God. "At the beginning God created heaven and earth." To begin with needs is a sign of man's pitiful perspective.

Religion is spiritual effrontery. Its root is in our bitter sense of inadequacy, in a thirst which can only be stilled by greater thirst, in the embarrassment that we really do not care for God, in the discovery that our religious need is utterly feeble, that we do not feel any need for God.

We must beware of converting needs into ends, interests into norms. The task is precisely the opposite: it is to convert ends into needs, to convert the divine commandment into a human concern.

Religion is not a way of satisfying needs. It is an answer to the question: Who needs man? It is an awareness of being needed, of man being a need of God. It is a way of sanctifying the satisfaction of authentic needs.

It is an inherent weakness of religion not to take offense at the segregation of God, to forget that the true sanctuary has no walls. Religion has often suffered from the tendency to become an end in itself, to seclude the holy, to become parochial, self-indulgent, self-seeking; as if the task were not to ennoble human nature but to enhance the power and beauty of its institutions or to enlarge the body of doctrines. It has often done more to canonize prejudices than to wrestle for truth; to petrify the sacred than to sanctify the secular. Yet the task of religion is to be a challenge to the stabilization of values.

II

The mind of the prophets was not religion-centered. They dwelt more on the affairs of the royal palace, on the ways and views of the courts of justice, than on the problems of the priestly rituals at the temple of Jerusalem.

We today are shocked when informed about *an increase* in juvenile delinquency, or *an increase* in the number of crimes committed in our city. The normal amount of juvenile delinquency, the normal number of crimes does not cause us to be dismayed. At this very moment somewhere throughout the nation crimes are being committed.

The sort of crimes, and even the amount of delinquency that fill the prophets of Israel with dismay do not go beyond that which we regard as normal, as a typical ingredient of social dynamics. A single act of injustice—to us it is slight, to the prophet it is a disaster.

Turning from the discourses of the great metaphysicians to the orations of the prophets, one may feel as if he were going down from the realm of the sublime to an area of trivalities. Instead of dealing with the timeless issues of being and becoming, of matter and form, of definitions and demonstrations, one is thrown into orations about widows and orphans, about the corruption of judges and affairs of the market place. The prophets make so much ado about paltry things, employing the most excessive language in speaking about flimsy subjects. So what if somewhere in ancient Palestine poor people have not been treated properly by the rich? So what if some old women found pleasure and edification in worshipping "the Queen of Heaven"? Why such immoderate excitement? Why such intense indignation?

Their breathless impatience with injustice may strike us as hysteria. We ourselves witness continually acts of injustice, manifestations of hypocrisy, falsehood, outrage, misery, but we rarely get indignant or overly excited. To the prophets a minor, commonplace sort of injustice assumes almost cosmic proportions.

> Be appalled, O heavens, at this,
> Be shocked, be utterly desolate, says the Lord.
> For My people have committed two evils:
> They have forsaken Me,
> The fountain of living waters
> And hewed out cisterns for themselves,
> Broken cisterns that hold no water.
>
> Jeremiah 2:12–13

They speak and act as if the sky were about to collapse because Israel had become unfaithful to God.

Is not the size of their indignation, is not the size of God's anger in disproportion to its cause? How should one explain such moral and religious excitability, such extreme impetuosity?

The prophet's words are outbursts of violent emotions. His rebuke is harsh and relentless. But if such deep sensitivity to evil is to be called hysterical, what name should be given to the deep callousness to evil which the prophet bewails? "They drink from bowls of wine, and anoint themselves with the finest oils; but they are not pained by the crushing of Joseph" (Amos 6:6).

The niggardliness of our moral comprehension, the incapacity to sense the depth of misery caused by our own failures, is a fact which no subterfuge can elude. Our eyes are witness to the callousness and cruelty of man, but our heart tries to obliterate the memories, to calm the nerves, and to silence our conscience.

The prophet is a man who feels fiercely. God has thrust a burden upon his soul, and he is bowed and stunned at man's fierce greed. Frightful is the agony of man; no human voice can convey its full terror. Prophecy is the voice that God has lent to the silent agony, a voice to the plundered poor, to the profaned riches of the world. It is a form of living, a crossing point of God and man. God is raging in the prophets' words.

The prophets had disdain for those to whom God was comfort and security; to them God was a challenge, an incessant demand. He is compassion, but not a compromise; justice, but not inclemency. Tranquillity is unknown to the soul of a prophet. The miseries of the world give him no rest. While others are callous, and even callous to their callousness and unaware of their insensitivity, the prophets remain examples of supreme impatience with evil, distracted by neither might or applause, by neither success or beauty. Their intense sensitivity to right and wrong is due to their intense sensitivity to God's concern for right and wrong. They feel fiercely because they hear deeply.

The prophets tried to overcome the isolationism of religion. It is the prophets who teach us that the problem of living does not arise with the question of how to take care of the rascals, of how to prevent delinquency or hideous crimes. The problem of living begins with the realization of how we all blunder in dealing with our fellow men. The silent atrocities, the secret scandals, which no law can prevent, are the true seat of moral infection. The problem of living begins, in fact, in relation to our own selves, in the handling of our emotional functions, in the way we deal with envy, greed, and pride. What is first at stake in the life of man is not the fact of sin, of the wrong and corrupt, but the neutral acts, the needs. Our possessions pose no less a problem than our passions. The primary task, therefore, is not how to deal with the evil, but how to deal with the neutral, how to deal with needs.

The central commandment is in relation to the person. But religion today has lost sight of the person.

Religion has become an impersonal affair, an institutional loyalty. It survives on the level of activities rather than in the stillness of commitment. It has fallen victim to the belief that the real is only that which is capable of being registered by fact-finding surveys.

By religion is meant what is done publicly rather than that which comes about in privacy. The chief virtue is social affiliation rather than conviction.

Inwardness is ignored. The spirit has become a myth. Man treats himself as if he were created in the likeness of a machine rather than the likeness of God. The body is his god, and its needs are its prophets. Having lost his awareness of his sacred image, he became deaf to the command: to live in a way which is compatible with his image.

Religion without a soul is as viable as a man without a heart. Social dynamics is no substitute for meaning. Yet, the failure to realize the fallacy of such substitution seems to be common in our days.

Perhaps this is the most urgent task: to save the inner man from oblivion, to remind ourselves that we are a duality of mysterious grandeur and pompous dust. Our future depends upon our appreciation of the reality of the inner life, of the splendor of thought, of the dignity of wonder and reverence. This is the most important thought: God has a stake in the life of man, of every man. But this idea cannot be imposed from without it; it must be discovered by every man; it cannot be preached, it must be experienced.

When the Voice of God spoke at Sinai, it did not begin by saying, "I am the Lord your God Who created heaven and earth." It began by saying "I am the Lord your God who brought you out of the land of Egypt, out of the house of bondage." Judaism is not only deliverance from external slavery, but also freedom from false fears and false glories, from fashion, from intellectual will-o'-the-wisps. In our souls we are subject to causes; in our spirits we are free, beholding the uncompromising.

The most commanding idea that Judaism dares to think is that freedom, not necessity, is the source of all being. The universe was not caused, but created. Behind mind and matter, order and relations, the freedom of God obtains. The inevitable is not eternal. All compulsion is a result of choice. A tinge of that exemption from necessity is hiding in the folds of the human spirit.

We are not taught to feel accused, to bear a sense of boundless guilt. We are asked to feel elated, bred to meet the tasks that never end.

Every child is a prince; every man is obliged to feel that the world was created for his sake. Man is not the measure of all things, but the means by which to accomplish all tasks.

As a free being the Jew must accept an enormous responsibility. The first thing a Jew is told is: you can't let yourself go, get into harness, carry the yoke of the Kingdom of Heaven. He is told to bear loads of responsibility. He is told to abhor self-complacency, to enjoy freedom of choice. He has been given life and death, good and evil, and is urged to choose, to discriminate. Yet freedom is not only the ability to choose and to act, but also the ability to will, to love. The predominant feature of Jewish teaching throughout the ages is a sense of constant obligation.

We are taught to prefer truth to security, to maintain loyalty even at the price of being in the minority. It is inner freedom that gives man the strength to forgo security, the courage to remain lonely in the multitude.

Judaism is forever engaged in a bitter battle against man's deeply rooted belief in fatalism and its ensuing inertia in social, moral and spiritual conditions. Abraham started in rebellion against his father and the gods of his time. His great distinction was, not in being loyal and conforming, but in defying and initiating. He was loved by the Lord not for ancestral worship but because he taught his descendants "to keep to the way of the lord, to do righteousness and justice" (Genesis 18:19).

III

We all share a supreme devotion to the hard won freedoms of the American people. Yet, to be worthy of retaining our freedoms we must not lose our understanding of the essential nature of freedom. Freedom means more than mere emancipation. It is primarily freedom of conscience, bound up with inner allegiance. The danger begins when freedom is thought to consist in the fact that "I can act as I desire." This definition not only over-looks the compulsions which often lie behind our desires; it reveals the tragic truth that freedom may develop within itself the seed of its own destruction. The will is not an ultimate and isolated entity, but determined by motives beyond its own control. *To be* what one wants to be, is also not freedom, since the wishes of the ego are largely determined by external factors.

Freedom is not a principle of uncertainty, the ability to act without a motive. Such action would be chaotic and sub-rational, rather than free.

Although political and social freedom must include all this, even the freedom to err—its true essence is in man's ability to surpass himself, even to act against his inclinations and in defiance of his own needs and desires, to sacrifice prejudice even it if *hurts,* to give up superstition even when it claims to be a doctrine.

Freedom is the liberation from the tyranny of the self-centered ego. It comes about in moments of transcending the self as an act of spiritual ecstasy, of stepping out of the confining framework of routine reflexive concern. Freedom presupposes *the capacity for sacrifice.*

Although all men are potentially free, it is our sacred duty to safeguard all those political, social, and intellectual conditions which will enable every man to bring about the concrete actualization of freedom which is the essential prerequisite of creative achievement.

The shock of radical amazement, the humility born in awe and reverence, the austere discipline of unremitting inquiry and self-criticism are acts of liberating man from the routine way of looking only at those features of experience which are similar and regular and open his soul to the unique and transcendent. This sensitivity to the novel and unprecedented is the foundation of God-awareness and of the awareness of the preciousness of all beings. It leads from reflexive concern and the moral and spiritual isolation which is the result of egocentricity to a mode of responding to each new and unique experience in terms of broader considerations, wider interests, deeper appreciation and new, as yet unrealized values.

As the object of divine transitive concern man is; knowing himself to be the object of divine concern and responding through acts of his own transitive concern *he is free*.

The meaning of freedom is not exhausted by deliberation, decision, and responsibility, although it must include all this. The meaning of freedom presupposes an openness to transcendence, and man has to be *responsive* before he can become *responsible*.

Man's true fulfillment cannot be reached by the isolated individual, and his true good depends on communion with, and participation in, that which transcends him. Each challenge from beyond the person is unique, and each response must be new and creative. Freedom is an act of engagement of the self to the spirit, a spiritual event.

Loyalty to freedom means loyalty to the substance of freedom. But such loyalty must be actualized again and again. Here our way of living must change: it must open the sight of sublime horizons under which we live.

Refusal to delegate the power to make ultimate decisions to any human institution, derives its strength either from the awareness of one's mysterious dignity or from the awareness of one's ultimate responsibility. But that strength breaks down in the discovery that one is unable to make a significant choice. Progressive vulgarization of society may deprive man of his ability to appreciate the sublime burden of freedom. Like Esau he may be ready to sell his birth-right for a pot of lentils.

A major root of freedom lies in the belief that man, every man, is too good to be the slave of another man. However, the dynamics of our society, the cheapening and trivialization of existence, continues to corrode that belief. The uniqueness and sacred preciousness of man is being refuted with an almost cruel consistency. I do not mean the anthropological problem whether we are descendants of the monkeys. What I have in mind is the fact that we are being treated as if there were little difference between man and monkey. Much that is being done, e.g. in the name of entertainment is an insult to the soul. What is involved is not demoralization; much of it may be morally neutral. What is involved is dehumanization; so much of it is a continual process of intellectual deprivation. Sensitivity to words is one of the many casualties in that process.

Words have become pretexts in the technique of evading the necessity of honest and genuine expression. Sometimes it seems as if we were all engaged in the process of liquidating the English language. But words are the vessels of the spirit. And when the vessels are broken, our relationship to the spirit becomes precarious.

To be free one must attain a degree of independence. Yet, the complexities of society have enmeshed contemporary man in a web of relationships which make his independence most precarious.

Inherent in man is the desire to be in agreement with others. Yet, today with a mass of miscellaneous associations and unprecedented excitements, it is a grim task, indeed, to agree with all and to retain the balance of integrity.

Loaded with more vulnerable interests than he is able to protect, bursting with fears of being squeezed by a multiplicity of tasks and responsibilities, modern man feels too insecure to remain upright.

Good and evil have always had a tendency to live in promiscuity, but in more integrated societies man, it seems, found it easier to discriminate between the two, while in our turbulent times circumstances often stupefy our power of discernment; it is as if many of us have become value-blind in the epidemics of needs.

The glory of a free society lies not only in the consciousness of my right to be free, and my capacity to be free, but also in the realization of my fellow-man's right to be free, and his capacity to be free. The issue we face is how to save man's belief in his capacity to be free. Our age may be characterized as the *age of suspicion*. It has become an axiom that the shortest way to the understanding of man is to suspect his motives. This seems to be the contemporary version of the Golden Rule: *Suspect thy neighbor as thyself.* Suspicion breeds suspicion. It creates a chain-reaction. Honesty is not necessarily an anachronism.

The insecurity of freedom is a bitter fact of historic experience. In times of unemployment, vociferous demagogues are capable of leading the people into a state of mind in which they are ready to barter their freedom for any bargain. In times of prosperity hidden persuaders are capable of leading the same people into selling their conscience for success. Unless a person learns how to rise daily to a higher plane of living, to care for that which surpasses his immediate needs, will he in a moment of crisis insist upon loyalty to freedom?

The threat to freedom lies in the process of reducing human relations to a matter of fact. Human life is not a drama anymore, it is a routine. Uniqueness is suppressed, repetitiveness prevails. We teach our students how to recognize the labels, not how to develop a taste. Standardization corrodes the sense of ultimate significance. Man to his own self becomes increasingly vapid, cheap, insignificant. Yet without the sense of ultimate significance and ultimate preciousness of my own existence, freedom becomes a hollow phrase.

The central problem of this generation is emptiness in the heart, the decreased sensitivity to the imponderable quality of the spirit, the collapse of communication between the realm of tradition and the inner world of the individual. The central problem is that we do not know how to think, how to pray, or how to cry, or how to resist the deceptions of the silent persuaders. There is no community of those who worry about integrity.

One of the chief problems of contemporary man is the problem: what to do with time? Most of our life we spend time in order to gain space, namely things of space. Yet when the situation arrives in which no things of space may be gained, the average man is at a loss as to what to do with time.

With the development of automation the number of hours to be spent professionally will be considerably reduced. The four-day week may become a reality within this generation. The problem will arise: What to do with so much leisure time? The problem will be *too much* time rather than too little time. But too much time is a breeding ground for crime. Idleness is unbearable, and the most popular method to solve the problem of time is to kill time. Yet time is life, and to kill time is murder.

The average man has not only forgotten how to be alone; he finds it even difficult to be with his fellow man. He not only runs away from himself; he runs away from his family. To children "Honor your father and your mother," is an irrational commandment. The normal relationship is dull; deviation is where pleasure is found.

The average man does not know how to stand still, how to appreciate a moment, an event for its own sake. When witnessing an important event or confronted with a beautiful sight, all he does is take a picture. Perhaps this is what our religious traditions must teach the contemporary man: to stand still and to behold, to stand still and to hear.

Judaism claims that the way to nobility of the soul is the art of sanctifying time. Moral dedications, acts of worship, intellectual pursuits are means in the art of sanctification of time. Personal concern for justice in the market place, for integrity in public affairs and in public relations are a prerequisite for our right to pray.

Acts of worship counteract the trivialization of existence. Both involve the person, and give him a sense of living in ultimate relationships. Both of them are ways of teaching man how to stand alone and not be alone, of teaching man that God is a refuge, not a security.

But worship comes out of wisdom, out of insight, it is not an act of insight. Learning, too, is a religious commandment. Learning is an indispensable form of purification as well as ennoblement. I do not mean memorization, erudition; I mean the very act of study, of being involved in wisdom, and of being overwhelmed by the marvel and mystery of God's creation.

Religion's major effort must be to counteract the deflation of man, the trivilization of human existence. Our religious traditions claim that man is capable of sacrifice, discipline, or moral and spiritual exaltation, that every man is capable of an ultimate commitment.

Ultimate commitment includes the consciousness of being accountable for the acts we perform under freedom; the awareness that what we own we owe; the capacity for repentance; that a life without the service of God is a secret scandal.

Faith in God cannot be forced upon man. The issue is not only lack of faith but the vulgarization of faith, the misunderstanding and abuse of freedom. Our effort must involve a total reorientation about the nature of man and the world. And our hope lies in the certainty that all men are capable of sensing the wonder and mystery of existence, that all men have a capacity for reverence. Awe, reverence precedes faith; it is at the root of faith. We must grow in awe in order to reach faith. We must be guided by awe to be worthy of faith. Awe is "the beginning and gateway of faith, the first precept of all, and upon it the whole world is established."

The grandeur and mystery of the world that surrounds us is not something which is perceptible only to the elect. All men are endowed with a sense of wonder, with a sense of mystery. But our system of education fails to develop it and the anti-intellectual climate of our civilization does much to suppress it. Mankind will not perish for lack of information; it may collapse for want of appreciation.

Education for reverence, the development of a sense of awe and mystery, is a prerequisite for the preservation of freedom.

We must learn how to bridle the outrageous presumption of modern man, to cultivate a sense of wonder and reverence, to develop an awareness that something is asked of man. Freedom is a burden that God has thrust upon man. Freedom is something we are responsible for. If we succeed, we will help in the redemption of the world; if we fail, we may be crushed by its abuse. Freedom as man's unlimited lordship is the climax of absurdity, and the central issue we face is man's false sense of sovereignty.

Tragic is the role of religion in contemporary society. The world is waiting to hear the Voice, and those who are called upon to utter the word are confused and weak in faith. "The voice of the Lord is powerful, the voice of the Lord is full of majesty" (Psalms 29:3). Where is its power? Where is its majesty?

A story is told about a community where a man was accused of having transgressed the seventh commandment. The leaders of the community went to the Rabbi and voicing their strong moral indignation demanded stern punishment of the sinner. Thereupon the Rabbi turned his face to the wall and said: "O, Lord, Thy glory is in heaven, Thy presence on earth is invisible, imperceptible. In contrast to Thy invisibility, the object of that man's passion stood before his eyes, full of beauty and enravishing his body and soul. How could I punish him?"

R. Simon said: "When the Holy One, blessed be He, came to create Adam, the ministering angels formed themselves into groups and parties, some of them saying, 'Let him be created,' whilst others urged, 'Let him not be created.' Thus it is written, Love and Truth fought together, Righteousness and Peace combatted each other (Psalms 85:11): Love said,

'Let him be created, because he will dispense acts of love'; Truth said, 'Let him not be created, because he is compounded of falsehood'; Righteousness said, 'Let him be created, because he will perform righteous deeds'; Peace said, 'Let him not be created because he is full of strife.' What did the Lord do? He took Truth and cast it to the ground. Said the ministering angels before the Holy One, blessed be He, 'Sovereign of the Universe! Why dost Thou despise Thy seal? Let Truth arise from the earth!' Hence it is written, Let truth spring up from the earth (Psalms 85:12)."

God had to bury truth in order to create man.

How does one ever encounter the truth? The truth is underground, hidden from the eye. Its nature and man's condition are such that he can neither produce nor invent it. However, there is a way. If you bury the lies, truth will spring up. Upon the grave of the specious we encounter the valid. Much grave digging had to be done. The most fatal trap into which religious thinking may fall is *the equation of faith with expediency*. The genuine task of our traditions is to educate a sense for the inexpedient, a sensitivity to God's demand.

Perhaps we must begin by disclosing *the fallacy of absolute expediency*. God's voice may sound feeble to our conscience. Yet there is a divine cunning in history which seems to prove that the wages of absolute expediency is disaster. We must not tire of reminding the world that something is asked of man, of every man; that the value of charity is not to be measured in terms of public relations. Foreign aid when offered to underdeveloped countries, for the purpose of winning friends and influencing people, turns out to be a boomerang. Should we not learn how to detach expediency from charity? The great failure of American policy is not in public relations. The great failure is in private relations.

The spirit is a still small voice, and the masters of vulgarity use loudspeakers. The voice has been stifled, and many of us have lost faith in the possibility of a new perceptiveness.

Discredited is man's faith in his own integrity. We question man's power to sense any ultimate significance. We question the belief in the compatibility of existence with spirit.

Yet, man is bound to break the chains of despair, to stand up against those who deny him the right and the strength to believe wholeheartedly. Ultimate truth may be hidden from man, yet the power to discern between the valid and the specious has not been taken from us.

Surely God will always receive a surprise of a handful of fools—who do not fail. There will always remain a spiritual underground where a few brave minds continue to fight. Yet our concern is not how to worship in the catacombs but rather how to remain human in the skyscrapers.

Chapter 11

THE RELIGIOUS BASIS OF EQUALITY OF OPPORTUNITY: THE SEGREGATION OF GOD

I

At the first conference on religion and race, the main participants were Pharaoh and Moses. Moses' words were: "Thus says the Lord, the God of Israel, let My people go that they may celebrate a feast to Me." While Pharaoh retorted: "Who is the Lord, that I should heed this voice and let Israel go? I do not know the Lord, and moreover I will not let Israel go."

The outcome of that summit meeting has not come to an end. Pharaoh is not ready to capitulate. The exodus began, but is far from having been completed. In fact, it was easier for the children of Israel to cross the Red Sea than for a Negro to cross certain university campuses.

Let us dodge no issues. Let us yield no inch to bigotry, let us make no compromise with callousness.

In the words of William Lloyd Garrison, "I will be as harsh as truth, and as uncompromising as justice. On this subject [slavery] I do not wish to think, to speak, or to write with moderation. I am in earnest—I will not equivocate—I will not excuse—I will not retreat a single inch—and I will be heard."

Religion and race. How can the two be uttered together? To act in the spirit of religion is to unite what lies apart, to remember that humanity as a whole is God's beloved child. To act in the spirit of race is to sunder, to slash, to dismember the flesh of living humanity. Is this the way to honor a father: to torture his child? How can we hear the word race and feel no self-reproach?

Race as a *normative* legal or political concept is capable of expanding to formidable dimensions. A mere thought, it extends to become a way of thinking, a highway of insolence, as well as a standard of values, overriding truth, justice, beauty. As a standard of values and behavior, race operates as a comprehensive doctrine, as racism. And racism is worse than idolatry. *Racism is satanism,* unmitigated evil.

Few of us seem to realize how insidious, how radical, how universal an evil racism is. Few of us realize that racism is man's gravest threat to man, the maximum of hatred for a minimum of reason, the maximum of cruelty for a minimum of thinking.

Perhaps this Conference should have been called *Religion or Race.* You cannot worship God and at the same time look at man as if he were a horse.

Shortly before he died, Moses spoke to his people. "I call heaven and earth to witness against you this day: I have set before you life and death, blessing and curse. *Choose life.*" (Deuteronomy 30:19). The aim of this conference is first of all to state clearly the stark alternative. I call heaven and earth to witness against you this day: I have set before you religion and race, life and death, blessing and curse. Choose life.

"Race prejudice, a universal human ailment, is the most recalcitrant aspect of the evil in man" (Reinhold Niebuhr), a treacherous denial of the existence of God.

What is an idol? *Any god who is mine but not yours,* any god concerned with me but not with you, *is an idol.*

Faith in God is not simply an *afterlife-insurance policy. Racial or religious bigotry* must be recognized for what it is: *blasphemy.*

In several ways man is set apart from all beings created in six days. The Bible does not say, God created the plant or the animal; it says, God created *different* kinds of plants, *different kinds* of animals (Genesis 1: 11–12, 21–25). In striking contrast, it does not say, God created different kinds of man, men of different colors and races; it proclaims, God created one single man. From one single man all men are descended.

To think of man in terms of white, black or yellow is more than an error. It is *an eye disease, a cancer of the soul.*

The redeeming quality of man lies in his ability to sense his kinship with all men. Yet there is a deadly poison that inflames the eye, making us see the generality of race but not the uniqueness of the human face. Pigmentation is what counts. The Negro is a stranger to many souls. There are people in our country whose moral sensitivity suffers a blackout when confronted with the black man's predicament.

How many disasters do we have to go through in order to realize that all of humanity has a stake in the liberty of one person; whenever one person is offended, we are all hurt. What begins as inequality of some inevitably ends as inequality of all.

In referring to the Negro in this paper we must, of course, always keep equally in mind the plight of all individuals belonging to a racial, religious, ethnic or cultural minority.

This Conference should dedicate itself not only to the problem of the Negro but also to the problem of the white man, not only to the plight of the colored but also to the situation of the white people, to the cure of a disease affecting the spiritual substance and condition of every one of us. What we need is an NAAAP, a National Association for the Advancement of All People. Prayer and prejudice cannot dwell in the same heart. Worship without compassion is worse than self-deception; it is an abomination.

Thus the problem is not only how to do justice to the colored people, it is also how to stop the profanation of God's name by dishonoring the Negro's name.

One hundred years ago the emancipation was proclaimed. It is time for the white man to strive for *self-emancipation,* to set himself free of bigotry, to stop being a slave to wholesale contempt, a passive recipient of slander.

II

"I saw all the oppressions that are practiced under the sun. Behold, the tears of the oppressed, they had no one to comfort them! On the side of the oppressors there was power, and there was no one to comfort them." (Ecclesiastes 4:1)

There is a form of oppression which is more painful and more scathing than physical injury or economic privation. It is *public humiliation.* What afflicts my conscience is that my face, whose skin happens not to be dark, instead of radiating the likeness of God, has come to be taken as an image of haughty assumption and overbearance. Whether justified or not, I, the white man, have become in the eyes of others a symbol of arrogance and pretension, giving offense to other human beings, hurting their pride, even without intending it. My very presence inflicting insult!

My heart is sick when I think of the anguish and the sighs, of the quiet tears shed in the nights in the overcrowded dwellings in the slums of our great cities, of the pangs of despair, of the cup of humiliation that is running over.

The crime of murder is tangible and punishable by law. The sin of insult is imponderable, invisible. When blood is shed, human eyes see red; when a heart is crushed, it is only God who shares the pain.

In the Hebrew language one word denotes both crimes. Bloodshed is the word that denotes both murder and humiliation. The law demands: one should rather be killed than commit murder. Piety demands: one should rather commit suicide than offend a person publicly. It is better, the Talmud insists, to throw oneself alive into a burning furnace than to humiliate a human being publicly.

He who commits a major sin may repent and be forgiven. But he who offends a person publicly will have no share in the life to come.

It is not within the power of God to forgive the sins committed toward men. We must first ask for forgiveness of those whom our society has wronged before asking for the forgiveness of God.

Daily we patronize institutions which are visible manifestations of arrogance toward those whose skin differs from mine. Daily we cooperate with people who are guilty of active discrimination.

How long will I continue to be tolerant of, even participant in, acts of embarrassing and humiliating human beings, in restaurants, hotels, buses, or parks, employment agencies, public schools and universities? One ought rather be shamed than put others to shame.

Our Rabbis taught: "Those who are insulted but do not insult, hear themselves reviled without answering, act through love and rejoice in suffering, of them Scripture says: 'They who love the Lord are as the sun when rising in full splendor.' " (Judges 5:31)

Let us cease to be apologetic, cautious, timid. Racial tension and strife is both sin and punishment. *The Negro's plight,* the blighted areas in the large cities, are they not the fruit of our sins?

By negligence and silence we have all become accessory before the God of mercy to the injustice committed against the Negroes by men of our nation. Our derelictions are many. We have failed to demand, to insist, to challenge, to chastise.

In the words of Thomas Jefferson, "I tremble for my country when I reflect that God is just."

III

There are several ways of dealing with our bad conscience. 1) We can extenuate our responsibility; 2) we can keep the Negro out of our sight; 3) we can alleviate our qualms by pointing to the progress made; 4) we can delegate the responsibility to the courts; 5) we can silence our conscience by cultivating indifference; 6) we can dedicate our minds to issues of a far more sublime nature.

1) Modern thought has a tendency to extenuate personal responsibility. Understanding the complexity of human nature, the inter-relationship of individual and society, of consciousness and the subconscious, we find it difficult to isolate the deed from the circumstances in which it was done. Our enthusiasm is easily stunned by realizing the ramifications and complexity of the problem we face and the enormous obstacles we encounter in trying to implement the philosophy affirmed in the 13th and 14th Amendments as well as in the 1954 decision of the Supreme Court. Yet this general tendency, for all its important correctives and insights, has often had the effect of obscuring our essential vision, aiding our conscience to grow scales: excuses, pretense, self-pity. The sense of guilt may disappear; no crime is absolute, no sin devoid of apology. Within the limits of the human mind, relativity may be true and merciful. Yet the mind's scope embraces but a fragment of society, a few instants of history; it thinks of what has happened, it is unable to imagine what might have happened. The qualms of my conscience are easily cured—even while the agony for which I am accountable continues unabated.

2) Another way of dealing with a bad conscience is to keep the Negro out of sight.

The Word proclaims: Love thy neighbor! So *we make it impossible for him to be a neighbor*. Let a Negro move into our neighborhood and madness overtakes the residents. To quote a recent editorial in the *Christian Century* (12–26–62):

> The ghettoization of the Negro in American society is increasing. Three
> million Negroes—roughly one-sixth of the nation's Negro population—are
> now congested in five of the greatest metropolitan centers of the north. The
> alienation of the Negro from the mainstream of American life proceeds
> space. The Negro is discovering to his sorrow that the mobility which he
> gained in the Emancipation Proclamation and the 13th and 14th Amend-
> ments to the Constitution nearly a hundred years ago merely enables him
> to move from one ghetto to another. A partial apartheid—economic, social,
> political and religious—continues to be enforced by the white people of the
> U.S. They use various pressures—some open, some covert—to keep the
> Negro isolated from the nation's social, cultural and religious community,
> the result being black islands surrounded by a vast white sea. Such enclaves
> in American society not only destroy the cohesiveness of the nation but also
> offend the Negro's dignity and restrict his opportunity. These segregated
> islands are also an embarrassment to white people who want an open
> society but are trapped by a system they despise. Restricted housing is the
> chief offender. So long as the racially exclusive patterns of suburban
> America continue, the Negro will remain an exile in his own land.

3) To some Americans the situation of the Negro, for all its stains and spots, seems fair and trim. So many revolutionary changes have taken place in the field of civil rights, so many deeds of charity are being done; so much decency radiates day and night. Our standards are modest; our sense of injustice tolerable, timid; our moral indignation impermanent; yet human violence is interminable, unbearable, permanent. The conscience builds its confines, is subject to fatigue, it longs for comfort. Yet those who are hurt, and He Who inhabits eternity, neither slumber nor sleep.

4) Most of us are content to delegate the problem to the courts, as if justice were a matter for professionals or specialists. But to do justice is what God demands of every man: it is the supreme commandment, and one that cannot be fulfilled vicariously.

Righteousness must dwell not only in the places where justice is judicially administered. There are many ways of evading the law and escaping the arm of justice. Only a few acts of violence are brought to the attention of the courts. As a rule, those who know how to exploit are endowed with the skill to justify their acts, while those who are easily exploited possess no skill in pleading their own cause. Those who neither exploit nor are exploited are ready to fight when their own interests are harmed; they will not be involved when not personally affected. Who shall plead for the helpless? Who shall prevent the epidemic of injustice that no court of justice is capable of stopping?

In a sense, the calling of the prophet may be described as that of an advocate or champion, speaking for those who are too weak to plead their own cause. Indeed, the major activity of the prophets was *interference,* remonstrating about wrongs inflicted on other people, meddling in affairs which were seemingly neither their concern nor their responsibility. A prudent man is he who minds his own business, staying away from questions which do not involve his own interests, particularly when not authorized to step in—and prophets were given no mandate by the widows and orphans to plead their cause. The prophet is a person who is not tolerant of wrongs done to others, who resents other people's injuries. He even calls upon others to be the champions of the poor. It is to every member of the community, not alone to the judges, that Isaiah directs his plea:

> Seek justice,
> Undo oppression;
> Defend the fatherless,
> Plead for the widow.
>
> Isaiah 1:17

5) There is an evil which most of us condone and are even guilty of: *indifference to evil.* We remain neutral, impartial, and not easily moved by the wrongs done unto other people. Indifference to evil is more insidious than evil itself; it is more universal, more contagious, more dangerous. A silent justification, it makes possible an evil erupting as an exception becoming the rule and being in turn accepted.

The prophets' great contribution to humanity was the discovery of *the evil of indifference.* One may be decent and sinister, pious and sinful.

The prophet is a person who suffers the harms done to others. Wherever a crime is committed, it is as if the prophet were the victim and the prey. The prophet's angry words cry. The wrath of God is a lamentation. All prophecy is one great exclamation; God is not indifferent to evil! He is always concerned, He is personally affected by what man does to man. He is a God of pathos.

6) In condemning the clergymen who joined Dr. Martin Luther King in protesting against local statutes and practices which denied constitutional liberties to groups of citizens on account of race, a white preacher declared: "The job of the minister is to lead the souls of men to God, not to bring about confusion by getting tangled up in transitory social problems."

In contrast to this definition, the prophets passionately proclaim that God Himself is concerned with "the transitory social problems," with the blights of society, with the affairs of the market place.

What is the essence of being a prophet? *A prophet is a person who holds God and men in one thought at one time, at all times.* Our tragedy begins with *the segregation of God,* with the bifurcation of the secular and sacred. We worry more about the purity of dogma than about the *integrity of love. We think of God in the past tense* and refuse to realize that *God is always present* and *never, never past;* that God may be more intimately *present in slums than in mansions, with those who are smarting under the abuse of the callous.*

There are, of course, many among us whose record in dealing with the Negroes and other minority groups is unspotted. However, an honest estimation of the moral state of our society will disclose: *Some are guilty, but all are responsible.* If we admit that the individual is in some measure conditioned or affected by the public climate of opinion, an individual's crime discloses society's corruption. In a community not indifferent to suffering, uncompromisingly impatient with cruelty and falsehood, racial discrimination would be infrequent rather than common.

IV

That equality is a good thing, a fine goal, may be generally accepted. What is lacking is a sense of the *monstrosity of inequality.* Seen from the perspective of prophetic faith, the predicament of justice is the predicament of God.

Of course, more and more people are becoming aware of the Negro problem, but they fail to grasp its being a personal problem. People are increasingly fearful of social tension and disturbance. However, so long as our society is more concerned to prevent racial strife than to prevent humiliation, the cause of strife, its moral status will be depressing, indeed.

The history of inter-racial relations is a nightmare. Equality of all men, a platitude to some minds, remains a scandal to many hearts. Inequality is the ideal setting for the abuse of power, a perfect justification for man's cruelty to man. Equality is an obstacle to callousness, setting a limit to power. Indeed, the history of mankind may be described as the history of the tension between power and equality.

Equality is an inter-personal relationship, involving both a claim and a recognition. My claim to equality has its logical basis in the recognition of my fellow men's identical claim. Do I not forfeit my own rights by denying to my fellow men the rights I claim for myself?

It is not humanity that endows the sky with inalienable stars. It is not society that bestows upon every man his inalienable rights. Equality of all men is not due to man's innocence or virtue. Equality of man is due to *God's love and commitment to all men.*

The ultimate worth of man is due neither to his virtue nor to his faith. *It is due to God's virtue, to God's faith. Wherever you see a trace of man, there is the presence of God.* From the perspective of eternity our recognition of equality of all men seems as generous an act as the acknowledgment that stars and planets have a right to be.

How can I withhold from others what does not belong to me?

Equality as a religious commandment goes beyond the principle of equality before the law. Equality as a religious commandment means *personal involvement,* fellowship, mutual reverence and concern. It means my being hurt when a Negro is offended. It means that I am bereaved whenever a Negro is *disfranchised.*

The shotgun blasts that have been fired at the house of James Meredith's father in Kosciusko, Mississippi, make us cry for shame wherever we are.

There is no insight more disclosing: *God is One, and humanity is one.* There is no possibility more frightening: God's name may be desecrated.

God is every man's pedigree. He is either the Father of all men or of no man. The image of God is either in every man or in no man.

From the point of view of moral philosophy it is our duty to have regard for every man. Yet such regard is contingent upon the moral merit of the particular man. From the point of view of religious philosophy it is our duty to have regard and compassion for every man regardless of his moral merit. God's covenant is with all men, and we must never be oblivious of *the equality of the divine dignity* of all men. The image of God is in the criminal as well as in the saint. How could my regard for man be contingent upon his merit, if I know that in the eyes of God I myself may be without merit!

You shall not make yourself a graven image or any likeness of God. The making and worshipping of images is considered an abomination, vehemently condemned in the Bible. The world and God are not the same essence. There can be no man-made symbols of God.

And yet there is something in the world that the Bible does regard as a symbol of God. It is not a temple nor a tree, it is not a statue nor a star. *The symbol of God is man,* every man. How significant is the fact that the term *tselem* which is frequently used in a damnatory sense for a man-made image of God, as well as the term *demuth*, likeness—of which Isaiah claims (48:18), no *demuth* can be applied to God—are employed in denoting man as an image and likeness of God. Man, every man, must be treated with the honor due to a likeness representing the King of kings.

> He who oppresses a poor man insults his Maker,
> He who is kind to the needy honors Him.
> Proverbs 14:31; cf.17:15

V

The way we act, the way we fail to act is a disgrace which must not go on forever. This is not a white man's world. This is not a colored man's world. It is God's world. No man has a place in this world who tries to keep another man in his place. It is time for the white man to repent. We have failed to use the avenues open to us to educate the hearts and minds of men, to identify ourselves with those who are underprivileged. But repentance is more than contrition and remorse for sins, for harms done. Repentance means a new insight, a new spirit. It also means a course of action.

Racism is an evil of tremendous power, but God's will transcends all powers. Surrender to despair is surrender to evil. It is important to feel anxiety, it is sinful to wallow in despair.

What we need is a total mobilization of heart, intelligence, and wealth for the purpose of love and justice. God is in search of men, waiting, hoping for man to do His will.

The most practical thing is not to weep but to act and to have faith in God's assistance and grace in our trying to do His will.

This world, this society can be redeemed. God has a stake in our moral predicament. I cannot believe that God will be defeated.

What we face is a human emergency. It will require much devotion, wisdom, and divine grace to eliminate that massive sense of inferiority, the creeping bitterness. It will require a high quality of imaginative sympathy, sustained cooperation both in thought and in action, by individuals as well as by institutions, to weed out memories of frustration, roots of resentment.

We must act even when inclination and vested interests should militate against equality. Human self-interest is often our Nemesis! It is the audacity of faith that redeems us. To have faith is to be ahead of one's normal thoughts, to transcend confused motivations, to lift oneself by one's bootstraps. Mere knowledge or belief is too feeble to be a cure of man's hostility to man, of man's tendency to fratricide. The only remedy is *personal sacrifice*: to abandon, to reject what seems dear and even plausible for the sake of the greater truth; to do more than I am ready to understand for the sake of God. Required is a breakthrough, a *leap of action*. It is the deed that will purify the heart. It is the deed that will sanctify the mind. The deed is the test, the trial, and the risk.

The plight of the Negro must become our most important concern. Seen in the light of our religious tradition, *the Negro problem is God's gift to America,* the test of our integrity, a magnificent spiritual opportunity.

Humanity can only thrive when challenged, when called upon to answer new demands, to reach out for new heights. Imagine how smug, complacent, vapid, and foolish we would be, if we had to subsist on prosperity alone. It is for us to understand that religion is not sentimentality, that God is not a patron. Religion is a demand, God is a challenge, speaking to us in the language of human situations. His voice is in the dimension of history.

The universe is done. The greater masterpiece still undone, still in the process of being created, is history. For accomplishing His grand design,

God needs the help of man. Man is and has the instrument of God, which he may or may not use in consonance with the grand design. Life is clay, and righteousness the mold in which God wants history to be shaped. But human beings, instead of fashioning the clay, deform the shape. God needs mercy, righteousness; His needs cannot be satisfied in space, by sitting in pews, by visiting temples, but in history, in time. It is within the realm of history that man is charged with God's mission.

There are those who maintain that the situation is too grave for us to do much about it, that whatever we might do would be "too little and too late," that the most practiced thing we can do is "to weep" and to despair. If such a message is true, then God has spoken in vain.

Such a message is 4000 years too late. It is good Babylonian theology. In the meantime, certain things have happened: Abraham, Moses, the Prophets, the Christian Gospel.

History is not all darkness. It was good that Moses did not study theology under the teachers of that message; otherwise, I would still be in Egypt building pyramids. Abraham was all alone in a world of paganism; the difficulties he faced were hardly less grave than ours.

The greatest heresy is despair, despair of men's power for goodness, men's power for love.

It is not enough for us to exhort the Government. What we must do is to set an example, not merely to acknowledge the Negro but to welcome him, not grudgingly but joyously, to take delight in enabling him to enjoy what is due to him. We are all *Pharaohs* or *slaves of Pharaohs*. It is sad to be a slave of Pharaoh. *It is horrible to be a Pharaoh.*

Daily we should take account and ask: What have I done today *to alleviate the anguish, to mitigate the evil, to prevent humiliation?*

Let there be a grain of prophet in every man!

Our concern must be expressed not symbolically, but literally; not only publicly, but also *privately;* not only occasionally, but regularly.

What we need is the involvement of everyone of us as individuals. What we need is *restlessness,* a constant awareness of the monstrosity of injustice.

The concern for the dignity of the Negro must be an explicit tenet of our creeds. He who offends a Negro, whether as a landowner or employer, whether as waiter or sales-girl, is guilty of offending the majesty of God. No minister of layman has a right to question the principle that reverence for God is shown in reverence for man, that the fear we must feel lest we hurt or humiliate a human being must be as unconditional as fear of God. An act of violence is an act of desecration. To be arrogant toward man is to be blasphemous toward God.

In the words of Pope John XXIII, when opening the Twenty-first Ecumenical Council, "divine Providence is leading us to a new order of human relations." History has made us all neighbors. The age of moral mediocrity and complacency has run out. This is a time for radical commitment, for radical action.

Let us not forget the story of the sons of Jacob. Joseph, the dreamer of dreams, was sold into slavery by his own brothers. But at the end it was Joseph who rose to be the saviour of those who had sold him into captivity.

Mankind lies groaning, afflicted by fear, frustration and despair. Perhaps it is the will of God that among the Josephs of the future there will be many who have once been slaves and whose skin is dark. The great spiritual resources of the Negroes, their capacity for joy, their quiet nobility, their attachment to the Bible, their power of worship and enthusiasm, may prove a blessing to all mankind.

In the words of the prophet Amos (5:24):

> Let justice roll down like waters,
> And righteousness like a might stream.

A mighty stream, expressive of the vehemence of a never-ending, surging, fighting movement—as if obstacles had to be washed away for justice to be done. No rock is so hard that water cannot pierce it. "The mountain falls and crumbles away, the rock is removed from its place—the waters wear away the stones." (Job 14:18 f.) Justice is not a mere norm, but a fighting challenge, a restless drive.

Righteousness as a mere tributary, feeding the immense stream of human interests, is easily exhausted and more easily abused. But righteousness is not a trickle; it is God's power in the world, a torrent, an impetous drive, full of grandeur and majesty. The surge is choked, the sweep is blocked. Yet the mighty stream will break all dikes.

Justice, people seem to agree, is a principle, a norm, an ideal of the highest importance. We all insist that it ought to be—but it may not be. In the eyes of the prophets, justice is more than an idea or a norm: justice is charged with the omnipotence of God. What ought to be, shall be!

Chapter 12

TO GROW IN WISDOM

I see the sick and the despised, the defeated and the bitter, the rejected and the lonely. I see them clustered together and alone, clinging to a hope for somebody's affection that does not come to pass. I hear them pray for the release that comes with death. I see them deprived and forgotten, masters yesterday, outcasts today.

What we owe the old is reverence, but all they ask for is consideration, attention, not to be discarded and forgotten. What they deserve is preference, yet we do not even grant them equality. One father finds it possible to sustain a dozen children, yet a dozen children find it impossible to sustain one father.

Perhaps this is the most distressing aspect of the situation. The care for the old is regarded as an act of charity rather than as a supreme privilege. In the never dying utterance of the Ten Commandments, the God of Israel did not proclaim: Honor Me, Revere Me. He proclaimed instead: Revere your father and your mother. There is no reverence for God without reverence for father and mother.

In Jewish tradition the honor for father and mother is a commandment, the perfect fulfillment of which surpasses the power of man. There is no limit to what one ought to do in carrying out this privilege of devotion (see "Children and Youth," p. 39). God is invisible, but my mother is His presence. . . .

Father and mother are always older, more advanced in years. But is being advanced in years to be considered an advance or a retreat?

Ours is a twin problem: the attitude of society to the old and old age as well as the attitude of the old to being old.

The typical attitude to old age is characterized by fear, confusion, absurdity, self-deception, and dishonesty. It is painful and bizarre. Old age is something we are all anxious to attain. However, once attained we consider it a defeat, a form of capital punishment. In enabling us to reach old age, medical science may think that it gave us a blessing; however, we continue to act as if it were a disease.

More money and time are spent on the art of concealing the signs of old age than on the art of dealing with heart disease or cancer. You find more patients in the beauty parlors than in the hospitals. We would rather be bald than gray. A white hair is an abomination. Being old is defeat, something to be ashamed of. Authenticity and honesty of existence are readily exchanged for false luster, for camouflage, sham, and deception.

A gray hair may destroy the chance for promotion, may cost a salesman his job, and inwardly alienate a son from his father. The fear of being considered old has become a traumatic obsession. Only very few people are endowed with the rare and supreme courage to admit their true age without embarrassment. With the rest of us, courage and honesty go underground when the question of age is discussed. The most delightful resolution the White House Conference on Aging could pass would be to eliminate from now on any mention of the date of birth from the birth certificate.

A vast amount of human misery, as well as enormous cultural and spiritual damage, is due to these twin phenomena of our civilization: the contempt for the old and the traumatic fear of getting old. Monotheism has acquired a new meaning: the one and only thing that counts is being young. Youth is our god, and being young is divine. To be sure, youth is a very marvelous thing. However, the cult of youth is idolatry. Abraham is the grand old man, but the legend of Faust is pagan.

A revision of attitudes and conceptions is necessary. Old age is not a defeat but a victory, not a punishment but a privilege. In education we stress the importance of the adjustment of the young to society. Our task is to call for the adjustment of society to the old.

By what standards do we measure culture? It is customary to evaluate a nation by the magnitude of its scientific contributions or the quality of its artistic achievements. However, the true standard by which to gauge a culture is the extent to which reverence, compassion, justice are to be found in the daily lives of a whole people, not only in the acts of isolated individuals. Culture is *a style of living compatible with the grandeur of being human*.

The test of a people is how it behaves toward the old. It is easy to love children. Even tyrants and dictators make a point of being fond of children. But the affection and care for the old, the incurable, the helpless are the true gold mines of a culture.

We maintain that all men are created equal, including the old. What is extraordinary is that we feel called upon to plead for such equality, in contrast to other civilizations in which the superiority of the old is maintained.

In our own days, a new type of fear has evolved in the hearts of men: the fear of medical bills. In the spirit of the principle that reverence for the old takes precedence over reverence for God, we are compelled to confess that a nation should be ready to sell, if necessary, the treasures from its art collection and the sacred objects from its houses of worship in order to help one sick man.

Is there anything as holy, as urgent, as noble, as the effort of the whole nation to provide medical care for the old?

This is one of the great biblical insights: the needs of suffering humanity are a matter of personal as well as public responsibility. The representatives of the community are held responsible for the neglect of human life if they have failed to provide properly for those in need. The ancient sages realized that it was not enough to rely upon individual benevolence, and that care for the sick was a responsibility of the community.

It is in accord with this tradition that all major religious organizations have endorsed the principle of government responsibility and the use of the Social Security mechanism as the most effective medium for dealing with the problem of medical care for the aged.

It is marvelous indeed that for the first time in history, our society is able to provide for the material needs of its senior citizens. Yet, in addition to the problem of material security, we must face the problem of psychological and spiritual security.

How to save the old from despondency, despair? How to lend beauty to being old? How to regain the authenticity of old age?

Old age is a major challenge to the inner life; it takes both wisdom and strength not to succumb to it. According to all the standards we employ socially as well as privately, the aged person is condemned as inferior. In terms of manpower he is a liability, a burden, a drain on our resources. Conditioned to operate as a machine for making and spending money, with all other relationships dependent upon its efficiency, the moment the machine is out of order and beyond repair, one begins to feel like a ghost without a sense of reality. The aged may be described as a person *who does not dream anymore,* devoid of ambition, and living in fear of losing his status. Regarding himself as a person who has outlived his usefulness, he feels as if he had to apologize for being alive.

The tragedy is that old age comes upon us as a shock for which we are unprepared. If life is defined exclusively in terms of functions and activities, is it still worth living when these functions and activities are sharply curtailed?

The tragedy, I repeat, is that most of us are unprepared for old age. We know a great deal about what to do with things, even what to do with other people; we hardly know what to do with ourselves. We know how to act in public; we do not know what to do in privacy. Old age involves the problem of what to do with privacy.

Among some primitive peoples the old were generally neglected and when helpless exposed to die. Today one can even be placed in a luxury hotel and be left to die.

While we do not officially define old age as a second childhood, some of the programs we devise are highly effective in helping the aged to become children. The popular approach is: "Keep alive a zest for living in the elderly, by encouraging them to continue old hobbies, or to develop new ones." Now preoccupation with games and hobbies, the overemphasis on recreation, while certainly conducive to eliminating boredom temporarily, hardly contribute to inner strength. The effect is, rather, a pickled existence, preserved in brine with spices.

Is this the way and goal of existence: to study, grow, toil, mature, and to reach the age of retirement in order to live like a child? After all, *to be retired does not mean to be retarded.*

What is the role of recreation in the life of the aged? Is it merely to serve as a substitute for work one has done in earlier years? It seems to me that recreation is serving a different purpose, and that an overindulgence in recreational activities aggravates rather than ameliorates a condition it is trying to deal with, namely *the trivialization of existence*. In the past it was ritual and prayer that staved off that danger.

For thousands of years human existence was not simply confined to the satisfaction of trivial needs. Through prayer and ritual man was able to remain open to the wonder and mystery of existence, to lend a tinge of glory to daily deeds.

Modern man has discarded ritual, failed to learn the art of prayer, but found a substitute for both in occupational routine. He severed relations to God, to the cosmos, even to his people, but became engrossed in the search for success. The excitement of success took the place of inspiration. Upon his retirement from labor or business, games and hobbies, the country club or golf take the place of church, synagogue, ritual, and prayer. This, then, is the fact: hobbies have become *a substitute for ritual,* not only for work. Should we not clearly distinguish between recreation as a substitution and recreation as a solution?

Authentic human existence includes both work and worship, utilization and celebration. We have a right to consume because we have the power to celebrate. The man of our time is losing the power to celebrate; instead of participating in spiritual celebration, he seeks to be amused or entertained. Upon reaching the summit of his years, man discovers that entertainment is no substitute for celebration.

What are the basic spiritual ills of old age?

(1) The sense of being useless to, and rejected by, family and society; (2) the sense of inner emptiness and boredom; (3) loneliness and fear of time. Let us analyze the root as well as the cure of these three ills.

1. The sense of being useless to, and rejected by, family and society

While it is vitally important to see man in his relation to society, we must not forget that society is *not* man's only and ultimate referent. In spite of the fact that our ideologies and institutions continue to imply that the worth of a person is equivalent to his usefulness to society, every one of us entertains the keen expectation that other people will not regard him merely because of what he is worth to them, because he is capable of satisfying other people's needs, but will regard him as a being significant and valuable in himself. Just as the grandeur of the sun or an oak tree is not reducible to the functions it fulfills, so is the grandeur of a human life not reducible to the needs it is capable of satisfying. Even he who does not regard himself as an absolute end, rebels against being treated as a means to an end, as subservient to other men. The rich, the men of the world, want to be loved for their own sake, for their essence, whatever it may mean, not for their achievements or possessions. Nor do the old and sick expect help because of what they may give us in return. Who needs the handicapped, the incurably sick, the maintenance of whom is a drain on the treasury of the state? It is, moreover, obvious that a person's service to society does not claim all of his life and can therefore not be the ultimate answer to his quest of meaning for life as a whole. Man has more to give than what other men are able or willing to accept. To say that life could consist of care for others, of incessant service to the world, would be a vulgar boast. What we are able to bestow upon others is usually less and rarely more than a tithe.

There are alleys in the soul where man walks alone, ways that do not lead to society, a world of privacy that shrinks from the public eye. Life comprises not only arable, productive land, but also mountains of dreams, an underground of sorrow, towers of yearning, which can hardly be utilized to the last for the good of society, unless man be converted into a machine in which every screw must serve a function or be removed. It is a profiteering state which, trying to exploit the individual, asks all of man for itself.

And if society as embodied in the state should prove to be corrupt and my effort to cure its evils unavailing, would my life as an individual have been totally devoid of meaning? If society should decide to reject my services and even place me in solitary confinement, so that I would surely die without being able to bequeath any influence to the world I love, would I then feel compelled to end my life?

Human existence cannot derive its ultimate meaning from society, because society itself is in need of meaning. It is as legitimate to ask: Is mankind needed? as it is to ask: Am I needed?

Humanity begins in the individual man, just as history takes its rise from a singular event. It is always one man at a time whom we keep in mind when we pledge: "With malice toward none, with charity for all," or when we try to fulfill: "Love thy neighbor as thyself." The term "mankind," which in biology denotes the human species, has an entirely different meaning in the realm of ethics and religion. Here mankind is not conceived as a species, as an abstract concept, stripped from its concrete reality, but as an abundance of specific individuals; as a community of persons rather than as a herd or a multitude of nondescripts.

While it is true that the good of all counts more than the good of one, it is the concrete individual who lends meaning to the human race. We do not think that a human being is valuable because he is a member of the race; it is rather the opposite: the human race is valuable because it is composed of human beings.

While dependent on society as well as on the air that sustains us, and while other men compose the system of relations in which the curve of our actions takes its course, it is as individuals that we are beset with desires, fears and hopes, challenged, called upon and endowed with the power of will and a spark of responsibility.

2. The sense of inner emptiness and boredom

Old age often is an age of anguish and boredom. The only answer to such anguish is *a sense of significant being*.

The sense of significant being is a thing of the spirit. Stunts, buffers, games, hobbies, slogans—all are evasions. What is necessary is an approach, a getting close to the sources of the spirit. Not the suppression of the sense of futility, but its solution; not reading material to while away one's time, but learning to exalt one's faculties is the answer; not entertainment but celebration.

To attain a sense of significant being we must learn to be involved in thoughts that are ahead of what we already comprehend, to be involved in deeds that will generate higher motivations.

There is a level of existence where one cannot think anymore in terms of self-centered needs and satisfactions, where the problem that cannot be silenced is: Who needs me? Who needs mankind? How does one relate himself to a source of ultimate meaning? The cry for such relatedness which gains intensity with old age is a cry for a referent that transcends personal existence. It is not experienced as a need from within but as a situation of being exposed to a demand from without.

Significant being is not measured by the amount of needs that agitate a person but by the intensity and depth of the response to a wisdom in relation to which *my* mind is an afterthought, by the discovery that the moment to come is an anticipation, an expectation, waiting to receive *my* existence. Significant being means experiencing moments of time as a comprehension which embraces *me*.

What a person lives by is not only a sense of belonging but also a *sense of indebtedness*. The need to be needed corresponds to a fact: something is asked of man, of every man. Advancing in years must not be taken to mean a process of suspending the requirements and commitments under which a person lives. To be is to obey. A person must never cease to be.[1]

Our work for the advanced in years is handicapped by our clinging to the dogmatic belief in the immutability of man. We conceive of his inner life as a closed system, as an automatic, unilinear, irreversible process which cannot be altered, and of old age as a stage of stagnation into which a person enters with his habits, follies, and prejudices. To be good to the old is to cater to their prejudices and eccentricities.

May I suggest that man's potential for change and growth is much greater than we are willing to admit and that old age be regarded not as the age of stagnation but as *the age of opportunities for inner growth?* The old person must not be treated as a patient, nor regard his retirement as a prolonged state of resignation.

The years of old age may enable us to attain the high values we failed to sense, the insights we have missed, the wisdom we ignored. They are indeed formative years, rich in possibilities to unlearn the follies of a lifetime, to see through inbred self-deceptions, to deepen understanding and compassion, to widen the horizon of honesty, to refine the sense of fairness.

One ought to enter old age the way one enters the senior year at a university, in exciting anticipation of consummation. Rich in perspective, experienced in failure, the person advanced in years is capable of shedding prejudices and the fever of vested interests. He does not see anymore in every fellow man a person who stands in his way, and competitiveness may cease to be his way of thinking.

At every home for the aged there is a director of recreation in charge of physical activities; there ought to be also a director of learning in charge of intellectual activities. We insist upon minimum standards for physical well being, what about minimum standards for intellectual well being?

What the nation needs is senior universities, universities for the advanced in years where wise men should teach the potentially wise, where the purpose of learning is not a career, but where the purpose of learning is learning itself.

Education for Retirement. The goal is not to keep the old man busy, but to remind him that every moment is an opportunity for greatness. Inner purification is at least as important as hobbies and recreation. The elimination of resentments, of residues of bitterness, of jealousies and wrangling is certainly a goal for which one must strive.

Only very few people realize that it is in the days of our youth that we prepare ourselves for old age.

This is an imperative we must be conscious of even in youth. Prepare spiritually for old age and learn how to cultivate it. The ancient equation of old age and wisdom is far from being a misconception. However, age is no guarantee for wisdom. A Hebrew proverb maintains: "A wise old man the older he gets the wiser he becomes, a vulgar old man the older he gets the less wise he becomes." People are anxious to save up financial means for old age; they should also be anxious to prepare a spiritual income for old age. That ancient principle—listen to the voice of the old—becomes meaningless when the old have nothing meaningful to say. Wisdom, maturity, tranquillity do not come all of a sudden when we retire from business. We must begin teaching in public schools about the virtues that come to fruition with the advance in years, about the wisdom and peace that arrive in old age. Reverence for the old must be an essential part of elementary education at school, and particularly at home. *Education for retirement* is a life-long process.

3. Loneliness and the fear of time

One of the major ills of old age as well as one of the roots of the general fear of old age is *the fear of time.* It is like living on a craggy ridge over a wide abyss. Time is the only aspect of existence which is completely beyond man's control. He may succeed in conquering space, in sending satellites around the moon, but time remains immune to his power; a moment gone by not even General Motors can bring back. Being used to dealing with things he can manage, the encounter with time is the most stunning shock that comes to man. In his younger years, he is too busy to react to it; it is in old age that time may become a nightmare. We are all infatuated with the splendor of space, with the grandeur of things of space. *Thing* is a category that lies heavy on our minds, tyrannizing all our thoughts. Our imagination tends to mold all concepts in its image. In our daily lives we attend primarily to that which the senses are spelling out for us; to what the eyes perceive, to what the fingers touch. Reality to us is thinghood, consisting of substances that occupy space; even God is conceived by most of us as a thing.

The result of our thingness is our blindness to all reality that fails to identify itself as a thing, as a matter of fact. This is obvious in our understanding of time, which being thingless and insubstantial, appears to us as if it has no reality.

Indeed, we know what to do with space but do not know what to do about time, except to make it subservient to space, or to while it away, *to kill time.* However, *time is life,* and to kill time is to murder (cf. "Religion in a Free Society," p. 19). Most of us seem to labor for the sake of things of space. As a result we suffer from a deeply rooted dread of time and stand aghast when compelled to look into its face. Time to us is sarcasm, a slick treacherous monster with a jaw like a furnace incinerating every moment of our lives. Shrinking, therefore, from facing time, we escape for shelter to things of space. The intentions we are unable to carry out we deposit in space; possessions become symbols of our repressions, jubilees of frustrations. But things of space are not fireproof; they only add fuel to the flames. Is the joy of possession an antidote to the terror of time which grows to be a dread of the inevitable death? Things, when magnified, are forgeries of happiness, they are a threat to our very lives; we are more harassed than supported by the Frankensteins of spatial things.

Most of us do not live in time but run away from it; we do not see its face, but its make-up. The past is either forgotten or preserved as a cliché, and the present moment is either bartered for a silly trinket or beclouded by false anticipations. The present moment is a zero, and so is the next moment, and a vast stretch of life turns out to be a series of zeros, with no real number in front.

Blind to the marvel of the present moment, we live with memories of moments missed, in anxiety about an emptiness that lies ahead. We are totally unprepared when the problem strikes us in unmitigated form.

It is impossible for man to shirk the problem of time. The more we think the more we realize that we cannot conquer time through space. We can only master time in time.

Time is man's most important frontier, the advance region of significant being, a region where man's true freedom lies. Space divides us,
time unites us. We wage wars over things of space; the treasures of time
lie open to every man.

Time has independent ultimate significance; it is of more majesty and
more evocative of awe than even a sky studded with stars. Gliding gently
in the most ancient of all splendors, it tells so much more than space can
say in its broken language of things, playing symphonies upon the
instruments of isolated beings, unlocking the earth and making it happen. Time is the process of creation, and things of space are results of
creation. When looking at space we see the products of creation; when
intuiting time we hear the process of creation. Things of space exhibit a
deceptive independence. They show off a veneer of limited permanence.
Things created conceal the Creator. It is the dimension of time wherein
man meets God, wherein man becomes aware that every instant is an act
of creation, a Beginning, opening up new roads for ultimate realizations.
Time is the presence of God in the world of space, and it is within time that
we are able to sense the unity of all beings.

Time is perpetual presence, perpetual novelty. Every moment is a new
arrival, a new bestowal. *Just to be is a blessing, just to live is holy. The
moment is the marvel;* it is in evading the marvel of the moment that
boredom begins which ends in despair.

Old age has the vicious tendency of depriving a person of the present.
The aged thinks of himself as belonging to the past. But it is precisely
the openness to the present that he must strive for. The marvel is
discovered in celebration.

He who lives with a sense for the Presence knows that to get older
does not mean to lose time but rather to gain time. And, he also knows
that in all his deeds, the chief task of man is to sanctify time. All it takes
to sanctify time is *God, a soul, and a moment. And the three are always here.*

It is still considered proper to expect that the first responsibility in
planning for the senior citizen rests with the family. Such expectation
presupposes the concept of a family which is not only an economic unit
but also an interplay of profoundly personal relations. It thinks of the
family not only as a process of living together but also of a series of
decisive acts and events in which all members are involved and by which
they are inwardly affected.

What is characteristic of the modern family is that on the level of profound personal experience, parents and children live apart. The experiences shared at home are perfunctory rather than creative. In the past, it was the role of the father to lead the children through moments of exaltation. Whatever stood out as venerable and lofty was associated with the father. Now we are entering a social structure in which the father is becoming obsolete, and in which there are only three ages: childhood, adolescence, and old age. The husband of the mother is not a father, he is a regular guy, a playmate for the boys, engaged in the same foibles and subject to similar impulses. Since he neither represents the legacy of the past nor is capable of keeping pace with the boys in the pursuit of the future, his status is rather precarious.

Children today experience their highest moments of exaltation in a children's world, in which there is no room for parents. But unless a fellowship of spiritual experience is re-established, the parent will remain an outsider to the child's soul. This is one of the beauties of the human spirit. We appreciate *what we share,* we do not appreciate *what we receive.* Friendship, affection is not acquired by giving presents. Friendship, affection comes about by two people sharing a significant moment, by having an experience in common. You do not attain the affection of your teen-age son by giving him an expensive car.

It is not necessary for man to submit to the constant corrosion of his finest sensibilities and to accept as inevitable the liquidation of the inner man. It is within the power of man to save the secret substance that holds the world of man together. The way to overcome loneliness is not by waiting to receive a donation of companionship but rather by offering and giving companionship and meaning to others.

The real bond between two generations is the insights they share, the appreciation they have in common, the moments of inner experience in which they meet. A parent is not only an economic provider, playmate, shelter, and affection. A human being is in need of security, he is also in need of inspiration, of exaltation and a transcendent meaning of existence. And to a child, the parent represents the inspiration, the exaltation, and the meaning. To my child, I am either the embodiment of the spirit or its caricature. No book, no image, no symbol can replace my role in the imagination and the recesses of my child's soul.

It is easy to speak about the things we are committed to; it is hard to communicate *the commitment itself.* It is easy to convey the resentments we harbor; it is hard to communicate the praise, the worship, the sense of the ineffable.

We have nearly lost the art of conveying to our children our power to praise, our ability to cherish the things that cannot be quantified.

This, then is a most urgent problem: How to convey the inexpressible legacy, the moments of insight, how to invoke unconditional commitment to justice and compassion, a sensitivity to the stillness of the holy, attachment to sacred words.

There is no human being who does not carry a treasure in his soul; a moment of insight, a memory of love, a dream of excellence, a call to worship.

In order to be a master one must learn how to be an apprentice. Reverence for the old, dialogue between generations, is as important to the dignity of the young as it is for the well-being of the old. We deprive ourselves by disparaging the old.

We must seek ways to overcome the traumatic fear of being old, the prejudice, the discrimination against those advanced in years. All men are created equal, including those advanced in years. Being old is not necessarily the same as being stale. The effort to restore the dignity of old age will depend upon our ability to revive the equation of old age and wisdom. Wisdom is the substance upon which the inner security of the old will forever depend. But the attainment of wisdom is the work of a life time.

> Old men need a vision, not only recreation.
> Old men need a dream, not only a memory.
> It takes three things to attain a sense of significant being:
>> God
>> A Soul
>> And a Moment.
> And the three are always here.
> Just to be is a blessing. Just to live is holy.

Part III

AN AFTERWORD: HESCHEL
REMEMBERED

Chapter 13

HESCHEL AS *MENSCH:* TESTIMONY OF HIS DAUGHTER

Susannah Heschel

There is a midrash that asks how Moses managed to gain access to Pharaoh when he first sought the release of the Israelite slaves. After all, how could just anyone march into the palace of a ruler, past the guards and advisors, and gain the ear of the Pharaoh? The midrash explains that when we speak truly from the heart, our words go directly to the heart of our listener. When Moses told the guards outside the palace what mission he had come to accomplish, the guards were so moved that they allowed him entry. Even Pharaoh was so touched by the heartfulness of Moses' message that he was ready to let the Children of Israel go, until God hardened his heart to make The Exodus a supernatural event.

People who read my father's books invariably say they feel deeply moved by what he is saying, that they have a religious experience when they encounter his writings or when they had the chance to hear him lecture or talk to him. That kind of reaction is not unexpected, because my father spoke very much from his heart. The description he gives of the religious life are genuine to him. He doesn't speak in a removed, analytic way, but very much out of his own, personal experience. In fact, he acknowledges this in *God in Search of Man* when he writes that the religious philosopher "is never a pure spectator. . . . His books are not responsa. We should not regard them as mirrors, reflecting other people's problems, but rather as windows, allowing us to view the author's soul."

We can get to know my father by reading his books, because they are a window into his own soul, into the life he led and the kind of person he was. He used to explain that different people understand his books in very different ways, depending on the kind of perspective they brought with them. But it is also true that he himself was a unique combination of a variety of backgrounds. *God in Search of Man,* one of his earliest major works, reflects his intellectual and spiritual experiences. We can see mirrored in the book the different civilizations my father himself experienced in his lifetime: East European Hasidism; German-Jewish thought; American Jewish life. There is something awe inspiring about the scope of my father's interests: poetry, scholarship, and theology, combined with his activism in political issues. In photographs of the 1960s and 1970s, he is a riveting figure, with his beard and bushy white hair. He is seen at demonstrations against the war in Vietnam; marching arm in arm with Martin Luther King, Jr.; standing next to Pope Paul VI at the Vatican. He cared about reaching both Jews and Christians, religious and secular. I remember the gentleness and respect with which he answered questions at his lectures and his intensity in speaking out against certain government policies. Sometimes organizations mistakenly thought they were inviting a gentle, meek rabbi to speak to them and then heard a powerful and charismatic challenge to their complacency.

My father wrote fluently and with grace in Yiddish, Hebrew, German, and English. His writings include technical studies of medieval Jewish philosophy and of the origins of Hasidism; a three-volume Hebrew study of rabbinic theology, which is striking in its scope and its method; numerous volumes of constructive Jewish theology; a doctoral dissertation, later expanded, on the religious consciousness of the biblical prophets. His last book was a two-volume study in Yiddish of the fascinating and eccentric Hasidic master of the nineteenth century, the Kotzker rebbe.

When my father died suddenly in his sleep in December 1972, it was a great shock. He was sixty-five, and I was still in college. When I was a child, storekeepers used to ask if he was my grandfather. That was painful, and I prayed he would live to see his own grandchildren. I always felt very close to him, with the certainty that he understood exactly how

I felt. People who are extraordinarily productive, like my father, often spend their lives hidden away, cut off from other commitments, devoting themselves exclusively to their writing. With my father, it was always the opposite. He worked long hours, yes, but stopped instantly when his family wanted his attention. More than that, he always looked up with a big smile and an enthusiastic "Susie!" At home, he was full of laughter, teasing, and affection, ready with jokes and hugs. With students and friends, he expressed his warmth verbally and with little gestures. For instance, he once found a police officer writing a ticket to a student who had parked his car illegally. My father tried to convince the police officer to change his mind, but when that failed, he went upstairs to his study and brought a set of books as a gift to the student, just to cheer him up. Those of us who have spent time in universities know how rare and precious such a professor is.

My father was born in Warsaw. His father was a Hasidic rebbe, Moshe Mordechai, born in Mezhbizh and known as the Mezhbizher rebbe of Warsaw, who died during an influenza epidemic when my father was only nine years old. His grave remains in the Jewish cemetery in Warsaw. My father's mother was Rivke Reizel Perlow, born in Novominsk, daughter of the Novominsker rebbe, a woman recognized for her deep piety. Her twin brother became the Novominsker rebbe and also came to live in Warsaw. She has no grave, having been murdered by the Nazis. Both of my father's parents were descended from long lines of Hasidic rebbes, dynasties of royalty in the Jewish world of Europe. My grandmother was a direct descendent of Rabbi Pinchas of Koretz and Rabbi Levi Yitzhak of Berdichev, while my grandfather descended from the Maggid of Meseritch, the Apter Rav, and the Rizhiner Rebbe. We have a photograph at home of each of my father's parents, and what is striking is the expressiveness of their faces. Each has large, dark eyes that make you feel they would sympathize with all your secrets. My father was the youngest of five children, so he was only three years old when his eldest sister, Sarah, married their first cousin, the Kopicziniczer rebbe (also named Abraham Joshua Heschel), and moved to Vienna. Their oldest son, Israel, became like a brother to my father. Eventually, Sarah and her husband and most of their children were able to escape to the United States in the late 1930s and spent the rest of their lives in New York City. My father had one older brother, Jacob, who became rabbi of an Orthodox congregation in a suburb of London. But my grandmother and three of my aunts, Devora Miriam, Esther Sima, and Gittel, were murdered by the Nazis. When I was a child, my father would tell me, with great pain, that nearly everyone who had known him in his growing-up years in Warsaw was dead.

My father's childhood education was traditional and rigorous in the study of Hebrew texts and immersed in the holiness of Hasidic life. Everyone assumed he would one day become a rebbe. His mind was recognized as extraordinary even when he was a child, and to honor his position as son of the rebbe, adults would rise when he entered the room, even when he was a small boy. But when he became a teenager, he decided to travel to Vilna, the capital of Lithuania, and study secular subjects. During the two years he spent in Vilna, my father became involved with a group of Yiddish poets, the "Jung Vilna," and published a volume of his poems in Yiddish, which he called *Der Shem Hameforash-Mensch*. Some of the poets from "Jung Vilna" have reminisced about him. While most of them were fiercely antireligious, they were touched by my father's piety. One of the surviving poets of that group, now living in Warsaw, wrote recently that during their walks together my father would put a hat on his head when they entered the forests around Vilna, explaining that this was a sacred place, filled with God's presence.

At the age of twenty-two, my father left Warsaw for Berlin to pursue a doctorate in philosophy at the Humboldt University. At the same time, he enrolled as a student in the Reform rabbinical seminary nearby, the *Hochschule fur die Wissenschaft des Judentums,* located just down the street from the Orthodox seminary, the *Hildesheimer Seminar.* He wanted the training in modern, scientific approaches to the study of Judaism from the Reform seminary, but also used to go back and forth, down the street to attend and deliver lectures at the *Hildesheimer Seminar.* He was one of the few students who felt comfortable in both worlds. At the University, several professors vied to have him as their student. He was considered unusually gifted, with his thorough mastery of Jewish texts and his critical, philosophical perspective. His doctoral dissertation at the University was a phenomenological study of the consciousness of the Hebrew prophets; he received his doctoral degree in February 1933—just a month after Hitler came to power. He remained in Berlin, teaching at the *Hochschule,* publishing articles on medieval Jewish philosophy as well as two books, biographies of the medieval Jewish philosophers Maimonides and Abravanel. Some of his correspondence from the 1930s managed to survive; it shows us the tremendous efforts he was making in those years to find a teaching position for himself outside Germany in the face of the terrible visa quotas.

His work was very well received, with book reviews appearing around the world. But all around him much older Jewish scholars were also struggling to escape Nazi Germany. In 1937 his friend Martin Buber asked my father to replace him as director of the *Lehrhaus* in Frankfurt, and my father accepted. Buber had decided to leave for Palestine; my father, for the time being, would have to remain in Germany. But he stayed in Frankfurt for only one year; in the fall of 1938, the Gestapo arrested him, in the middle of the night, and deported him, along with all Jews holding Polish passports.

The train trip back to Poland was a horror, and when the train arrived, the Poles refused to admit the Jews. They were placed in a detention camp on the border, but with some family help, my father was released and returned to Warsaw. There he spent a year teaching in an institute for Jewish studies, until he received word that the Hebrew Union College in Cincinnati was prepared to send him a visa. In July of 1939, just six weeks before the Nazis invaded, my father fled to England, where he founded an institute for adult Jewish studies similar to the *Lehrhaus* in Frankfurt. After a year, in 1940, he arrived in the United States, where he became an assistant professor at Hebrew Union College.

The five years he spent in Cincinnati were painful and lonely. His English was poor; he knew almost no one in the United States other than his sister and her husband, who were living in New York City. They all knew their family and the entire Jewish community in Europe were suffering terribly. Adding to my father's sense of isolation, the Hebrew Union College was adamantly Reform, with non-Kosher food in the cafeteria, and students and faculty who, with few exceptions, had little affection for the kind of Hasidic piety that was my father's background. There was little he would do, by himself, to help his family escape Europe, although he tried hard, and he was shocked by the complacency and even hostility toward the fate of the European Jews that he encountered among some American Jews. Some of the letters his mother and sister wrote to him from Warsaw during the war survived the Nazi censorship, and were wrenching for him. His mother was full of love and warmth, affection and concern for him, praying for a reunion, for peace, for his health. He received the news of her death and of the murder of his sisters before the end of the war, while he was still alone in Cincinnati.

The spiritual exile he felt during those first years in the United States was eased a bit by his friendships with some students, many of whom remained devoted to him throughout his lifetime. They were students who shared his love for Hasidism and traditional observance, and his concern for the inner, spiritual life. But the most significant encounter of those years was his meeting Sylvia Straus, a pianist who was studying in Cincinnati with the distinguished teacher Severin Eisenberger. There was an instant rapport between them; she had studied philosophy and literature and was a sensitive, religious person. He fell in love with her artistry, her mind, her gentleness, and her soul. In 1945 they met again in New York City—he, teaching at the Jewish Theological Seminary, she, studying with the pianist Eduart Steuermann—and soon were married.

My mother was born in Philadelphia and grew up in Cleveland, but her spirit was European. Her parents, Samuel Straus and Hannah Hochman, met on the Polish-Russian border en route to America. They had four children, three sons and a daughter, and raised them in an atmosphere full of the warmth, humor, and generosity that they brought with them from Europe. My grandfather was somewhat reserved, always reading, while my grandmother was spilling over with love and affection. Their home was a gathering place for friends and relatives. The sons—Reuben, Morris, and Jack—eventually moved to Los Angeles, and my parents and I spent nearly every summer there. We would sublet a house that had a piano for my mother, while my father studied every day in the library at UCLA. My mother's unusual musical talent had been recognized when she was a small child, by her parents and by her teachers, and when she became an adult, a significant career was assured. But the Depression, followed by her father's illness and then the war, made achieving that goal difficult.

It's hard for a child to write about her parents' marriage. Since I was the only child, my parents took me everywhere with them—to dinner parties, vacations, concerts, lectures. They even spent the summer with me during my one misadventure in camp. I felt we three were a unit, and couldn't imagine they had lives before I arrived. But I know their first years of marriage, before I was born, were important for their work. Only after his marriage did my father begin his theological writings.

Traditionally, Jewish men write religious books only after they are married. It makes sense: spirituality in Judaism requires a partnership, not an ascetic withdrawal. My father, too, needed a companion, someone who loved him and understood him, and someone he could love and be devoted to, before he could open his soul to the world in his books; indeed, he dedicated *God in Search of Man* to his new wife. My mother was a wonderful partner for him: she could discuss his philosophical ideas with him, and also explain the American religious context to him. She put my father in touch with music, which clearly had a profound effect on him as well: he suddenly starts using musical metaphors for religious life throughout *God in Search of Man.* As a new husband, he speaks of the mitsvot not as laws to be obeyed; rather, he says that Jews are violins on which the mitsvot are played. And I can hear my mother's voice in his sentence: The music in a score is open only to a person who has music in his or her soul, and the holiness of the mitsvah is open only to a person who knows how to discover the holiness in his or her own soul.

But it wasn't only their shared interests that brought my parents together; it was their temperaments. Both were very sensitive and expressive, full of affection and not hesitant to show it. My father always stressed that their values were the same. Growing up, I was amazed that they almost always had same opinions of other people and that they always wanted to spend their time in similar ways. In the evenings, after dinner, my father would write and my mother would play the piano. Then, before bed, they would drink tea, talk and laugh together. On Sabbaths and Jewish holidays they created an atmosphere that was peaceful and happy, described by my father in his classic book, *The Sabbath.* The trips we took to Israel were deeply moving for both my parents, spiritual homecomings which they shared. I think the inner religious life of Eastern Europe that my father describes in *The Earth Is the Lord's* is a description of the two of them as well: "Jewishness was more than a set of beliefs and rituals, more than what was compressed into tenets and rules. Jewishness was not in the fruit but in the sap that stirred through the tissues of the tree. Bred in the silence of the soil, it ascended the leaves to become eloquent in the fruit. Jewishness was not only truth; it was vitality, joy. The intellectual majesty of the Shema Yisrael, when translated into the language of their hearts, signified, 'It is a joy to be a Jew.' " Each of my parents found in the other something which was central to them: a religious soul who was close to God.

Both my parents were conscious of the preciousness of time and never wanted to waste a minute. Time is life, they would say, and to kill time is to commit murder. Occasionally, they would attend the theater, but only for a serious, important play, never just for amusement. My father would distinguish between entertainment, which is passive, and celebration, which involves people. In our home, the three of us made little celebrations for one another to mark all sorts of occasions. Words were also precious and powerful to my parents. They never swore and hardly ever used slang expressions. Words create worlds, my father used to tell me; each word has an impact, and you must be very careful what you say. He would write out phrases from rabbinic literature about the importance of language as epigraphs in my school notebooks. In conversation, the three of us would jokingly insist it was not necessary for us to waste words by finishing our sentences; we understood one another so well. This trait, too, seems similar to my father's description of Eastern Europe: "The East European Jews had a predilection for elliptic sentences, for the incisive, epigrammatic form, for the flash of the mind, for the thunderclap of an idea. They spoke briefly, sharply, quickly and directly; they understood each other with a hint; they heard two words where only one was said. Mentioning the more obvious of two premises was considered trite."

My parents' sensitivity to words extended also to listening. I remember being present many times when my mother and father were approached by people with problems, and I watched how they listened empathically, responding with compassion. My father used to tell people that old age is a pinnacle we reach, that we grow in wisdom throughout our lives, and that older people have so much to offer us. He also saw promise in young people. Even during the 1960s, when college students were closing universities with their demonstrations, my father approved of their intentions: "They are protesting the hypocrisy and mendacity of our government." Openmindedness was an important virtue to him; changing one's mind was a sign of intellectual growth. So when, as a small child, I would challenge my parents and my teachers with questions—Why can't a woman read from the Torah?—my father was pleased. He encouraged me, and told me he agreed with me. He even suggested that I study for the rabbinate. Knowing I had his support made a big difference to me when I began writing about Jewish feminism.

My father and mother created a home that was intensely Jewish and deeply spiritual. They entertained with elegance and formality, mainly over tea on Sabbath afternoons or Friday night dinner. Most of their friends were colleagues, professors or musicians. The conversations were full of Jewish jokes, Hasidic stories, reminiscences about European Jewish life, stories of people they had known. Nearly all their friends were also refugees from Europe, Jews with strong accents and definite customs. The German Jews were always punctual, hated it when we always arrived late, spoke carefully and distinctly and with great seriousness. But the East European Jews had personalities that fit their native tongue, Yiddish: they were always full of jokes, laughter, teasing, and exuberance. My father would tease my mother to be careful to whom she wished "Shabbat Shalom" (properly accented Hebrew for the German Jews and Israelis) and "Gut Shabbes" (Yiddish for the Eastern European Jews). While the East European Jews had no interest in Polish culture, the German Jews still were quoting Goethe and Schiller, praising German translations of Shakespeare, and lamenting the destruction of what they still believed to have been the greatest cultural life in the world. America, for these Jewish immigrants, was a great political refuge but was culturally vacuous. My father's feelings were less ambivalent: he almost never spoke Polish or German, and refused to travel to those countries. Once we were given tickets to the Metropolitan Opera, and my father was very uncomfortable when we arrived and found that the opera was Wagner's *Tristan und Isolde.* He wouldn't applaud and whispered to me from time to time, "Look what the Nazis made from this."

Gradually during the 1960s, in the years of my childhood and adolescence, my father became increasingly involved in social and political protest. Our guests began to include many of his colleagues from organizations he was involved with, including Clergy and Laity Concerned about Vietnam, which he helped to found. Conversations at home changed, too, with his increasing involvement in the civil rights movement, the anti-war movement, and the effort to elect George McGovern president. William Sloane Coffin, then chaplain at Yale University, was a favorite family friend. Coffin was active with my father in the anti-war movement and often visited us in New York. He has a vibrant personality and would burst into the room with exuberance and humor. We thought of his visits as a great treat, and I remember the excitement in the apartment when he was around.

On the Sabbath, of course, politics and money were not permissible conversation topics, but social issues continued as my father's constant passion. My parents rarely discussed detailed points of Jewish law or history, but spoke instead about the prophets, what they would have said and done about racism in America, or about how we can put the horror of the Holocaust into constructive action by opposing the war in Vietnam and supporting the State of Israel. My father used to tell me and my mother that he often studied at a library in Germany during the 1930s that was run by Jesuit priests. Once he asked them why they never spoke out against what the Nazis were doing to the Jews in Germany, and they told him, "Because the Nazis might close our library." "Can you imagine," he would say, "measuring books against human beings?" When other professors would sometimes criticize him for getting involved in social problems rather than writing scholarly books, he would refer to that Jesuit library. With all his love of books and his devotion to scholarship, people always came first.

When I was still a little girl, I remember, my father went to Chicago for several days, to speak at a conference on religion and race that was organized by the National Conference of Christians and Jews. It was the first of many times that he spoke at a conference with Martin Luther King, Jr. My father began his talk by stating that "At the first conference on religion and race, the main participants were Pharaoh and Moses. . . . The outcome of that summit has not come to an end. Pharaoh is not ready to capitulate. The exodus began, but is far from having been completed." He pointed out that it was easier for the Children of Israel to cross the Red Sea than it was for blacks to cross certain university campuses in the United States. The metaphor was powerful and original, and also very brave. My father never hesitated to be critical of his own community, as much as he was of others. He not only taught the Jewish community to identify with blacks in America seeking liberation, but also forced them to examine their own collusion with Pharaoh, with the forces of racism in white America. At the same time, both my father and Dr. King achieved their power by drawing on biblical language. They offered us pride in our religious traditions and in our Bible. For the Jewish community, my father offered his words as a balm to heal our wounds after the Holocaust.

My father's Jewishness infused everything he did: from the moment he woke up and prayed, with *tallis* and *tefillin,* to his work in the classroom at the Seminary, where he taught Jewish philosophy, Hasidism, and Kabbalah. His theological writings and his political work both were his Judaism. Being opposed to the war in Vietnam was for him a religious conviction and a political statement. Indeed, to him, the two were inseparable. In an essay, "Why I Oppose the War in Vietnam," which he wrote in the last months of his life, my father described his growing involvement in political affairs that occurred after the writing of his book on the prophets: "The more deeply immersed I became in the thinking of the prophets, the more powerfully it became clear to me what the lives of the prophets sought to convey: that morally speaking, there is no limit to the concern one must feel for the suffering of human beings, that indifference to evil is worse than evil itself, that in a free society, some are guilty, but all are responsible." What he describes of the prophets was reflected in his own person, in a quality of empathy that fills his writings and speeches, and that filled his life. Whatever the issue, whatever the situation, he responded with his heart, empathically. About the war he wrote: "Vietnam is a personal problem. . . . To be human means not to be immune to other people's suffering. . . . The question addressed to every one of us personally and collectively is this: What shall *I* do to stop the killing and dying in Vietnam?"

Of course, my father's involvement in social issues did not always bring him the support of the Jewish community. On the contrary, he was often fiercely opposed for the positions he took. It hurt to read articles in the local Jewish newspapers attacking him. Years later, many in the Jewish community who had opposed my father learned to take pride in the famous photographs showing him marching in the front lines in demonstrations with Martin Luther King, Jr. I remember vividly when he left home one Saturday night for the famous Selma-to-Montgomery march. The telegram from Dr. King asking my father to join the demonstrators arrived at home on Friday afternoon. There was a flurry of activity, arranging of flights and packing, before the Sabbath began. When it became dark on Saturday and the Sabbath ended, we went downstairs to see my father off. I remember kissing him goodbye, watching him get into the yellow Checker cab and drive off, and wondering if I would ever see him again. Both my mother and I worried terribly the next days. Demonstrations in the South at that time were fierce and dangerous. We used to see Sheriff Bull Connors of Birmingham, Alabama, on the television news, unleashing dogs and aiming water hoses at demonstrators. My father was not young and not able to protect himself physically. When he finally came home, we were relieved and proud. My math teacher, the only black teacher in the school, took me aside and told me what a wonderful thing my father had done. Later, my father told us how he had experienced the march: he said, "I felt my legs were praying."

My father's genius was to say the unusual and unexpected, and yet have what he said resonate deeply with his listeners. Actually, his writings are quite controversial and radical. The very title, *God in Search of Man,* is a jolt. In Martin Buber's work, for instance, we are accustomed to discussions of "encounters" with God. In Protestant theologian Karl Barth's writings, we hear about the Word thundered from heaven. And we commonly speak of our own search for God. But in my father's writings there is gentle upheaval. My father opens to us, in his writings, his own soul, the piety of a religious Jew. Imagine with him that it is God who is searching for us. We might ask, How can God be in search of human beings? What for? Isn't God all-knowing, perfect, unchanging? Why would God need to search for us? Doesn't God already know where we are, the state of our souls?

This starting point, that God is in search of us and in need of us, is the central concern of my father's writings. In his doctoral dissertation on the prophets, my father first developed his interpretation of the consciousness of the prophets as the way to understand what it means to be a religious person and what God is trying to convey through the Torah. To my father, the Bible is not a human book about God but, rather, God's book about human beings, and its central message is God's pathos. My father writes, "The decisive thought in the message of the prophets is not the presence of God to human beings but rather the presence of human beings to God. This is why the Bible is God's anthropology, rather than humanity's theology." What, he asks, is the pathos of God but that God is deeply affected by what human beings do. The prophets, in his view, came to teach us that God cares deeply about human suffering, that God is involved in human life. My father used to say, "Whatever I do to another person, I do to God. When I hurt a human being, I injure God. If you want to understand the meaning of God, sharpen your sense of the human."

Imagine, in the formal world of philosophical theology, saying that God could possibly be concerned with the pettiness of human beings, let alone be hurt by human misdeeds. It seems to contradict everything we conventionally assume about God's nature. But, my father emphasized, God's concern with human beings is precisely what constitutes our greatness. My father writes: "To be is to stand for, and what human beings stand for is the great mystery of being God's partner. God is in need of human beings." My father shattered our assumptions by rejecting the Aristotelian description of God as the "Unmoved Mover." Instead, he described God as the "Most Moved Mover." Traditional Jewish philosophy has accepted the rubrics of Aristotelian philosophy, and has taught us that God cannot possibly be affected by any other being. According to most Jewish philosophers, God is beyond affection and change. The great medieval Jewish philosopher Moses Maimonides taught that the various descriptions of God that appear in the Bible and the Talmud should not be taken literally as attributes of God's essence, but rather as human ways of understanding God's works. When God is called compassionate, this does not mean, according to Maimonides, that God feels compassion, but that God does things to and for human beings and the natural world that are similar to those things we human beings do when we feel compassionate. And, for Maimonides and other Jewish philosophers, the same holds true of the other adjectives used to describe God—pain, sorrow, even love.

But a second, equally important tradition exists within Judaism, even more ancient and just as powerful. This tradition holds that God is deeply affected by human deeds, that God suffers and rejoices as our history unfolds. For instance, we read in the Bible that a person who oppresses the poor blasphemes God, but one who is gracious to the needy honors God. We are told in the Talmud that God cried as the Temple in Jerusalem went up in flames. And, in a striking midrash, God says, I am God and you are my witnesses; if you are not my witnesses, then I am not God.

My father's theology is an outgrowth of this tradition in Judaism, a tradition he reviews schematically in his three-volume Hebrew study, *Torah min HaShamayim b'Espakloriah shel HaDorot*. My father sees the prophets and all religious people as just such witnesses who allow God to be God. Understood this way, God is never neutral, never beyond good and evil. On the contrary, my father says, the Bible shows us a relationship of reciprocity, of the engagement of God to individuals.

The Bible does not simply describe a commitment by people to God. Human beings are not the end products of creation, placed on this earth and left to their own devices. God is involved in the lives of individuals, affected by what people do. When we commit evil acts, we put God into exile, unable to bring about redemption. Faith requires a leap of action, accepting the responsibility that is ours for creating a just society, for bringing an end to war and to evil, for making possible our redemption and the end of God's captivity.

These ideas of my father's will strike a chord of recognition in those readers familiar with Kabbalah, Jewish mysticism. For Jewish mystics, God is in captivity, having gone into exile with the Jewish people. In captivity, God is not whole, but divided; the *Shechinah,* the female aspect of God, is cut off from the other divine attributes and remains here in this world, accompanying us into exile. The Kabbalists spoke of a *Tzorech Gavoha,* a divine need, which could be filled through our good deeds and inner, spiritual direction. Each mitsvah, each divine commandment that we perform with the proper intention, is able to give strength to God, to bring about at least a temporary union of the *Shechinah* and the Holy One of Blessing. Ultimately, through our good deeds, we can make that reunion permanent and experience the redemption of the world and of God. Conversely, our misdeeds weaken God and give strength to the forces of evil in the world. In Kabbalistic and Hasidic writings, evil is understood to entrap sparks of divinity that lie scattered throughout the universe, awaiting redemption.

The idea that good and evil are often intermingled is developed in my father's writings. In a section of *God in Search of Man* entitled "The Confusion of Good and Evil," he writes that evil thrives in the disguise of the good and pious, that "the holy and the unholy do not exist apart, but are mixed, interrelated and confounded." Indeed, my father draws on a strong Kabbalistic current when he writes that "there is a holy spark of God even in the dark recesses of evil. If not for that spark, evil would lose its power and reality, and would turn to nothingness." The confusion of good and evil is personal as well. In our own lives, my father recognizes, and increasingly in modern times, which have witnessed terrible crimes, we are easily confused by the mixture of good and evil. Our ability to distinguish between right and wrong is often blurred, leaving us horrified at our loss of the sense of horror.

What, then, should be the human response to evil? My father, after all, had lived through a calamitous evil in the life of the Jewish people and in his own life. He writes without specific reference to the Holocaust, although it is clearly present on every page. We may not know how to solve the problem of evil, he writes, but we can do something about evils, and we are never alone in that struggle. Our task is to separate good from evil, to recognize the distinction between them. "At the end of days," he writes, "evil will be conquered by the One; in historic times, evils must be conquered one by one." We are responsible for the kind of world we make, for fighting injustice and establishing righteousness. Yet evil is not the ultimate problem we face, according to my father. Our ultimate problem is our relation to God. The biblical answer to evil, my father writes, "is not the good but the holy. It is an attempt to raise human beings to a higher level of existence, where we are not alone when confronted with evil." Our ability to overcome evil comes through the power of love and holiness given us by God. God is present in every mitsvah, in every holy deed, as the Kabbalists taught, and so our response to evil in the performance of mitsvot is not impersonal and lonely. Our deeds are the divine in disguise: "*Shechinah* is the mitsvah." Redemption of the world begins with human efforts to overcome evil by committing holy acts. Yet this does not mean that redemption is entirely in our hands, that the messianic age is a human invention. After all, if human resources were sufficient by themselves to do what is good, we would not have been given the promise of messianic redemption, my father says. The point of messianism is that good deeds alone will not redeem history, and, at the same time, redemption will not come about through a magical act of God's grace. Our tasks, our faith and works, my father explains, are preparations for the ultimate, divine redemption: "Our task is to make the world worthy of redemption." Similarly, he writes in his book *Quest for God* that prayer does not save us, but may make us worthy of being saved.

How should we understand my father's writings? He hardly strikes us as a conventional philosopher, presenting long, drawn-out logical arguments, and yet it is clear that he has thought through some central questions of religious philosophy and has developed systematic responses to them. And while his work is deeply appreciated by Christian readers, it is, obviously, firmly rooted in classical Jewish sources, particularly Kabbalah and Hasidism. He has created a new context for religious thought, with important answers to those for whom God has no reality apart from human power, as well as to those for whom God is an impassible, transcendent Wholly Other. The historian of philosophy Richard Rorty makes a helpful distinction between systematic and edifying philosophy in his book *Philosophy and the Mirror of Nature.* Systematic philosophers, Rorty writes, "want to put their subject on the secure path of a science. Edifying philosophers want to keep space open for the sense of wonder which poets can sometimes cause—wonder that there is something new under the sun, something which is not an accurate representation of what was already there, something which (at least for the moment) cannot be explained and can barely be described."

My father is precisely one of those edifying philosophers Rorty is describing. Rather than engage in ponderous arguments or present a theology rooted in the categories of formal logic, he offers images and metaphors, aphorisms that read like prayers but that nevertheless are part of a sustained system. Often, he weaves biblical phrases into his writing in such a flowing way that his voice and the psalmist's merge. The mood of his books is not one of confrontation or intellectual challenge but of loving, gentle evocation. *God in Search of Man* is filled with love for human beings. The book reflects the sense of alienation and pain we all experience at times, and tries to lift us out of it by showing us new dimensions of our own humanity. The book is not a defense of traditional religion but a guide to finding the religious dimension within ourselves. Rather than try to convince the nonbeliever with arguments, my father presents the consciousness of the person of faith. Rather than ask what we can say about God, he teaches that the Bible is God's book about us. The structure of the book itself is a lesson: God, Revelation, Response. How we can find ways to God's presence, how we can each find in ourselves a religious path, precedes his discussion of how God relates to us. First, we have to develop ourselves. Then we can explore what Judaism teaches us about God, Torah, and mitsvot.

The first third of *God in Search of Man* is a description of the inner, spiritual life and the path a religious person takes to reach God's presence. There are no exercises in meditation, no calls for retreat from the world, no mantras to recite. Rather, my father speaks about human sensibilities, qualities within ourselves that we can cultivate in response to the world around us. I remember as a child walking with my father along Broadway, in dirty, noisy, grimy streets, and then turning the corner to go home, walking down the hill toward Riverside Drive, and seeing before us the Hudson River and, sometimes, a magnificent sunset. My father would describe what we were seeing, the wonder of God's miracles in nature, the beauty of a sunset which reminds us of God's presence in the world. I realized later, when I read his books, how the words of his writings and his speech were one and the same.

Perceiving God's presence is our task, he writes, and he lived his life with that constant awareness. He writes in *God in Search of Man* that "the Bible is a seed, God is the sun, but we are the soil. Every generation is expected to bring forth new understanding and new realization." The understanding he brought forth through his life and work are immeasurable gifts. What a miracle that his life was spared. How blessed are we who knew him.

INDEX

Index to Biblical References